# ETHNOGRAPHY AND PROSTITUTION IN PERU

D0783149

# Anthropology, Culture and Society

Series Editors:
Dr Richard A. Wilson, University of Sussex
Professor Thomas Hylland Eriksen, University of Oslo

# ETHNOGRAPHY AND PROSTITUTION IN PERU

LORRAINE NENCEL

Pluto Press
LONDON • STERLING, VIRGINIA

First published 2001
by PLUTO PRESS
345 Archway Road, London N6 5AA
and 22883 Quicksilver Drive,
Sterling, VA 20166–2012, USA

www.plutobooks.com

Copyright © Lorraine Nencel 2001

The right of Lorraine Nencel to be identified as the author of this work has
been asserted by her in accordance with the Copyright, Designs and
Patents Act 1988.

British Library Cataloguing in Publication Data
A catalogue record for this book is available from
the British Library

ISBN 0 7453 1662 X hardback
ISBN 0 7453 1661 1 paperback

Library of Congress Cataloging in Publication Data
Nencel, Lorraine.
  Ethnography and prostitution in Peru / Lorraine Nencel.
    p. cm.
— (Anthropology, culture, and society)
  ISBN 0–7453–1662–X (hard)
  1. Prostitution–Peru. 2. Women–Peru–Social conditions. I. Title.
II. Series.
  HQ181.A5 N46 2001
  306.74'0985–dc21
                                                                00–009132

        10   09   08   07   06   05   04   03   02   01
        10    9    8    7    6    5    4    3    2    1

Designed and produced for Pluto Press by
Chase Publishing Services, Fortescue, Sidmouth EX10 9QG
Typeset from disk by Stanford DTP Services, Northampton
Printed in the European Union by
TJ International, Padstow, England

# CONTENTS

PART II    DAY AND NIGHT

# ACKNOWLEDGEMENTS

Acknowledgements are generally written when a book is nearly finished. Yet, paradoxically, they are placed at the beginning, as if they have been waiting there all along, while in fact they are part of a moment of nostalgia. The author fondly reflects upon all the people or institutions that have contributed to the whole. In these acknowledgements I want to thank those who helped me at different phases of this project as well as share with them the joy and satisfaction I felt when I realized that the last sentence had just slipped out of my fingertips and onto the screen. Thus, these acknowledgements are a show of my appreciation as well as a list of the people I mentally danced with at the party held in my imagination.

To begin with this project would not have existed without the financial contributions made by the Netherlands Foundation for the Advancement of Tropical Research (WOTRO) and the Belle van Zuylen Institute (previously Onderzoek Zwaartepunt Vrouwenstudies). From 1990–4, I received a grant from WOTRO and from 1990–3 from the Belle van Zuylen Institute. I am extremely indebted to the CEDLA (Center for Latin American Research and Documentation) at the University of Amsterdam for the use of their fine facilities, which gave me the possibility of creating a think-tank for myself from the beginning until the very end of this project. My thanks to my then supervisor, now colleague and friend Joke Schrijvers, for being able to crawl into my skin and make interesting and constructive comments from the perspective of this book, for her dedication, her comments and the time she took to read thoroughly the different versions of this manuscript. I would also like to recall in fond memory the late Professor Dr Gerrit Huizer, for the solidarity that he showed throughout this project. Further, I would like to thank Anna Aalten for, among other things, introducing me to JB, and Geert Banck for his supervision at CEDLA. I am doubly thankful to Ton Salman and Cees de Groot for their comments on different chapters. Gerdien Steenbeek and Magdalena Villarreal also gave their comments on different aspects and thoughts found in this book. I am especially thankful to Anke van Dam for all she has done, and for the fact her vocabulary does not include the word no. Rafael Calvo has accompanied me almost from the very beginning and has shared his extraordinary insight into his own culture with me. Finally, a special thanks to Eduardo Archetti for his 'public relations' abilities.

Going westward over the ocean, there are so many people who have helped to make this research project a success. During my two episodes of fieldwork I was a visiting researcher at the Faculty of Social Sciences of the Pontificia Universidad Católica and at the non-governmental organization (NGO) Flora Tristán. I am grateful to both institutions for providing their services and affiliation, and specifically to the Research Section of Flora Tristán where I shared an office and thoughts during the first period of fieldwork. Gina Vargas, as well as many other women of Flora Tristán, supported my work from the outset of this project in 1988, when I did a preliminary investigation. Another feminist NGO, Manuela Ramos, was extremely supportive of my work and helped in solving some logistical problems. I am specifically grateful to Charo Cardich, Frescia Carrasco and Susanna Galdos; to Mujer y Sociedad and their then presiding director Zoila Hernández for their enthusiasm and contacts; to CENDOC for the use of their facilities and their enthusiasm; to Germinal, for sharing space and time with me to talk about prostitution and sexuality as I could nowhere else, and for giving me the opportunity to meet a very special person, and especially to Francisco Basili for his creative insight into matters of sexuality; to MHOL (Movimiento Homosexual de Lima) for supplying the condoms needed during this project and for supporting my ideas, particularly Rebecca Sevilla and Kique Bossio Montellanos. Thanks are due to Dr Manuel Luján and Marco Aurelio Denegri, and a special thanks goes to the movement EL POZO and to each of their members who opened their organization to me and helped me on my way, to Veronica de Kwant for being a good friend, and, finally, to those who supported me in the research process: the late Claudio Bashuk, Roberto Bielich Thiessen who helped in many different aspects involved in the research process, Mariella Guillén whose magic fingers got the transcripts out quickly and accurately and Herminia Alayza for her help in the archives.

It is a usual occurrence to thank the people who wear the label of research subject because obviously without their help, cooperation and belief in the research and researcher's commitment, the researcher would never have been able to complete the project. However, in this case I find it difficult to display my gratitude with any enthusiasm. As will become clear in the course of this book, the word cooperation is not the most adequate one to describe our relationship. Nevertheless, I am still grateful. Grateful that I got to know and cherish a very special heterogeneous group of women no matter how difficult it may have been. And despite the (un)intentional turbulence my project and their reactions caused, I am appreciative to all of them for letting me come close – maybe not as close as I would have liked to, but close enough to open my eyes to a part of their life experiences and pass on this knowledge to the reader in the following pages.

Lorraine Nencel
November 2000

# INTRODUCTION
## Zooming in on the Locality

It happened one night during the premiere of a new television talk show, modelled after the successful Hispanic American talk show *Christina* which in turn is modelled on the various American-style talk shows. In each, invited guests are interviewed and audience participation is stimulated. Day-to-day problems are discussed; controversial themes or people are examined. The Peruvian show's first episode concerned the subject of prostitution. First, a documentary presented the 'facts and figures', followed by interviews with six prostitutes who sat in a row, wearing disguises to protect their identities.[1] The predictable questions were posed concerning the whys and whats and the women responded with the expected answers. And then it happened ... One of the women stepped out of the mould. She did not talk of guilt or shame, she admitted she liked her work, enjoyed her work and took pride in it. No, she replied, she would not go back to working in an office, why should she? She sat there listening courageously to the audience's remarks, questioning her state of mind, calling her sick and degenerate. She appeared calm, letting each remark bounce off her gently. I admired her. In all my experiences in Lima with women-who-prostitute, I never spoke to a woman who did not make excuses for what she did, and no one ever defended themselves like this woman did. However, the show was not over until the host cut her arguments to pieces and tried to force her to promise to get out of the business.

Prostitution in Peru is a subject that appears frequently in the media, be it radio, television, newspapers or magazines. However it appears – as a police item, human interest story, tabloid gossip or short (quasi) documentary in an informative television programme – no more is said than what is already known. The significance of prostitution in Peruvian society is not my own invention, rather it is an issue dealt with regularly. It is part of the social context, albeit a problematic component, but something the population of Lima is frequently confronted with.

SCENE TWO

During a one-day workshop concerning 'prostitution as a microcosm of women's oppression', the organizers showed a video from Brazil about prostitution. The participants in this workshop were members of different non-governmental organizations (NGOs), religious orders working with prostitutes, teachers, but the majority came from the health sector who work directly with prostitutes at one of the government-run health centres which provide the obligatory medical check-up required by law. The video vividly showed the bitter-sweet life of the prostitutes in a lower-class district. It showed their strengths, their weaknesses, the ways they dealt with their situation. Afterwards, the participants were divided into groups and asked to reach some general conclusions concerning prostitution, relying on the video for information.

Different interview excerpts were used to illustrate the prostitutes' condition. One health worker considered the prostitutes' acceptance of their work to be a sign of their loss of shame. Another person compared the women's decision to continue in the trade to an addiction similar to that of a drug addict. Finally, when one of the prostitutes was asked if she feared Aids, she answered bitterly, 'I fear hunger more than Aids.' This was interpreted as a sign of her irresponsibility and illustrated the lack of good information for high-risk groups.

These three comments can be looked at from another angle. The prostitutes' so-called loss of shame can be considered the capacity to cope with and manage their situation. Rather than a sign of addiction, their alleged dependent behaviour could be regarded as the enactment of their identity as prostitutes. Lastly, the prostitute's 'ignorance' concerning Aids shows what things are given priority in her life. Hunger is felt daily while Aids is not. Additionally, it did not cross the minds of any of the participants in the seminar that the woman might be practising safe sex and had little to worry about.

These two scenarios serve excellently to introduce the reader to the cultural specificity of this subject and touch on diverse issues approached in this book. They express the ordinariness of prostitution's existence in society and immediately give a good idea of several conflictive and repressive standpoints that women-who-prostitute are up against.

The woman interviewed who boldly claimed to like her work received comments particularly specific to the Lima context. If this same woman had made the same remark in a Western context, the chance that her comment would be accepted without many problems would be greater. In the last two decades a specifically Western discourse has developed which, among other things, supports the rights of prostitutes, recognizes their work as a profession and uses the term 'sex worker' instead of 'prostitute' (Bell 1987, 1994; Delacoste and Alexander 1987; Pheterson 1989, 1996). In her postmodernist analysis, Shannon Bell claims '[p]ostmodernism opens the feminist terrain to prostitute feminist discourse and to differences among prostitute discourses' (1994: 6). The idea that a feminist discourse of prostitution, generated from prostitutes, could exist in Peru, is unthinkable. The Peruvian feminist prostitution discourse is founded on notions of sexual slavery and sexual exploitation, and comes from the women's movement not the prostitutes. Here the possibility of recognizing prostitution as a profession is fervently rejected. Furthermore, there are few signs from the women themselves that they are willing to step out of the discursive mould, appropriating and embodying the notions the different discourses produce. Prostitution might be described as 'a job like any other', but that is more often to counteract the notion of promiscuity entangled in the construct of the prostitute, rather than a sign of professional recognition.

Likewise, the idea that different prostitute discourses have the right to exist side by side is also impossible to envision in the Peruvian context. Not only do those who uphold the feminist standpoint refute alternative discourses, but those who adhere to the hegemonic discourse of prostitution take the same position, indicating the regulation of prostitution as the only feasible manner to solve the 'prostitution problem'. Prostitution's inevitability, its function as a necessary evil and control of the prostitute play crucial roles in defining the space allotted to the women involved in this trade.

In Lima, it is virtually inconceivable that a woman who prostitutes would openly admit to liking her work. According to the supporters of the various discourses prostitutes are suffering and forced into these circumstances. The idea that they might be working out of free will is totally out of sync with all the existing gender imagery. Moreover, the majority of prostitutes disclaim the possibility of enjoying this work. They experience it as a sacrifice.

Finally, the idea that prostitutes might be considered as sex workers has not gone over at all well in the context of Lima. Attempts have been made to recognize registered prostitutes as sex workers, but when this label is spoken out loud it often is accompanied by a disbelieving smirk. Additionally, the women-who-prostitute do not call themselves sex workers and do not recognize the dimension of empowerment encapsulated in the term. They use the word 'prostitute' without any problem. My use of the term 'sex workers' quickly diminished and eventually the word was removed from my vocabulary. Calling Peruvian prostitutes sex workers (with all its political implications) would be a misrepresentation of their social reality. Without any qualms I use the term 'prostitute', the name they call themselves. This is alternated with the term 'women-who-prostitute' in an attempt to accentuate the women and not the way they earn a living.

The second scenario gives us a different glimpse into the world of prostitution. Prostitution is a concern of many different people who are members of various types of organizations: the medical establishment (at different levels), police and government authorities. As the scenario shows, it is very difficult to talk about prostitution in Peru (or for that matter anywhere else) without morality and ethics getting in the way. And morality and ethics – whether they arise from the regulationist or the feminist discourse (the two predominant discourses in Peru) – straitjacket women into conforming to representations produced by these discourses. The illustrations taken from the Brazilian documentary exemplify this extremely well. My co-participants made me realize that those who work with prostitutes or are interested in their well-being cannot escape from appropriating a discourse embedded with gender meanings that is predestined to contribute to the marginalization or stigmatization of women-who-prostitute.

As this brief contextual sketch reveals, prostitution is a loaded subject in Lima. Discussion is permeated with different moral standpoints which causes do-gooders to lose whatever objectivity they originally possessed. Moreover, these value-laden discourses effect women's agency profoundly and are tightly woven into their performances as prostitutes. Finally, the possibilities for change, and improvement in the situation, are limited to alternatives prescribed in the discourses. Any alternatives – political, social or emotional – that fall outside this space are generally deemed immoral. In its entirety this greatly affected the possibilities and decisions made in this project, and led to the development of particular concepts designed to capture the sensations involved in being a woman who prostitutes in this specific context. These will be elaborated below.

## THE CONCEPTUAL PLOT

This book is about three different groups of women-who-prostitute in Lima. It narrates a particular moment in their lives when they were confronted with the presence of a female anthropologist (myself) who intended to approach the lives of women-who-prostitute holistically, through the analysis of gender meanings and how they are (re)produced in different institutions, structures and cultural elements, as well as approaching the women as both prostitutes and women, attempting to depict the enactment and embodiment of different gender meanings from different subject positions.

From the outset, I expected to encounter a range of diversity in regard to how women-who-prostitute enacted their gender identities: from the women who take pride in their work, and regard it as a profession, to the women who feel guilty, victimized and forced into prostitution or those who act out a little of both. Yet, despite the existing differences, I was surprised by the degree of uniformity in their enactments and projections of their gender identities, which were both highly informed by and constantly interacting with the gender notions produced primarily in the hegemonic discourse.

In the field, this profoundly influenced my research methodology and brought into question several epistemological principles concerning the notion of intersubjectivity and all its related tangents, the collection of life stories and the significance of truths and lies in the fieldwork setting (see

Chapter 5). In the writing up process, this led to the development of certain concepts to symbolize the processes involved in the construction of gender identities for this group of women-who-prostitute in Lima.

The first concept is what I have come to call 'gendered enclosures'. This term came into being after several careful readings of the historical and contemporary material collected. I had to find a term that would capture several sensations transmitted from the material. The first was the repetitive, virtually mechanical reproduction of events and gender meanings that have influenced the lives of women-who-prostitute similarly throughout history. The notion of enclosures suits this objective well. Enclosures are defined as shaped and fabricated forms that are not identical but similar, and are continually produced to serve the same purpose. Second, an enclosure is something that immures the women – their mobility, their space for manoeuvring and negotiating – in other words, that restricts their agency. Enclosures incessantly surround prostitutes with gender notions and meanings that contribute to their stigmatization and give very little leeway in transgressing gender boundaries.

The idea of enclosure as a theoretical concept became stronger after reading Corbin's description of the French system of regulation of prostitution in the late 1800s, proposed by Parent-Duchâlet, one of its founding fathers. Here, the regulation system was defined by three principles based on the notion of enclosure.

1. It is essential to create an *enclosed milieu*, invisible to children, honest women, and even prostitutes outside the system; enclosure makes it possible to carry marginalization to the limit and to contain extramarital activity; it constitutes a dike to prevent any spillover.
2. This enclosed milieu must remain constantly under the *supervision of the authorities*. Invisible to the rest of society, it is perfectly transparent to those who supervise it ...
3. In order to be sufficiently supervised this milieu must be strictly *hierarchized and compartmentalized*; by avoiding as far as possible the mixing of age groups and classes, observation is facilitated and, by the same token, the grip of the authorities is tightened.

    The history of regulationism was to be that of a tireless effort to *discipline* the prostitute, the ideal being the creation of a category of 'enclosed' prostitutes, on the analogy of the enclosed orders of nuns, who would be good 'workers', aspiring to the condition of automata, and who above all would not enjoy their work. (Corbin 1990: 9–10)

The notion of enclosure stood for a system that aimed to marginalize and control the prostitute. Although the Peruvian system did not set out to marginalize prostitutes, its predominant aim was and still is control. Since it was established in 1910 it has functioned as an enclosure that has perpetuated the marginalization of prostitutes. Furthermore, it is one of the

most culturally specific features that contributes to creating a 'no-way-out
situation' for women-who-prostitute, which goes hand in hand with a notion
of gender identity as appearing fixed. Both of these assertions are central to
the arguments in this book.

Women's agency, their enactment and embodiment of gender meanings
are also referred to as the performance of gender identity, in which different
versions of the prostitutes are performed.[2] Although the notion of
performance carries for some an inference of intentionality, an offstage and
an onstage way of doing things, in Butler's terms this is far from the truth.
Butler states 'gender proves to be performative – that is, constituting the
identity it is purported to be. In this sense gender is always a doing, though
not a doing by a subject who might be said to preexist the deed' (1990a: 25).
In this notion of the performance of gender, there is no distinction between
on- or offstage; gender is always being performed and constructed in
interaction. Butler's definition provides the necessary coefficient that
removes any traces of determinism implied in the notion of gendered
enclosures.

For obvious reasons, these enclosures are gendered because they are sites
where meanings of femininity and masculinity are constructed and
expressed. Thus, the concept 'gendered enclosures' symbolizes a two-fold
process: the (re)production of gender meanings particularly but not
exclusively in discourses, and the performance of gender identities which
include the reworking of the gendered enclosure meanings into experience-
based or subjective meanings by women as agents.

To proceed, these concepts are meant to serve the reader as guidelines to
facilitate his or her understanding of the complexity of the situation of
women-who-prostitute in Lima. In addition, they helped in structuring and
organizing this book.


WOMEN-WHO-PROSTITUTE: A STORY IN NINE PARTS

This book is divided into two parts. Each part represents one of the processes
constituting the construction of gender identities. The first part,
'(En)gendered Enclosures', is comprised of the chapters which delineate the
creation of gendered enclosures and the fabrication of gender meanings.
Thus Chapter 1 traces the historical development of prostitution, the institutionalization of the regulation of prostitution, and gender meanings and
how they were historically reproduced in the image of the prostitute. Chapter
2 seeks to continue this analysis from the contemporary situation, choosing
the media's representation as the most adequate source for dismantling the
value-laden gender imagery. Read together, these chapters give volume and
content to the assertion that women-who-prostitute are entangled in a no-
way-out situation. Chapter 3 makes an intimately related detour. It is a
detailed analysis of the construction of male sexuality. Few prostitution

studies include an analysis of male sexuality which does not predefine it. Moreover, the theoretical conclusions concerning prostitution's position in the configuration of male sexuality normally replicate the author's standpoint towards prostitution. This chapter is intended to bridge this theoretical gap and concomitantly make sense of prostitution as a cultural expression of the construction of men's sexual selves.

Part II, 'Day and Night', embraces the fieldwork context in all its epistemological, methodological and empirical complexity. The body of the second part is an ethnographic narrative which stems from the ordinariness of the women's lives during the fieldwork period. Moreover, it depicts the subjective performance of the women's gender identities and the experience-based interpretation of the meanings produced in the gendered enclosure. The first chapter introduces the ethnographic narrative. Besides serving as a contextual backdrop, it treats epistemological and methodological issues which came up during fieldwork and analyses them for the cultural meanings they produce. In addition, it stresses the importance of reflexivity in the field and the writing up process. It is an indispensable section, without which many of the stylistic and methodological decisions taken during the writing process would be extremely difficult to decode. Chapters 5 and 6 relate the story of women-who-prostitute who work during the day on one particular street in one of the oldest neighbourhoods of Lima. It aims to express the ordinariness of their working lives and the construction of their gender identities as prostitutes and as ordinary women. It illustrates the tricky balance that exists between representing oneself and sharing commonalities with a larger population of female urban poor while at the same time having more in common with the women-who-prostitute on this particular street than with any others. Chapter 7 and 8 retell the stories of the women working at night in a particular middle-class leisure centre. Chapter 7 concerns street prostitutes and Chapter 8 women working in a club. It attempts to transmit the nightly sensations entangled in their work, being members of a world that exists while the majority of the people of Lima sleep.

Read separately, the first part can be regarded as the historical and contemporary development of the 'social representation' of prostitutes' gender identity, and the second part, the construction of the 'subjective representation or self-representation' (Moore 1994) of gender identity. Thus, to a certain extent, each part tells a different story. However, read in its entirety the book expresses the dynamics and tensions constituting the relationship between 'how the social representations of gender affect subjective constructions and how the subjective representation or self-representation of gender affects its social construction' (Moore 1994: 53), or, to rephrase it, the interaction and motion of the gendered enclosures and women's agency. These processes are synthesized in the final chapter.

The subject of prostitution and the story of the women-who-prostitute are narrated and orchestrated by myself. It is not a fictive story, but neither is it a purely scientific venture, which sets out to prove or disclaim some hypotheses on the subject and promote verifiable generalizations.

With the arrival of postmodernism in anthropology, the line between fiction and ethnography has been blurred or strengthened, depending on which side of the debate the author stands. This narrative has used some literary stylistic conventions, but it is not fiction. In the first place, it is based on a true story. There are those who will counter this statement by asserting that realist fiction is also based on the truth. However, the fine line which differentiates the two is stated by Carrithers:

> Whereas the canon of a fictional realist might be to achieve verisimilitude, ethnographers adhere to quite a different standard. In their writing the touchstone must be fidelity to what they experienced and learned about others, and much of what they write has to be verifiably true ... a very different matter than the plausibility of inner harmony we ask of realist fiction. (quoted in Wolf 1992: 57)

Thus, I may have decided to piece conversations together to weave a story, placing one incident that occurred closer to another than it was in reality, nevertheless the incidents occurred and the conversations did take place. Wolf is worried about the effect of the literary turn on the audience claiming:

> [i]n the end, our readers will have no basis to judge whether they are reading about a culture very different from their own or whether they are reading the product of a mind very different from their own, or both. (1992: 60)

Although her warning is valid if reflexivity is taken to the furthest extreme, between this extreme and traditional ethnography lies a range of ethnographic options (Behar 1993; Abu-Lughod 1993; Stoller 1989), which may even include Wolf's (1992) *A Thrice-Told Tale*.

This ethnographic narrative situates itself amongst the ethnographies that lie between the two poles. First, it attempts to transmit sensations which are felt in the field, through silence, the tone used to say something, the expression on someone's face, or even the smell of the place where it took place. These sensations are difficult to convey through scientific language and are important in trying to portray and evoke a cultural context. Narrative conventions work well for this objective. Therefore unlike Wolf who says, '[f]iction can evoke a setting, a social context, an involvement of all the senses in ways that enhance understanding. But it is no substitute for a well-written ethnographic account ...' (1992: 59), I think a well-written ethnographic account must attempt to include, as difficult as it may be, a dimension that evokes sensations.

Second, this ethnographic account seeks to find a satisfactory form to combine what are often considered juxtaposed tendencies, namely my interpretations as an anthropologist and my record of the conversations and incidents as they occurred, so they can speak for themselves. In Chapter 4, I deal with this subject in detail. Suffice it to say that the inclusion of myself in this book is not merely a reflexive decision. I am not only a protagonist in the narrative because I was present, but I have bestowed upon myself the role of interpreter because, in the Peruvian context of prostitution, I would be running the risk of doing more harm than good if I let the conversations and actions go unaccompanied. They could bolster already existing stereotypes rather than dismantle them. Thus, I try both to make sense of things for myself, as well as transmitting the cultural sense of the field to the reader, both of which are essential in writing ethnography.

**PART I**

# (EN)GENDERED ENCLOSURES

# 1  A HISTORICAL NARRATIVE OF PROSTITUTION

A striking resemblance exists between the Peruvian history of prostitution and other cross-cultural histories of prostitution. This is not a coincidence but rather a consequence of the manner in which prostitution is conceptualized.[1] Prostitution is considered to be the same universally. The fact that a woman offers sexual services in exchange for material compensation is considered sufficient to erase cultural difference. Numerous articles in the Peruvian literature accentuate its alleged universal character by presenting an evolutionist history of prostitution which commences in Ancient Greek and Roman times and ends in contemporaneous Peru.[2] Although thousands of years and miles separate the different realities, this line of argumentation is used to justify the existence of prostitution. The conceptualization of prostitution as universal goes hand in hand with other essentialist notions. In their entirety these notions have informed the actions taken towards prostitution and have deeply marked its historicity.

One of the core notions behind the hegemonic discourse of prostitution is its inevitability. It is considered inevitable, first, because it is a universal phenomenon and, second, because of its intrinsic relation to what has been called the necessity to satisfy human needs or in plain English: the satisfaction of male sexual desire. Male sexuality is depicted as insatiable, instinctual and uncontrollable, reducing it to an essentialist universal notion. Because of this, society is faced with a moral dilemma: how can male sexual desire be soothed without dishevelling society's moral fabric? Prostitution's existence is legitimized as a 'necessary evil', tying tightly together the idea of inevitability and male sexuality. Approached as a moral problem, it was condoned for the sake of society's well-being. It was only when the relationship between prostitution and venereal diseases was discovered, that it began to be regarded as a fully-fledged problem in need of a solution. Solutions to the prostitution problem were borrowed from previous European attempts, which had been confined to deciding whether it would be wiser to regulate or abolish it. The regulationist discourse departed from the aforementioned notions, claiming that this alleged social disease must be controlled,[3] and sought to introduce legislation to implement a regimen of control. Their abolitionist adversaries, however, rejected all arguments derived from the regulationists' discourse, and replaced them with others, calling prostitution an 'illicit act', a sign of society's injustice, and calling for its total disappearance. Each discourse produced unyielding and narrow concepts which have continually been reproduced throughout the course of history.

The approach taken towards prostitution has also been greatly determined by the social position of the experts who produced the discourse in the multitude of articles and theses on the subject. Most of the Peruvian literature was written by male doctors and lawyers, or students of these disciplines, predominantly from the upper classes. The majority of this moral vanguard were of European descent. Accordingly, their ideas concerning education, their attitudes and their customs were closer to those of their 'European cousins' than their compatriots who lived in urban slum dwellings.

The historical narrative presented in this chapter has been deeply informed by the understanding of these aspects of the discourse on prostitution, which have contributed to creating a partial history that emphasizes some occurrences while silencing others. It is a chronicle of the making of the first gendered enclosures and how they profoundly affected the agency of women-who-prostituted.

THE CALL FOR REGULATION (1858–1909)

The first[4] call for the regulation of prostitution, written by L. Villar, was published in the *Gaceta Medica de Lima* in 1858. Villar spoke frankly to his public when he asked them to find a solution if not for prostitution then at least for the prevention of syphilis. His answer to this problem was to 'establish a sanitary vigilance by proceeding with the regulation of prostitution for the women who have entered into the market and lost their honour disgracefully' (1858: 186).[5] To avoid accusations of immorality, he reminds the reader of the reality: 'In proposing this measure we are not trying to establish prostitution in a country which is not acquainted with it. If prostitution did not exist in Lima and we were engaged in establishing it, thus offering society to drink from the cup of perversion, it would be justifiable to accuse us of being immoral. Since we see that it exists and its existence is inevitable, in spite of religion and laws, it is necessary to attenuate its consequences and tolerate the lesser of the evils' (1858: 186). Villar was not alone in his call for regulation to prevent the spread of venereal diseases. Other articles published later on included various justifications that legitimized this standpoint.

Regulationists have underlined the importance of prostitution's control by stressing the notions of inevitability and male sexuality. Muñiz refers to the act of copulation as being as necessary to the individual[6] as food, liquids and sleep (1887: 458). The inactivity of the genitals at the age when the sexual appetite is awakened is one of the causes of pathological states and can bring the individual into grave dangers. 'Thus, rightfully it can be sustained that, whether or not prostitution is a morbid inherent phenomenon of our species, it is an evil necessity. It is a plague, if you wish, derived naturally from what we are. If it must exist and it has to exist, then the most logical and natural way is to regulate and watch over it to avoid its dangers. It is better to tolerate it and watch over it than abandon it to itself' (1887: 460). Barrios et al. give a variation on this theme, but relay the same message. 'Prostitution ... is the security valve for the honour of families and it is as necessary in societies as garbage dumps, drainage and sewer systems, etc. ... With the same right the authorities have to watch over the purity of food and beverages, regulating the sale of dangerous substances ... with the same right it can and must impede that prostitution should be the direct cause of the propagation and development of venereal diseases ...' (1892: 208–9). Despite the assumptions made about male sexuality, the authors refrain from passing judgement on men's behaviour, or from proposing measures to constrain their lust. Male sexuality is not the problem here. The problem lies in how society can keep men's sexuality rid of venereal diseases without repressing it.

An interesting twist in the argumentation for regulation is found in an article written by Valdizán Medrano. He adds to the list of usual reasons cited for prostitution's inevitability women's disadvantageous position in society. 'If we examine any of our present social organisms, despite the high level they occupy in the scale of civilization, we find the unconsoling truth that, in a large number of cases the woman sees herself obliged to choose between misery which is a crisis of desperation and pain, and prostitution. Good or bad, it offers relative abundance for the exchange of the theoretical concept called honour.

'To follow the first way is to follow the path of heroism, a path that only those can follow whose souls own an unyielding faith. They hope to be recompensed in their spiritual life for their efforts. But since heroism is not common and hunger is not a good adviser, the natural and usual thing to do is choose the second' (1909: 148). Valdizán Medrano painted a relatively compassionate picture seldom encountered in the literature on women-who-prostitute. As we will see further on, this same argument, namely women's disadvantageous economic position which forced them into losing their honour, was also used by the opponents of regulation.

Since the beginning of the debate, women's economic situation has been acknowledged as a key push factor for entering prostitution. Needless to say, this recognition has not been very influential in swaying public opinion in the prostitutes' favour.

The call for a regulation of prostitution was not met with total acceptance. Disapproval was voiced and prohibition urged. The pages of the *Crónica Médica de Lima* – a monthly medical journal – functioned briefly as a sparring ring for the opposing opinions.

At the beginning of the 1890s the Sub-Prefect of the province of Lima, Pedro Enrique Muñiz, presented a project for an ordinance regulating prostitution. Avendaño (1892),[7] a physician who was in the vanguard of the fight for regulation and happened to be chief editor of the *Crónica Médica de Lima*, mentions the project in his article. He runs through the predictable reasons given to support the regulation and announces the project's endorsement by the Section of Public Medicine of the National Academy of Medicine. In the following issue an article was published written by the Attorney General (*Fiscal de la Nación*) in response to the project.

In the first place, he claimed, the project reproduces earlier models applied in various American and European cities and is not attuned to Peruvian reality. Second, it obliges all women to carry a certificate of health. He objected to the damage that this would cause women working as prostitutes. 'Concerning the women of the life of little honesty, that for honour or other motives elude the mandatory inscription, obtain the certificates and submit to medical check-ups, a series of denouncements, persecutions and fines are established to force them to register, reducing all those women to the condition of public prostitutes, even when they have not arrived to that extreme of lewdness and it is only poverty or seduction which accidentally leads them to practice acts suspicious of prostitution' (Galvez 1892: 66).

The second criticism he launches concerns the measure included to concentrate all prostitutes in one area to facilitate control, avoid disorder and scandals, and prevent venereal diseases. He objects to this utopian idea on the grounds it would disgrace the majority of the women to register with the police. '[O]nly the extremely disgraced who have lost all notion of honour and shame, or the innocent ones seduced by misery to beg their bread in a house of tolerance, would submit to getting a card and submit to the check-ups. All the rest would openly commence a fight with the authorities ...' (1892: 66–7). The Attorney General's criticism is based on the negative consequences for women working as prostitutes. Here once again women's economic situation is seen as an essential factor behind her willingness to lose her honour. However, unlike Valdizán Medrano, who uses this argument to underscore prostitution's inevitability and the need for its control, the Attorney General claims society would be institutionalizing what had been until that moment women's temporary disgraceful position.

Finally, he calls attention to the ineffectiveness of mandatory medical control, emphasizing that any woman who has received a clean bill of health could contract a venereal disease with the first man she attends after she completes her check-up.

In summary, one of his strongest motivations for rejecting regulation was the degradation it would cause women. Voluntarily or forced it would be the 'bloodstain which could not be erased and impedes the rehabilitation of those who registered ...' (1892: 68). He pleads for the total prohibition of prostitution: 'you do not regulate vices, you prohibit them no sooner than they affect the order and morality' (1892: 68).

The Attorney General met with opposition. In the issues that followed, his report was criticized on several accounts. The discussion here is confined to the position given to women-who-prostitute.

Medina (1892), a proponent of the regulation, sketches a different picture of the women's predicted fate. '[T]hus, when a woman is placed on the fatal slope of vice, she completely turns around. When she has arrived at the extreme to look to satisfy the passions of others, as an indispensable element of her existence, making her body merchandise which can be bought with a fistful of money; given her depraved life, the degradation of her moral being and the perversion of her feelings, we find none of these noble impulses which hearten the spirit. She has completely lost all notions of dignity ...' (1892: 94–5).

Another reply to the Attorney General's report was written by members of the Fourth Section of the Academy who served as advisers for the proposal. One of the arguments justifying regulation is found in the following representation of the prostitute. 'The priestesses of Venus who deal with their bodies generally come from the lowest social sphere. Disgraced women without education nor instruction, without the slightest notion of morality, indolent, lazy, neglected ... and those miserable beings who have in some cases even lost the consciousness of their personality. Would they be worried to repair the tracks that continual carnal use imprints in their organism? Very few of them would take care. On the contrary, many would use their cruel disease as a means of revenge against an honourable society which has rightly rejected them from its bosom' (1892: 209).

It appears the Attorney General had the last word. There were no further publications on the subject until some time later. Reference to the project's outcome is found in an article written for a Buenos Aires journal. The author, a Peruvian physician, describes the situation. 'Among us, regulation does not exist. Years ago, the current Minister of war, General Muñiz who was the Prefect[8] of Lima, presented a laudable project for the regulation of prostitution. It failed because of the Attorney General's opposition, basing his opinion on issues I call romanticism. Since then, no one has attempted to insist in its necessity. Nonetheless, the majority think prostitution should be regulated' (quoted in Dávalos y Lissón 1909: 41).


THE STATE OF AFFAIRS AND THE NEED TO REGULATE


'An insignificant number of prostitutes, the youngest and noisiest grouped in those dens of thieves, drunkenness and corruption called brothels, and the older ones or the experts who work from their domiciles, surrender to the vocation without any hygienic prescriptions ... How much disorder and crime is born in those places? ... How many diseases are contracted there which have been the seed of terrible suffering in the bosom of the family!

How many tears have been shed and are shed, for the abandoned husband, the son, the father in those so-called houses of tolerance!

'... All types of disorders (alcohol, thievery, etc.) arise in those houses of tolerance. Their population is indiscriminately recruited by the irresponsible owners, making their actual conditions of existence incompatible with the demands of a capital in a civilized country.

'Thus, in Lima, prostitutes who exist in ad hoc houses, those who have their own domicile and the streetwalkers do not offer any guarantee' (Muñiz 1888: 19–20).

Muñiz does not call for the prohibition of prostitution, rather he calls for measures to meet higher sanitary standards. He offers the regulation as the solution.

Although many articles of the time gave the impression they would present an informative report on prostitution, very few deal with it in detail. One of the few exceptions is a book commissioned by the Ministry of the Government – Office of the Police (Ministerio de Gobierno – Dirreción de Policía) on 2 December 1907. Their motive in commissioning this study was to investigate the plausibility of regulating prostitution.[9] Pedro Dávalos y Lissón was entrusted with the task and given 90 days to report his findings. The result was a book entitled *La Prostitución en la Ciudad de Lima* which describes the actual situation in Lima. Four different types[10] of prostitution were distinguished, each type attracting different women and clients. Despite the diversity, Dávalos y Lissón managed to whittle down the character traits of the women into a general stereotype of 'the prostitute'.

'Almost 90 per cent of prostitution in Lima consists of Peruvian women.[11] The majority are white, intelligent, imaginative and resistant to unnatural eroticism, alcohol and tobacco. The youngest is 17 years old and the oldest 40. Almost half of them are mothers and support their children with the fruits of their business. They are not nymphomaniacs and it is only idleness, bad example, poverty or abandonment by their lovers, which has driven them to this state of abjection ... They do not know how to earn money nor spend it. They always live on the edge of poverty, letting themselves be exploited and they die in destitution ... They never expose their flesh and their modesty goes to the extreme of not washing themselves – a great health hazard – until after the visitor has left. They are neither thieves nor pickpockets. Although their lovers have treated them barbarously before they entered the life, as soon as they are spoken to about love and settling down they willingly return to their primitive state. They are religious, go to mass, have saints and lamps in their rooms ... Suicide, frequent among these women in Chile, Cuba and Argentina, is not found among Peruvian prostitutes' (1909: 9–10).

Dávalos y Lissón appears to be fighting an imaginary battle with those who accuse prostitutes of being immoral, hedonistic and criminals. Within the context of this era, his description is relatively sympathetic. Nevertheless, he cannot avoid seeing them as harmful to society. 'In their large majority the Peruvian prostitute is not a miserable woman. Inclination has driven her to enter into the vice. She possesses elements of moral resurrection. She does not consider "the life" the end of her career and aspires to rehabilitation and pardon. You must pity her: in no way feel contempt or hate her. The state is obliged to regenerate her and in cases where this is not possible, incorrigible ones should be watched over to the point that she does the least harm to society' (1909: 46).

The author maps out the different types of prostitution in Lima. Three are bounded to locations: the brothel, the street and the bordello.[12] The fourth is not defined by location but by character traits inherent in a person: the hidden prostitute. Generally they live among honourable people, many of them in the bosom of the family. 'They are not always beautiful, these prostitutes, although they are young. What the clientele pays for is the delight produced by the mystery that surrounds them ...' (1909: 23). This type of prostitution is for bread and luxuries for their home and 'to calm the erotic furore of these hysterical beings' (1909: 24).[13]

The woman's possibilities and the type of life she leads is determined by the location where she works. The brothel, probably the most common location for prostitution in this period, is divided into three different categories. The lowest category is found in the poorest sections of Lima and is frequented by the lower classes of society, the least knowledgeable of matters of hygiene who only use *curanderos*' (traditional healers) medicines to cure a venereal disease. Syphilis is probably common in this neighbourhood (1909: 13).

The brothels are shabby, smelly, dismal dwellings, lacking any form of hygienic facilities and barely furnished. They are only used at night, the prostitute returning to her own house when she is not working. It is common for these prostitutes to live with a pimp who probably introduced her to the business. Although one can encounter women of all ages and races working in these brothels: 'As a rule they are *mestizas*,[14] of white and Indian mixture who have fallen in this social sewer ... they have lost, if they ever had it, the smallest trace of beauty. They live in the mire of complete impassiveness. They are ignorant, superstitious, selfish, quarrelsome. They use coarse language, do not have the least notion of hygiene and are consumptives or on their way to becoming so' (1909: 15).

The second category of brothels is small houses possessing kitchens, water and plumbing. The majority contains simple furnishings and clean sheets and towels. The women working here are 'generally white, averaged age, respectful and with some culture' (1909: 17). They are more refined than their counterparts who work in the first category of brothels. 'They do not exhibit themselves in the street door nor do they call to passers-by. Normally they sit at their windows behind the blinds. From there they observe the men but do not make any insinuation if they are not acquainted with them' (1909: 18). They select their clients according to certain criteria. The majority of their clientele are clerks and army officers or government bureaucrats.

These women possess modesty and discreet dignity. 'In their hearts there are feelings of honour, affection and diffuse romantic hopes and happiness. Many talk about widowhood, their obligation to support their children and mother. In many cases this is certain, poverty is the principal cause of their actions. Since they are useless as seamstresses and still young with some beauty, and determined not to sink to the level of servant, they enter into prostitution as a trade and are as honest as it is possible to be in such a dishonest profession' (1909: 19).

Women-who-prostituted in the third category are young and beautiful. They distinguish themselves from the second category by their level of culture, manners and customs. They work in luxuriously furnished houses and are very much in demand as mistresses (1909: 20–2). 'Few of them wear hats, the majority use mantas,[15] and they wear it gracefully and flirtatiously. They do not use rouge nor flashy dresses. However, there is something about them which makes it easy, very easy to recognize them even when they are among a thousand people' (1909: 21).

Whereas brothel prostitution appears to be well established, street prostitution is portrayed as a relatively new phenomenon commencing approximately seven years earlier. Street prostitution is described as the most degrading form, attracting women from the bottom of society (1909: 26–8). The two types are distinguished racially. The first are Indian women or 'at the most *mestizas*, the second are white. The first class is younger than the second and more ignorant about the things that women in this life know. Some of them are pregnant which shows how relatively new they are to the trade. Although they are young, they are not known for their beauty, not even for their lovely figures' (1909: 27). They are depicted as poverty-stricken and undernourished, showing signs of physical poverty. They live in neighbourhoods situated at a distance from where they work and lack any real notion of hygiene. The second class knows as little as the first, but they are generally older and possess more acceptable features and figures (1909: 28).

'Street prostitutes are not very discreet. If a person passes by their side and looks interested, they address him at that moment' (1909: 28–9). Their clients are taken to hotel rooms which only contain a bed and where a knock on the door ten minutes later tells them their time is up. Others are taken to slightly more comfortable hotels, where they change the sheets nightly.

The discrepancies that exist between the author's general description of the Limanian prostitute and his description of each category are interesting. The contrasts between the two reflect the ruling elite's ethnic and class preferences. The whiter the prostitute's complexion, the less she calls attention to herself, and the higher her class, the closer she fits the humble prototype of the Limenean prostitute.

Dávalos y Lissón's investigation concluded that, in all their diversity, the majority of the locales do not live up to sanitary standards required to control venereal diseases. With the exception of higher-class prostitutes, most of the women practising this profession were either unaware of measures used for prevention or practised forms that were partially or totally ineffective. Dávalos y Lissón joined the ranks of those before him, urging the sanitary regulation of prostitution. His report was decisive in getting the machinery working to implement the regulation of prostitution in Lima.

REGULATION TAKES ROOT (1910–1930s)

In 1910 a system of regulation of prostitution was put into effect. This solid assertion of fact shakes at its foundation when we try to find out what the regulation actually entailed. A factor contributing to the chaos is that the regulatory system was put together piecemeal, over a lengthy period. It is not a single law but rather a conglomeration of decrees, resolutions, orders originating from different governmental levels (Ministry, Prefect and Municipality). The two most significant components concern the health statutes and registration/licences. Each of these will be dealt with in turn.

On 1 June 1910 a Supreme Resolution was proclaimed to organize the Sanitary Services of Prostitution.[16] It states:

Taking into consideration:
that it is the State's duty to attend to the prophylaxis of venereal diseases, that more than the harm it occasions in individuals who contract it, it also attacks the interest of the society and the race; that universal experiences have proven the inefficiency of police regulations of prostitution for the prophylaxis of these diseases;
that experience has also proven, the measures most efficient in this sense are those referring to sanitary inspections and vigilance of public women, houses of tolerance and free medical treatment in adequate dispensaries for the sick, infected with a venereal disease;
that in order to organize duly the sanitary service of prostitution it is expedient to place it under the subordination of the Office of the Director Public Health (La Dirección de Salubridad Pública) and make use of those physicians' services that cooperate with the government;
that the local institutions should equally lend their cooperation for anti-venereal prophylaxis service to the population where it is deemed necessary, inasmuch that they try to improve the condition of health of said populations.

It has been resolved:
Art. 1. The Office of Public Health is in charge of the organization and functioning of the sanitary services of prostitution, and will be in charge of all related issues of said service. It will formulate as briefly as possible, the corresponding sanitary regulation and for now proceed to install health dispensaries designated for venereal disease in the cities of Lima and Callao[17] and afterwards in the rest of the Republic when it is deemed necessary. (quoted in Chavez 1955: 59–60)

The remaining four articles concern implementation, designating specific roles to police and medical authorities and declaring all medical treatment gratis. In 1911 the Special Licences department was established, a special police unit with the responsibility for administering licences to houses of prostitution and registering the women working or wanting to work in these establishments.[18]

Three different types of locales are listed (a) houses of tolerance (*casas de tolerancia*) where one or more women exercise prostitution, permanently or temporarily, and where music, dance and purchase of alcohol are permitted (art. 29); (b) brothels (*prostíbulos*) refer to the same kind of establishments except dancing, music and alcohol are prohibited (art. 30); (c) hotels or pensions strictly for appointments (*casas de citas*) that rent rooms strictly to couples, by the hour, 24 hours a day. Their licence prohibits dance, music and the purchase of alcohol, and that the women should stay in the hotel for long intervals. Only adult women are permitted to run houses of prostitution. Direct or indirect intervention of men in these businesses is subjected to the penalty of the law. This last article is aimed at eliminating relations of exploitation between individuals such as pimps and the prostitutes.

The rules governing the location of *casas de tolerancias* and *prostíbulos* are stipulated in the regulation, designating them to 'where the moral rights of the poor are not offended' (art. 33).

Several articles in the procedures of the Department of Venerology[19] restrict prostitutes' movements and liberty. However, it is unlikely that they were systematically enforced. Article 31 states that those who fail to go for their medical checkup will be 'obliged to' by the police. Article 33 prohibits a registered woman from changing her residence without previously notifying the respective section of the Department of Venerology (Chavez 1955: 68). Article 36 concerns the steps to be taken in order to remove oneself from the police register: 'The registered women who wishes to eliminate her name from the "prostitution register" should send her written request to the chief of the Venereal Department expressing, if possible her motives. It should be countersigned by two honourable neighbours. Then it will be communicated to the police authorities' (Chavez 1955: 69).[20]

Chavez asserts that in 1914 the Prefect of Lima ordered (through a Prefectoral Order) all prostitutes to register, and compelled them to have a weekly medical check-up. Between 1910 and 1920 the location of the weekly medical check-up changed three times. First it was located in a hospital but it was removed from these premises because mixing prostitutes and 'the decent people' was considered inconvenient. Without any place to go it was decided in 1916 to move the inspection to Public Assistance, where free medical aid was given to women and children (Chavez 1955: 61). In all likelihood this was considered an unsatisfactory solution because in 1920 the Anti-Venereal Clinic (Dispensary) was established through a Supreme Resolution of the Ministry. In 1923 the *Sifilicomio* was established, a hospital providing mandatory treatment of prostitutes with venereal disease (Solano 1943: 290).

At this same time, police authorities ordered all houses of prostitution to be transferred to the street XX de Setiembre – later to be known as Jirón Huatica – in the district of La Victoria, a popular neighbourhood in Lima inhabited by families of modest condition (1943: 290).

The year in which the regulation firmly took root was 1924. Several articles of the Penal Code (Law no. 4868, and Law no. 4891 – the vagrancy law), ratified by Congress, supported this process.

Article 206 of the Penal Code deals with prostituting a minor of either sex with or without their consent. Article 207 of the same law penalizes those who dishonestly exploit prostitutes' earnings or are kept totally or partially by her.[21] Article 390 concerns offences against public order. A fine and imprisonment is imposed on different categories of people, including those who publicly offend honour, with words, songs, merriment or obscene gestures. The vagrancy law (no. 4891 art. 3) specifically names those committing the criminal offence of vagrancy as: (3) those who carry out, promote and exploit professional prostitution and (7) women who, being professional prostitutes, elude working in licensed establishments for prostitution and evade police regulation, and health and hygiene defences and mock public order.[22]

Two substantial developments stemmed from the institutionalization of the regulation of prostitution. A new category of prostitution was constructed – clandestine prostitution or unregistered prostitutes. The second occurrence was the growing popularity of the abolitionist current resulting in the foundation of the National Abolition Committee of Peru (NACP) in 1936. The existence of an organization for the abolition of prostitution can be considered evidence of the authoritative power granted to the regulation. For if it had not been becoming more institutionalized, there would be no reason to formalize a committee to oppose it.

## ABOLITION AND SOCIAL CHANGE: THE OTHER SOLUTION TO THE PROSTITUTION PROBLEM

The origins of the NACP can be traced to the National League of Social Hygiene and Prophylaxis, founded in 1923. The league's concern grew out of their preoccupation with venereal diseases and its negative effects on the race. On 6 September 1935, it organized a debate on prostitution. A vote was taken as to whether they should endorse a policy of regulation or abolition. The abolition doctrine won. Several members of the League were interested in spreading the abolitionist doctrine and, on 30 January 1936, the NACP was founded. In the initial period, they dedicated the majority of their efforts to lectures promoting sexual education (Solano 1937: 304), an instrumental component of their abolitionist campaign.

The NACP's centre was located in Lima. Its goal – to spread the abolitionist doctrine nationally – was to be carried by working on the following objectives stated in their founding statutes:

(a)  Make propaganda to organize the country's material and moral resources to prevent prostitution and permit the rehabilitation of the female prostitute;
(b)  Take steps to attain that the Sanitary Code includes the prophylaxis and treatment of the venereal ill according to the general norms of hygiene and assistance.
    Prostitution should be considered illicit and dangerous ... (Solano 1936: 246) .

On 26 August 1936, a Supreme Decree authorized by the Ministry of Health declared 6 September Anti-Venereal Day. The abolitionists proudly considered this an accomplishment. Peru was the first Latin American country which officially recognized this day (Bambarén 1937: 270). The activities were sponsored by the League. The papers presented on this day were published in the *Crónica Médica de Lima* which, at some point in the preceding years had changed hands and had become the voice of the League and the abolitionists. The Chief Editor, Carlos Bambarén was treasurer of the League and one of the founding members of the NACP. The League and the NACP were linked together not only by their ideas but also by their officials. Several members held positions in both organizations.

In the opinion of both organizations, three subjects converged in the issue of prostitution: prophylaxis of venereal diseases, abolition of prostitution and eugenics. The League organized the Second Peruvian day of Eugenics in 1944. The connection between the three different systems of thought is illustrated by a quote taken from an article written by Susana Solano, Secretary of the League and Secretary General of the NACP.[23] 'How can the men of government improve the physical condition of the people if they cling to a erroneously adapted sanitary policy?, if they sustain the legitimacy of prostitution as a means of subsistence for women punished by the inequalities of the economic-political-social system, if they authorize the uncurbed functioning of the brothel and stimulate male youth's sexual initiation in those dens of corruption, where they are contaminated and degenerated, infecting and debauching their flesh, mind and feelings with frequent usage of the mercenary dealers of love ...' (1944: 291). In the abolitionist perspective, regulation was ineffective in fighting the spread of venereal diseases. Registered prostitutes evaded their medical check-ups; the system did not reach clandestine prostitutes; and, a point repeatedly stated, the one-sided medical check-ups were ineffective. There was no guarantee that men were not causing the spread of venereal diseases.[24] In the abolitionists' eyes, the regulation system had failed on all counts. They aimed to eradicate the regulation and propagated a view of prostitution as an illicit act.

Strangely enough, their harsh attitude towards prostitution did not contradict the philanthropic tenor encountered in their analysis of the prostitute. Society's injustice, the inequality between the sexes, low wages and scarce employment opportunities were the factors to blame for women's motivations for entering prostitution. There was an urgent need to redeem these women. 'The proponents of the regulation say that prostitution always existed since man is man. But the antiquity of the evil does not justify its adoption. Christ never thought of giving regulations when the Magdalenes presented themselves nor did he suggest confining them to special places, like the women accused of adultery ... The Nazarene transformed them into honourable and dignified persons and he sent them into the world to complete their high mission as true women' (Montaño 1943: 278). Needless to say, their stance towards the prostitute was far from tolerant: '[P]rofessional prostitution is intolerable because it is not an honest means to earn a living for which abolitionist countries oblige the prostitutes to readapt to the moral norms' (Higginson 1941: 123). Measures of prevention and re-adaptation were stipulated in their proposal for an Anti-Venereal Law, an essential weapon designed for their battle (Solano et al. 1941: 137).

Art. 8. To prevent and repress prostitution there is to be established:
(a) a 'Women's Hostel', to accommodate young females who arrive at the capital in search of work;
(b) a 'Work Exchange for Women', to facilitate adequate occupations for the female sex;
(c) the 'Profilactorium', to receive the prostitutes who desire their social re-adaptation, after this law is put in effect ... (Solano et al. 1941: 137)

Solano (1943) considered the Women's Hostel a pragmatic and effective means to prevent girls recently arrived in the city from entering prostitution. The hostel would simultaneously function as a vocational school, which would give lodgers skills in an industrial trade or domestic arts. This would increase their possibilities on the labour market. The Profilactorium would 'cure the prostitutes ... and re-adapt them to a normal life by habitual work and a moral and social re-education conforming to the principles used in the Socialist Republic of Russia' (1943: 293).[25]

The abolitionists focused a relatively large amount of attention on men's contribution to the permanent existence of prostitution and its increase. Men were a part of the problem, albeit not the predominant worry. Their search for solutions included the area of men's problematic sexual behaviour, beginning with adolescents' sexual initiation.

'At the beginning of puberty sexual instinct begins to manifest itself imperatively. In this period, in which all energies are awaken, the attraction to the opposite sex begins to make the youngster anxious ... For the male youth everything is love and love is the most beautiful illusion of the youth. In this special state of mind the adolescent is surprised by his initiation into his sexual life and almost always this initiation takes place in official prostitution. What a brutal shock between reality and fantasy!; the illusion of love dreamt about for so long converts into a bitter and filthy maceration. What a disenchantment suffered by the initiated youth!; what malaise, displeasure and sadness. And, without doubt, it would have been truly beautiful to love and the initiation so different if true love had brought the adolescent to the woman ... The most rational system to regulate the sexual function is matrimony and early matrimony, the matrimony of the youth' (Higginson 1937: 300–1).

Bustamante Ruiz sees the solution not only in an anti-venereal battle that prescribes hygienic rules, but above all in the study of factors favouring prostitution and their destruction using criteria exalting the cult of the family (Bustamante Ruiz 1941: 133).

Structural changes were only a partial solution to the problem, ideational changes were also demanded. Sexual education would '[i]n effect advocate one sexual morality which would not place women in current masculine practices of uncontrolled liberty, but purify the customs of both sexes referring to what is called sexual instinct' (Bambarén 1937: 272).

The NACP's social impact was, to say the least, minimal. MacLean y Estenós characterized the abolitionist movement as a weak current, which declared prostitution illegal and those dedicated to it as delinquents (1942: 358). Their efforts did not lead to modification of the system of regulation. In fact, it became more institutionalized. The question remains, why did the abolitionist continue their battle?

Perhaps the answer lies in the fact that certain regulationist measures, such as the opening of Anti-Venereal Dispensaries were considered abolitionist victories. This measure was also promoted in the Anti-Venereal Law. According to Solano, abolitionist institutions were being incorporated into the regulation of prostitution without anyone being aware of it (1943: 291–2). Thus, the abolitionists' optimism seemed to be supported by their subjective interpretation of the events, changing regulationist measures into abolitionist successes. The NACP continued their fight until at least 1962.[26]

## JIRÓN HUATICA – ABOLITION OR REGULATION? THE CAMPAIGN OF THE MAGAZINE *¡YA!* (1949)

Peru was a very religious country until more or less 1930. Its religiosity was *sui generis*, basically founded on the idea 'What will the neighbours say?' ... So prostitution always had to be clandestine. But from a certain time, prostitution flourished openly in Jirón Huatica. It was not just one street, it was the whole avenue, all the blocks. There were prostitutes of all prices. The most expensive were Chilean and French. Well, they called them French because they were white and blonde. Most probably they were Chilean or Argentinean. There was a corner with a brand new house. Anyway, it wasn't anything out of this world but the women were white, tall and caught your attention – the prices they charged! On the side streets there were national prostitutes with other prices. The prices ranged from 5–10 *soles* and there were those who charged 25. There were also brothels and there were also those who worked independently. You went to dance and suppose you got together with one of them, you went to a room, paid, that was ... everything concentrated in one neighbourhood. (Doctor of Immunology working in the Callao Aids programme)

If you ask any man above the age of 50 about Jirón Huatica, a metamorphosis occurs. Generally, they get starry-eyed and begin to reminisce about the good old days when Jirón Huatica existed. They tell of its glory, never forgetting to include the fact that there were foreign women working there – 'Chilean' and 'European' women whose prices were higher than the nationals, insinuating their services were better, too. Many men initiated their sexual lives in one of the establishments of Jirón Huatica.

Jirón Huatica came into being in 1923 through a government ordinance ordering all houses of prostitution to be moved to this avenue, in the newly established neighbourhood of La Victoria – then thinly populated by families of working- and lower middle-class origins. In this era, La Victoria was situated at the city limits. It quickly transformed into an over-populated neighbourhood close to the heart of Lima housing the poorer strata of the working class.[27] Schools, churches and businesses sprang up, and several of them were located at a short distance from Jirón Huatica. Jirón Huatica, which originated as a 'red-light district' on the outskirts, gradually grew to become a part of La Victoria's centre.

On 8 February 1949, a bimonthly magazine appeared on the market entitled *¡Ya!*. In the eight months that followed it went on a journalistic crusade intended to move public and political opinion in favour of transferring Jirón Huatica's business to a less populated area. Every edition contained a column entitled 'Abolition or Regulation'? It presented letters, interviews from worried neighbours, school authorities, clergymen and even several prostitutes. In short, the column is interesting because it is one of the few spaces where you see how the prostitution problem is dealt with in practice. It illustrates the reproduction of prostitution discourse on a community level. It also exemplifies how the prostitute's image is moulded when her presence in society is no longer a theoretical abstraction but rather a part of the daily-life experiences of a community.

The magazine had a firm standpoint in relation to the occurrences in Jirón Huatica. It demanded the removal of this *barrio alegre* (wanton or merry neighbourhood) to a less populated area. Its intentions are clearly stated in the first issue.

If prostitution is impossible to eliminate, than at least these unhappy women should be obliged to exercise their profession in a place where they do not give such a repugnant example, where they do not tarnish the happiness of many families nor impair the reputation of a whole Capital. It would not be difficult to find a place. Inclusively, they could construct locales endowed with all the implements required by hygiene. Police control would be more rigorous, to combat the grave offence of men who are dedicated to exploit them. Also, they could establish sanitary offices specializing in attention and control ... We ask the authorities for comprehension and human feelings, and to think about the situation, and in the shortest period possible change the location of the women who presently 'work' at Jirón Huatica, so that the families can live peacefully and their children can go out on the streets. (1949: 1[1])

The proposed locale was to be called the *unidad roja* (the red unit). History appeared to be repeating itself. The magazine demanded the same thing that brought the women to Jirón Huatica in the first place. They wanted them removed because they were practising prostitution in a populated area and in inadequate hygienic conditions.

It should come as no surprise that the community, which on several occasions had complained to the authorities, was enthusiastic about the magazine's campaign. Their praises rang through every interview published by the magazine. One of their main concerns was the influence these activities had on their children. Children's innocence was at stake when they had to cross the street to run an errand or go to school. Male adolescents' curiosity could no longer be soothed with vague replies to their questions. It was considered dangerous for children to play on the streets of Huatica, but their cramped quarters did not allow for any other possibility. Girls were in need of protection from the bad example given by the women who worked there. A 'painful paragraph of a letter from a father' is published:

With the excuse of equivocation, they knock on the doors and make shameful propositions. Girls cannot cross the street freely and the boys blur their retinas with improper and repugnant scenes because these women overflow on to the pavement. Those who live on the west side of the district and are forced to cross Jirón Huatica are obliged to be a spectator to the scandals of these people ... (1949: 1[8])

The articles do not conceal the contempt felt for the prostitutes. The column ridiculed them. Quotation marks were placed sarcastically around words such as 'work' or 'profession'. On various occasions women working at Huatica went to the magazine's office to offer a statement. These encounters were published. They show the women's desire to collaborate with the campaign and the journalists' cynicism towards the women. In one interview a woman says, 'You know sir, I work at Huatica. I earn my living there.' The written reply was 'and we thought, and your death ...' (1949: 1[16]). Another issue reprints the conversation held with a prostitute in which the journalist's prejudices were apparent throughout and made her feel uncomfortable.

A woman arrived at the office who could have represented the majority of them. She came in the early evening. She was so thin she appeared weak. She was wearing an exaggerated amount of make-up. As a whole she gave the impression she was a convalescent who made herself up with brisk brush strokes, trying to cover the last signs of a long illness. She was very shy.

Could I talk with one of the editors of the magazine *¡Ya!*?

We are here to serve you. How can we help you?

You know ... I want to talk a bit about your campaign in the neighbourhood La Victoria.

A concerned mother, oh really?[28]

She became more shy. Our question made her feel disconcerted. She appears to regret she came here. We see the bags under her eyes, her long polished nails, the excessive amount of powder which almost falls in her daring neck-line.

Speak freely. What do you want?

I am a woman who works there ... I don't even know how I got into this. But I would like to tell you a few things. (1949: 1[9])

She tells them about the women's situation. How they are exploited and forced to pay exorbitant prices for their rooms. The women agree with the campaign in the hope of being less exploited. The passage ends with '[s]he leaves the office in her loud dress, high heels and a timidness we did not believe existed in these women' (1949: 1[9]).

The accompanying photographs demonstrated another dimension of the insolence displayed towards the prostitute. Every article had a picture portraying a typical street scene on Jirón Huatica, which always included prostitutes. The women feared the encounters with the magazine because they did not want their picture or their names to be published. As one woman put it when a journalist approached her, 'You are from the magazine ... I will answer your questions but don't take my picture. We also have friends who do not know about our lives. Then our pictures are printed and you can imagine ...' (1949: 1[3]). In one issue they tried to find an answer as to why the women received the photographer so aggressively 'with the most ridiculous expressions of slang ... and coarse words in other languages.[29] One more reason to pity those who have fallen so low. Another reason to insist on this battle' (1949: 1[6]).

The women approved of the campaign despite their treatment by the reporters. Basically, they promoted their own removal to improve their working conditions. Unfortunately, to a certain extent they also agreed with image of the prostitute being projected. The following letter illustrates both tendencies.

I am a woman who works at Huatica. I am one of the many wretched ones who have fallen into this disgrace to be exploited by foreign women. Living in constant martyrdom, pointed to by everyone, with the constant worry of falling ill at any moment. When one of us becomes ill they take away our identification card. Then we have to go to the Health Centre every day until they discharge us. Many days go by going back and forth until we recover.

In the street where we perform they charge 20–30 *soles* for each 'room'. In each locale three or four women exercise this sad trade. In some cases up to six.

I would like to say with all my heart that the campaign 'Abolition or Tolerance' should triumph, to put an end to the exploitation over the rooms. So that we are less exposed to catch diseases. So that there are better medical services. Basically, so that the numerous children are not exposed to the moral and material infection ...

In reference to moving the neighbourhood. All of us or almost all of us agree that it would be better to move us to a separate area. What we do not agree with is abolition because Lima would become filled with people attacked by venereal disease. (1949: 1[12])

Since the community, clergy, school authorities and even the prostitutes were in agreement, it should have been very easy to put the proposal into action. However, the magazine's later issues show that the removal of the prostitutes would take some time. The journalists dedicated one of the columns to an interview with the mayor of La Victoria, who of course totally agreed with their initiatives and showed the reporters that he had not been sitting around idly. He named all the important authorities he had talked to find a solution. It would take some time before the *unidad roja* could be realized and a lot of money and cooperation is needed from various municipalities. Meanwhile, the mayor offers a temporary solution which he is aware will not cure the problem but at any rate it will alleviate the symptoms. He suggests:

To avoid the shameful spectacle, we are thinking of blocking off each of the transversals of Jirón Huatica. I have talked to the Traffic Office. As soon as I obtain the superior authorization, the works will commence. We also hope that many of the well-off neighbours of the district will collaborate with us. We will raise brick walls. Important avenues like 28 de Julio will be totally blocked off; there will be no exit. The other streets' walls will have portals, but will be closed off for traffic. With this measure, the street will be isolated until the moment the removal becomes reality, which is the most important goal we are pursuing. (1949: 1[14])

The mayor's proposal was rejected by all sides including the prostitutes. They claimed that exploitation would increase if the street was closed off. This proposal is an excellent example of the 'anything goes' policy towards the prostitution problem, and of the ludicrous extremes people are willing to go to impede prostitution's bad influence and to make it invisible.

The closure of all the establishments of Jirón Huatica had to wait until a Municipal Ordinance came into effect on 12 August 1956. The street was renamed Renovación (Renovation) in an attempt to breath new life into it. Huatica's closure was the end of designated areas for prostitution. However, not even the abolitionists could have predicted that Lima would no longer have one red-light district but instead, as they say, it turned pink, as prostitution spread throughout the whole city.

The campaign of *¡Ya!* might have contributed to Jirón Huatica's closure but might also just have been another of the many moments in history when the prostitution problem flares up because of a group of concerned citizens or authorities, only to subside and lie dormant until the following episode.


PATTERNS OF REPETITION AND GENDER MEANINGS

The history of prostitution can be read as a giant enclosure orchestrated by two systems of thought. Far from being uneventful, much has taken place throughout the course of history. Yet, surprisingly, the historical events described in the previous pages share a likeness. Behind the historical development of prostitution are repetitive patterns which fabricate gender meanings that mould almost identical social representations of gender identities.

The Peruvian history of prostitution has basically flowed steadily in the direction of regulation. The brief moments of dissent provoked by the abolitionist alternative were not strong enough to make it change direction. Nonetheless, despite their outward appearances, the two discourses share fundamental similarities which can partially be ascribed to the privileged position of the authors, who started from the same notions of contemporary morality. The prostitute as an individual, her activities and her sexuality were the mirror image of what was considered correct and proper behaviour for a lady. The abolitionists may have given different reasons for the causes of prostitution and proposed contrasting solutions to those of the regulationists, but both discourses pinpointed the prostitute as the core of the problem and the key to its solution. In other words, the prostitute was constructed as the element which could be manipulated to produce the desired result. This result might be desirable for the 'establishment', but generally brought negative consequences to the prostitute. For instance, during the period in which the articles concerning Jirón Huatica were published, two solutions were proposed for solving the prostitution problem. Both involved measures which would directly repress the prostitute. Since the earliest stages of its development, the regulationist discourse has contributed to marginalizing women-who-prostitute. Another component which contributes to this process of marginalization is the frequent use of dualities to describe prostitution and the prostitute. Degradation versus vice, poverty versus lust, honour versus shame are just a few examples that permeate the publications of the regulationist discourse. This repetitive pattern tightly seals the gendered enclosure and indicates the beginnings of the making of a fixed identity for women-who-prostitute.

# 2 READ ALL ABOUT IT
## Gender Meanings and the Written Press

A DISCURSIVE EXPLOSION: 'THE TORMENTED PASSION BETWEEN THE MAGNATE AND THE COURTESAN'[1]

On 19 August 1990, the naked corpse of a woman, with one high-heeled shoe on her foot and the New Testament at her side, was found on a patio of one of the most affluent hotels in Lima, the Sheraton. It appeared she had fallen from one of the balconies. The remains of this unidentified body were transferred to the Central Morgue where her body remained unclaimed. Strangely enough, it was kept in one of the few functioning refrigerated cells, an unusual occurrence for a corpse which had not been identified or claimed. In addition, the funeral costs had been paid anonymously in advance.

For approximately three months, the death of this unidentified woman who would eventually be called Marita Alpaca filled the country's newspapers. The story that unfolded came to represent more than just the tragic death of a young, attractive woman. It reflected the Limanian reality – the power of the rich and the impotence of the poor, police corruption, women's position in society and the public's thirst for sensationalism. All the ingredients were present for a television soap opera. However, this drama was not fiction, it actually took place.

Marita Alpaca had been the lover or partner (depending on the version) for the past nine years of an extremely powerful man, Leandro Reaño, vice-president of one of the most influential Peruvian banks. They dined together frequently and took up residence regularly in various high-class hotels in Lima. On the night of her death, they returned to the hotel and, as the hotel attendants explained, there seemed nothing abnormal in their behaviour. The police investigation concluded the death was suicide. Partially due to the pressure exerted by her family, certain inconsistencies concerning the case surfaced.

Marita entered the morgue unidentified, but her name was released after the magnate had safely left the country, which, it was rumoured, he accomplished with help from some government officials. He was the anonymous person who paid the funeral costs. Procedural faults discovered in the police investigation suggested police corruption. Burn marks were found on her clothing, blood was found on the mattress lying on the floor, her pocketbook with her identification had mysteriously disappeared and the autopsy was undeniably incomplete. All of these details suggested that violence had taken place in the hotel room and something was being covered up. Reaño maintained throughout that it was suicide and he was 'the witness of the self-elimination of a person he loved'. Marita's mother was convinced it was murder. Further investigation was called for. Several of the original police officials were dismissed from the case and the investigation continued.

The blood found in the hotel room was said to have come from an abortion. Marita was pregnant. Her mother said she had gone to Reaño to tell him she was planning to keep the baby and end the relationship. Reaño denied ever knowing she was pregnant, but, somewhere along the line, the suggestion spread that he wanted to keep the baby and she did not, giving a motive for suicide. The body was exhumed to complete the autopsy. However, her uterus had inexplicably disappeared, bringing this track of the investigation to a dead end.

Until the end of September, the image painted of Marita was of a very attractive woman who, as a single mother, worked as a ground-stewardess and aspired to be a model. Just as it was becoming more credible that her alleged suicide was murder and things were beginning to look bad for Reaño, a new bit of information surfaced. Marita had been picked up by the police in a raid on an illegal brothel in Miraflores in 1985 and registered as a clandestine prostitute. Her record with her photograph was published in the newspapers.

It cannot be determined with certainty who was behind this information leak. A possible culprit is Reaño's lawyer, who may have deliberately given this piece of information to the press, to taint her image and sway public opinion in favour of his client. Who was behind it is less relevant than how the media's coverage shifted when Marita was pronounced to be a clandestine prostitute. This prompted an outpouring of speculations and thoughts concerning the subject.

Was Marita a prostitute or not? Her mother fervently denied it and was certain the document was forged to defile her daughter's memory. A credible explanation, considering the anterior practices of corruption cited in this case. In an interview, her mother claimed that Marita was invited to a party by Reaño who never mentioned it was to take place in a brothel – an incredible story. As one journalist suggested, if Reaño was present he would not have had a problem arranging with the police to let her go. If she was prostituting, the only thing that can be said is that on this particular occasion she was prostituting. Since the police have no way of keeping track of clandestine prostitutes unless they are arrested, no conclusions can be reached concerning whether she prostituted before or after this date. Yet, there is one assertion that can be made with certainty: women-who-prostitute are vulnerable and unprotected. The ease with which this document, forged or not, was released to the press, demonstrates how readily the police archives can be used against prostitutes.

Various positions were presented in the media in regard to Marita's presumed occupation. Reaño, who was temporarily residing in Buenos Aires, Argentina, stated in an exclusive televised interview that he wanted to call it to the media's attention that what they were doing was harming their children (his own child and Marita's). He states, 'I had a Jesuit education and I must say that there are two things that Jesus does not pardon, scandalizing children and humiliating women.' Further on, after expounding on Jesus' understanding for Mary Magdalene, he was asked his opinion concerning the publication of Marita's record in the papers. He replied, 'I already said that Jesus gave a message of love and pardon and he is merciful. We are merciless when we are obliged to correct a person. Will this contribute to Marita coming back? She is gone' (*Página Libre*, 1 October 1990). Reaño's answer is open to different interpretations. He does not deny she was a prostitute, although he does not blatantly admit it either. He appropriates the Bible teachings to reproach the media and sends a message implying that he was fulfilling Christian duty. Marita might have been a 'fallen woman' but she deserved to be saved.

Postulations concerning Reaño's innocence or guilt were derived from different interpretations of the significance of Marita being a prostitute. In Reaño's hearing, his lawyer stated that Marita's suicide was evoked by a chain of frustrations she experienced in her life, one of them being that, as a prostitute, she 'had sexual relations without love and affection' (*La República*, 10 November 1990). In *Página Libre* the hypothesis of suicide is disputed because being a prostitute implies that Marita was not the innocent, unfortunate woman whose body fell or was thrown from a balcony, as the media led the public to believe, but rather that she was a woman with five years' experience in a 'risky profession practised in secrecy and danger. Marita Alpaca was a woman who knew what she was doing and not a naive person at the mercy of the circumstances' (24 September 1990). This train of thought continues in a later article. The fact that Marita was a prostitute taints Reaño's lawyer's hypothesis of suicide. 'Would a prostitute commit suicide because her lover wanted her to have an abortion? It is unlikely' (*Página Libre*, 1 October 1990).

A final interpretation was found in a folder left by MRTA (Movimiento Revolucionario Tupac Amaru – one of the subversive movements active in Peru at the time) after the bombing of one of Reaño's family businesses. They state, the case of Marita is: 'not an exception, but a frequent occurrence that shows one of the aspects of the situation of women in our country. In summary, a single mother out of necessity can arrive at prostitution. This is something which is occurring more frequently, especially for the women of our country whose situation is a response to the suffocating economy ... and the decomposition of present society ... There are many Marita Alpacas in

Peru who are submitted to the power of the rich and the exploiters' (*La República*, 21 October 1990). According to MRTA Marita was exploited not only as a prostitute but also in a relationship with a rich and powerful man. She was a victim of the system.

Reaño returned to Lima for his trial. In March 1991, the charges were dropped for lack of evidence and he was freed. The circumstances leading to his conditional freedom are not relevant for the further developments of this chapter. What is of great importance is the way prostitution was used to manipulate public opinion and the judicial system. The fact that Marita Alpaca may have been a prostitute was debated and torn apart in an attempt to locate its relevance for the alleged murder. Her actions as a prostitute were not under discussion, but, rather, attention was focused on the implications of what it meant to be a prostitute.

The discursive explosion which took place around the death of Marita Alpaca is one of the present day illustrations of how women-who-prostitute are constructed to be a version of the Other in their own society and how the notion of promiscuity underpins this construction. Different interpretations of the circumstances were given, but all of them took as their point of departure that a woman who prostitutes is no ordinary woman. Branded a prostitute, everything a woman does and thinks is filtered through this lens, transforming her means of making money into her gender identity.

This anecdote serves as an excellent introduction for a chapter aimed at disentangling the gender meanings which construct the prostitute's identity because it succinctly exposes various meanings of femininity, sexuality and the prostitute from different social perspectives.

Women-who-prostitute are trapped in gendered enclosures constructed by this imagery. Once a woman becomes a prostitute, her prospects of improving her situation are limited. The only accepted alternative proposed by an array of social institutions is 'rehabilitation', 'reinsertion', 're-education', all of which are different terms for the same alternative. Women who cannot or do not choose to leave the profession behind them, find themselves in a no-way-out situation.

The discussion in the following pages concentrates predominantly on the written representation of prostitution. It will use information taken from two distinct sources: the media and Peruvian feminist documents. The choice of analysing the media's representation of prostitution is intimately related to certain of its attributes. It reflects the positions of authorities. It not only intends to inform the public, it amplifies public opinion. At times it crosses the border into sensationalism. Nevertheless, sensationalist accounts present crystal-clear imagery. This discussion is followed by an analysis of the counter-discourse produced from within the feminist movement. It is the only accepted alternative to the hegemonic discourse. In its own particular way, each discourse produces notions and strategies fortifying the walls of the gendered enclosures.

## (MIS)REPRESENTATIONS OF PROSTITUTION AND THE PROSTITUTE IN THE WRITTEN MEDIA

The subject of prostitution appears in the media on a regular basis. During the period of my investigation, I reviewed approximately 100 articles on the subject, taken from the 'serious' press rather than the sensationalist tabloids. The earliest was published in 1972 and the most recent in 1993.

There are four different, intricately related themes, which construct imagery of the prostitute and prostitution. The first concerns the regulation of prostitution. The second is directly related to working conditions and hazards such as crimes or protest actions. The third group has increased substantially in the past five years with the growing concern for what has been referred to as 'the plague of the century' – Aids. Finally, the largest group of articles found on the subject are contextual ones in which (a type of) prostitution or the prostitute is illuminated. This discussion is limited to an analysis of a selected number of articles, events and representations which illustrate the imagery used in relation to prostitution most lucidly.

### Control and the Notion of Danger

The image of the prostitute is intimately linked with the notion of control. This relationship can be traced back to the establishment of the regulation of prostitution, which organized it around standardized norms, thereby permitting its control. Accordingly, the prostitute becomes the essential cog for guaranteeing the successful functioning of the system of regulation.

The media's general posture towards prostitution resonates with the hegemonic discourse indicating regulation as the only viable solution to the prostitution problem. The articles report on infractions such as tax evasion by owners of hotels used for clandestine prostitution, police raids of illegal establishments or on the streets, and campaigns to clamp down on the mafia who are in control of the illegal establishments. All the articles show that the police are doing their job to eliminate all forms of prostitution not conforming to the norms stipulated by the system of regulation. Although these articles could also be read as evidence of the malfunctioning of this system – for example, illegal brothels are proof that there are types of prostitution that function outside its jurisdiction – the media rarely comment on this. The only critique voiced is intended to expose ineffective components of the system in need of repair and urge their treatment.

The acceptance of the regulation of prostitution signifies the uncritical endorsement of the categories of registered and clandestine prostitutes. This division is ingrained in the Peruvian perception of prostitution. As in the past, these notions and assumptions brought into existence by the system of regulation determine the representation of the clandestine prostitute in all areas. The controlled prostitutes (registered) and the uncontrolled (clandestine) are portrayed differently. Registered prostitutes are treated relatively more fairly than their clandestine colleagues. They are more often assumed to be hardworking health-conscious mothers as opposed to the disease-infested clandestine prostitute who is more ignorant and more inclined to self-indulge in drugs or alcohol. Hence, the media buttresses the notion that clandestine prostitution should be targeted as the domain in need of control. Articles written on clandestine prostitution often use metaphors depicting its uncontrollable growth. Subsequently, the clandestine prostitute is considered a danger to society's well-being. The notions of danger and control are inseparable and function to legitimize any type of action taken to impede the growth of clandestine prostitution.

Talk of cleaning up the streets of clandestine prostitution is a recurring theme among municipal officials. During the period researched, I encountered two initiatives which were taken to resolve the problem of clandestine prostitution.

In 1972, the Prefect of Lima proposed a project for the construction of four large brothels each 'having the capacity to hold 600 women'. This brothel complex, planned to be located on the outskirts of Lima, would provide health and other services, such as rehabilitation workshops for *mujeres de la vida* (women of the life)(*Ojo*, 24 September 1972). The announcement of this plan caused a momentary discursive explosion in the press.

The Catholic Church responded to this proposal with indignation. An official communiqué was published in various newspapers stating their objections and their position with regard to prostitution. The solution proposed to eradicate clandestine prostitution was considered, in all its components, degrading to women. It was implausible that this project would rehabilitate them. The Church was convinced the prostitutes would sink even deeper into their situation. The existence and propagation of prostitution was considered a frontal attack on Christian morality. 'We believe ... to legalize prostitution would not be humane.[2] To marginalize women would not be just. To convert them into merchandise would not be promoting a person's dignity and instead of liberating women they would be degraded' (newspaper article without source). Thus, their solution to the prostitution problem was abolitionism. New wind was blown briefly into the old debate of regulation versus abolition. *Ojo* published another article with responses to the Church's communiqué from prominent male citizens. Three out of the four men interviewed entirely agreed with the Prefect's proposal. As a psychiatrist stated: 'I completely agree with the construction of modern and separate *barrios rojos* (red-light districts). This will avoid the proliferation of venereal diseases. Nonetheless, there is a negative aspect which concerns moral values and customs: prostitution cannot be a source of work. I think that in the new establishments these women must be re-educated' (24 September 1972).

The silence after the initial clamour proved this project would go down in history as another unsuccessful attempt to curb clandestine prostitution. No establishments were built nor was there talk of their construction in the years to come. However, that this was considered the only viable solution to eradicate clandestine prostitution was proven again in 1993 when a council-woman of the Municipality of Lima proposed a similar plan. Her concern for the 'deplorable conditions in which clandestine prostitution operates feeding the propagation of Aids ...' led her to propose an 'audacious initiative' to move the women to the outskirts of Lima creating *zonas rosas* (pink zones) where they would be controlled on a regular basis' (*Caretas*, 16 December 1993).[3] Additionally, a new law would be needed to establish sanctions against the illegal practice of prostitution. This new turn would ultimately discourage clandestine prostitution, making it undesirable.[4] Moving clandestine prostitutes to a legally controlled establishment would also have economic advantages: new sources of work, such as new lines of public transport to the establishment and the possibility for the municipality to receive new sources of income with its incorporation in the formal sector (*Caretas*, 16 December 1993). Thus, the removal of clandestine prostitutes from the centre of Lima would not only resolve a part of the prostitution problem, but was a modernist twist in neo-liberal plans for urban development. Like the previous initiatives, the 1993 plan has not been realized.

How short is the collective memory of a society? Had it already forgotten the experience of Huatica earlier in this century? Huatica was chosen for its advantageous location at the outskirts of the city. Rapidly, it became incor-porated into urban life. If anything this experience should have caused the initiators of both plans to be cautious in suggesting a similar undertaking. Any area momentarily situated on the outskirts, in a blink of an eye could be incorporated inside the city's boundaries. Putting practicalities aside, these nearly identical plans illustrate that if regulation is regarded as the only viable solution, there are few alternatives for achieving the control of the prostitute. Thus the only acceptable solutions will be replicas of the original plan. This is one of the clearest examples of how regulation and the notions of control/danger are repeatedly reproduced throughout the course of history. There are few indications this will change in the future.

The discursive explosion which was provoked by the Prefect's plan in 1972 reveals another intricacy tied up in the discourse of prostitution. This was expressed most clearly in the statement given by the psychiatrist. His words reflect the double-edged moral tightly woven into the regulation. Prostitution is sanctioned because it is a 'necessary evil'. Prostitutes are needed so that men can satisfy their insatiable sexual desires. Yet the women who work as prostitutes are an affront to society's morals and customs, and need to be re-educated. As necessary as it is for the government to control prostitution, this same control should not stimulate its propagation. The system of regulation is founded on a schism: solutions proposed for prosti-tution are incompatible with the solutions proposed for prostitutes. What would become of prostitution if all prostitutes were to be re-educated?

Following this line of thought, it is not surprising that there is no solution to the prostitution problem.

*Working Women*

Just as it is customary for newspapers to present prostitution as a problem, so it is equally unusual to find any recognition of the problems prostitutes encounter in their work. Prostitution is rarely conceptualized as a profession, with good, bad or dangerous working conditions.

Articles sporadically appear which report on crimes committed against prostitutes, the majority of whom are clandestine. Working as a clandestine prostitute is riskier than working in a legal brothel. However, it is not this dimension of danger that is referred to in the discussions of clandestine prostitution.

Various articles have reported on collective protests organized by registered prostitutes to improve working conditions. Although one would expect these incidents to be newsworthy, the media does not pay much attention to them. The articles use the women's actions as a starting point to expound on more general issues.

One of these protests occurred in the first half of 1982. It appears it was a tumultuous time for the women at the brothels of Callao (the port of Lima). The exact circumstances are difficult to abstract from the few published articles. The Prefect of Callao ordered the closure of all the brothels with entrances on the Avenida Centenario. The brothels El Trocadero, La Salvaje, El Botecito and Mi Jardín were closed. The first three brothels were re-opened shortly afterwards, having moved their entrance to a different avenue, but Mi Jardín remained closed.[5] An article published on 15 February begins by stating: 'not all of the problems which effect the "sellers of love" of the brothels of Callao have been resolved. At 10 o'clock in the morning today, a delegation of "these workers" [from Mi Jardín] met with the president of the Commission of the Family of the House of Representatives to expound on their problems.' According to the group, their continued closure was a result of a power game played by the owner of the other three brothels, who wanted to buy Mi Jardín. However, the owner of Mi Jardín decided to give the women and employees the opportunity to buy the brothel. This decision made the other brothel-owner furious and, being a woman with important connections, she used her influence to keep it closed.

The employees and the prostitutes decided to form a cooperative and requested a one-year term to pay for the location which would permit them to secure the maintenance of their children.[6] They planned to run the brothel in an orderly fashion and divide the income equally amongst the members. The cooperative would also be willing to contribute a part of its revenue to the *pueblo jóven* (squatter settlement/shantytown) situated nearby which called for the brothel's closure. As one of the members said: 'We are willing to give a part of our monthly revenues to this community for good works. With that money they would be able to construct their parish church and a police station. Hopefully, they will comprehend we are mothers of families and do not have any other work or a husband to watch over us' (*Ojo*, 15 February 1982).

That things had not quietened down for all the women who worked in Callao became clear with the publication of an article in *El Diario*, a socialist newspaper. The article was the first in a five-day series. The articles presented a Marxist-feminist analysis of prostitution (22–26 February 1982). Prostitution was conceptualized as exploitation and the regulatory system was explained and criticized, as well as the role of the state in its propagation. The articles relied heavily on sources and interviews provided by a feminist organization which works with clandestine prostitutes, and departs from the standpoint that prostitution is a form of sexual slavery. This will be discussed in detail later. The incident which ignited the newspaper's concern was described briefly in the first article. Approximately 500 prostitutes occupied the brothels of Callao protesting 'their maltreatment, their social abandonment and the abuses they receive as victims of the mafias which control the prostitution business' (22 February 1982). A commission constituted by members of the House of Representatives went to the brothels to talk with the women. The article continues, '[t]his explosive protest will be extinguished promptly. Perhaps certain measures will be taken. But the problem at the bottom, the generator of prostitution continues unyielding at the base of present-day society' (*El Diario*, 22 February 1982). This was the only mention of their protest in the series of articles. Their demands and their negotiations with this commission were not reported.

However, there is evidence that the women's protest made a momentary impact. Two articles which appeared during this period quoted government officials on the subject. The Minister of the Interior announced that a multi-sector commission would be established to study the 'problem of prostitution in the country and to establish regulatory standards. It will also look for ways to tend to their rehabilitation and rescue the many women who are victims of such a vice' (*La Prensa*, 25 February 1982).[7] Another article, entitled 'Prostitution in Peru' presented an interview with Guisti La Rosa, who was a member of the commission who went to visit the prostitutes. The representative stated that 'nobody would like to see their fiancée, their daughter, their sister or mother subjected to prostitution. From a humanistic perspective, the presence of prostitution is repugnant' (*Perspectiva*, 14 March 1982). He pointed out that several constitutional articles opposed its existence and that '[t]he majority are abandoned single mothers and would leave this work if they found something else. These women find themselves obliged to prostitute to provide their children with bread' (*Perspectiva*, 14 March 1982).

Is this the type of response the women envisaged? Is this what they were trying to achieve with their protests? Unfortunately, there is no clear reply.

Certainly, they wanted society to show more comprehension for their situation and to recognize they did not prostitute for pleasure but because it was their only means of making money. But did they expect that comprehension would provoke statements which called for their rehabilitation and the abolition of prostitution? There are clues which suggest they were searching for answers in a different direction.

On 16 June, *El Diario* published an interview with the leader of the union of *El Trocadero*. Several months later, the newspaper returned to visit to inquire if they had been able to organize a union representing the four brothels. They reprinted the conversation they held with one of the leaders, named Fanny Dusek.

Fanny told them that the desire to organize had subsided after the initial crisis. Nevertheless, the women and employees of her brothel started procedures to unionize and in 25 days the union would be officially established. She hoped it would serve as an example for other women.

The union collected dues and was planning to open a bank account. The money would be used for all types of emergency which would arise. They tried to make an appointment with the owner to talk about the problems, such as the hygienic conditions of the workplace, the state of their rooms and the abrupt dismissal of personnel, but the owner refused (*El Diario,* 16 July 1982).

This brief review of the events shows the efforts of a group of prostitutes to improve their working conditions. The women had specific demands and plans for the future. Yet the media paid very little attention to what they were trying to accomplish. Their representation of the events disempowered the women's collective actions. The newspapers confined their reports to a few essential facts and counterbalanced this with interviews, analysis and opinionated statements addressing the broader issues concerning the existence of prostitution, or how control could be improved, or how to make it disappear. The use of expressions such as 'sellers of love' or 'those workers' in the description of the women's actions discredits their struggle as workers. In keeping with the Marxist tradition, *El Diario* did present the women as *luchadoras* (fighters, strugglers), but this was counterpoised with testimonies of women who described the hardship of their lives, their hatred for their work and their guilty feelings. The newspapers' coverage contributed to the victimization of the prostitute. To a large extent, the women have internalized the public image and enact it. The gesture of the women of Mi Jardín who offered to give money to the nearby community reflects their preoccupation with convincing society that they are good at heart and not promiscuous. They reject the way they earn a living, but as mothers they are left with no other choice than to prostitute. Their statements endorse the discursive portrayal of the prostitute. If they stepped out of their position in the discourse, they would run the risk of losing the only respectable image given to them – the abandoned mother who is a victim of her circumstances and hates what she does to earn a living. However, their recognition of prostitution as work – like any other job – and their desire that society should recognize it as such, could be interpreted as a crack in the discourse. Unfortunately, this angle was of no interest to the media. In fact, the media contributed to silencing these moments, either by not reporting them or by transforming them into idiosyncratic instances in their working lives. Any potential improvements or permanent changes which could have resulted from these actions disappeared as quickly as they arose.

## The Vector of Illness

Since the appearance of the first recognized case of Aids in 1983, prostitution has been indicated as one of the principal vectors of this illness, along with homosexuals, transvestites and the category of the bisexual. The association of prostitution with Aids is not a distinguishing characteristic of the Peruvian context. Since the pandemic outbreak, women-who-prostitute have been earmarked globally as a 'risk group' (e.g. Day 1988; Brock 1989). Obviously, this is related to the inherent nature of their work – having a multitude of sexual partners. What should be defined as risky sexual practices is generally confused with promiscuity. In this setting, there is another element which strengthens the association of prostitutes with Aids. Prostitution's association with illness originates from the discovery that venereal diseases are sexually transmitted and regulatory measures were designed to combat them. Although the media has recently shifted its attention from this 'risk group' to the other three, prostitution's association with Aids, and in particular, the association of clandestine prostitution with Aids, remains intact.

There is one aspect which makes the situation in Lima different from that in many other countries. The percentage of prostitutes who are carriers of the HIV virus is less than 1 per cent.[8] In other words, the prevalence of the HIV virus amongst this group of women is extremely low. I am not suggesting that this is sufficient to let down one's guard. However, the actual situation does not merit the media's approach to the subject, which, as we will see below, has constructed a discourse of panic instead of initiating a campaign of prevention, which would be more appropriate under the circumstances.

A 1987 article entitled 'Commission Declares War on Aids. Prostitutes and Gays Will be Checked' states that: '[out of] 200 ladies of the night, less than 1 percent are passive carriers of the Aids virus. Although this amount appears to be low, it is alarming if a projection is made that every one of these women goes with ten men a week ... These women have contracted this illness because of their promiscuous way of life, because of anal and vaginal lesions and their contact with foreigners' (*Hoy*, 17 September 1987).

The magazine *Gente* felt it was its duty to warn the public of the impending threat which awaits the visitors to the brothels. It was estimated that eight out of 1,000 prostitutes were carriers of the virus. 'The love nests have converted into hostels of death' (7 June 1990). In particular, clandestine prostitutes were indicated as the most difficult group to reach and the most menacing in terms of contagion.

> The task [of prevention] is even more difficult with the women who work on the streets. Clandestine prostitutes are brought by force to those Anti-Venereal Centres by the National Police. They raid the places where women of all ages congregate who do not carry out health control and are predisposed to be infected and propagate the Aids virus. The terrible thing is that they do not understand the danger of this illness. In general they feel persecuted which makes it impossible to subject them to the test, advice and recommendations.
>
> They are women who have six to eight children and are used to society's hostility. They do not trust the authorities. Many of them complained of being subjected to extortion by corrupt police who abuse their authority to ask for sexual favours or money. Unfortunately, it is not possible to carry out an inspection. The majority do not give their real names and it is nearly impossible to find them again, given that they never stay in one specific place.
>
> Another lamentable fact is that these women do not take care of themselves. The money they receive from each client is destined for their children's nutrition or for their vices, forgetting about their own health. (*Gente*, 7 June 1990)

The article urges the Ministry of Health to take measures because the Anti-Venereal Centres do not have enough resources. 'Do we have to wait until the mortality statistics increase before the central government will take measures?' (*Gente*, 7 June 1990).

The notion of the uncontrollable clandestine prostitute takes on greater significance in relation to an incurable disease. The system of regulation is unable to control the spread of clandestine prostitution and therefore it is unable to control the spread of Aids in society at large. This has reinforced the already existing claim that, unless forced, clandestine prostitutes will not take responsibility for their own health, turning every clandestine prostitute into a walking death trap. Despite public and state preoccupation with the 'danger' this group presents to society, there are no studies available which treat the subject seriously, particularly with regard to health and sexual attitudes and practices. Statistics may show a higher rate of venereal diseases among this group, but the only thing this proves is the need for more work on prevention. It does not disclose anything concerning the steps they undertake to cure themselves. It is assumed that clandestine prostitutes would not seek professional medical help if they were not forced to. This assumption is unsubstantiated and founded on regulationist hearsay. It will remain unfounded until more efforts are taken to work with this group of prostitutes.

Yet, the existence of the regulation makes it difficult to develop effective prevention campaigns for clandestine prostitutes which could help change their sexual practices. Posters have been put up in prostitution establishments, and there was a plan to bring a unit of the Anti-Venereal Centre to these unauthorized establishments for testing and prevention information.[9] However, the development and success of integrated programmes of prevention are impeded by the contradiction enwrapped in the regulation. How can state agencies work with a group they label illegal, and whose growth they seek to inhibit? Hence, if the number of HIV carriers among this group does increase in the future, the blame will lie partially with the workings of the system of regulation.

The discourse of Aids has moved faster than the actual situation, and has been fed by notions engendered within the constraints of the regulation. In this sense, it adds another dimension to the images which construct a gendered enclosure around women-who-prostitute.

## *The (De)Contextualized Prostitute*

The media's coverage of the subject of prostitution produces snapshot images which arouse compassion, sexual excitement or aversion. A tension exists between the whore – the sellers of love, the ladies of the night – and the abandoned and/or unwed mother who does it for her children. The depiction of the prostitute oscillates between these two extremes and encompasses all prostitutes; that is, all those who do not engage in this activity for pleasure or to buy luxuries. This latter group is the antithesis of the average prostitute working in Lima.[10] How is it possible for the same woman to be promiscuous, immoral and at the same time virtuous in fulfilling her vocation of motherhood? Yet, these images are placed side by side in the media's representations with an assumed and unexplained logic. One article I encountered illustrates this excellently. A photo covering two pages introduces the article. A middle-aged woman who is wearing a bathing suit is stretched out in a provocative position on a disarranged bed. The walls are plastered with pin-ups of semi-naked young women. The title of the article reads, 'Three Fifty-Year-Old Tigresses Tell Their Story: Women of the Life' (*Sí*, 12 March 1990). The article tells the story of these three women, the hardships they endured as mothers which gave them the final push into prostitution. The photos and a few comments about the good old days when they earned good money, suggest they are in their decline. Their sex appeal has dried up but they still try (with little success) to keep up appearances. The most striking element of this article is the discord existing between the sensationalist photographs and the ordinary testimonies of the women.

The motivation for many women to prostitute is profoundly related to their civil status as single mothers. In fact, many prostitutes are aware of the ideological weight this contains and use it strategically in their dealings with clients. Some childless women are suddenly struggling mothers of two and a mother of two is suddenly a mother of four. Whether this was done to evoke more compassion, make them seem credible, or was intended as a hidden form of ridicule of the client, is hard to say; nonetheless, it illustrates their astute awareness of society's expectations.

Nevertheless, their social reality is often reduced to this one dimension and the related hardships. In this context, being an abandoned/single mother reinforces the exploited, victimized image. Their agency is channelled into this sanctioned social identity.

The media maintains two hypersexual images of the prostitute.[11] Both images are underscored with a large doses of promiscuity. The first is the appealing sensual whore alluded to in expressions or labels highlighting sexual pleasure. This transmits the message that her sensuality is second nature instead of acknowledging it as an acquired trick of the trade. To be able to distinguish the other hypersexual version of the whore one must be in possession of the knowledge of the sexual qualities that constitute a sensual whore. The flip side – the negative qualities associated with the notion of promiscuity contains one or more of the following attributes: (1) she is a cheap imitation of the real thing; (2) she possesses unattractive, vulgar sexual qualities which she shamelessly flaunts as if they were not; (3) she is physically beyond being considered desirable – being either too ugly or too old or both – but disgracefully attempts to prove otherwise; and (4) she does not recognize all of the above and kids herself that she can continue. In their entirety these characteristics de-eroticize the whore. The article on the 'Three Fifty-year-old Tigresses' is an illustration of this tendency.

An unofficial consensus exists with regard to the expectations of a whore. This was articulated in an article as followed: 'The most requested women, whether it be for their attractive figure, for their pretty face or their pleasant treatment ... have regular customers ... The ugly ones' style is mechanical, semi-computerized, cold, without affection, without a greeting. The client enters and leaves without any form of human communication' (*Semana 7*, 30 September 1990). This description presents a paradox. According to public opinion a woman who prostitutes is not supposed to like her work. Any signs of pleasure could bring her into the category of a prostitute who works to buy luxuries or for pleasure. However, when a woman treats prostitution like any other job or shows indifference, she is accused of being a bad whore. A prostitute has to make the client feel good and cannot show she is faking it. Women-who-prostitute are in an extremely difficult situation; it appears they cannot do anything right.

In sum, the articles intended to provide a context to the public – to let them know who is the woman behind the prostitute and what her work entails – do not deviate from the discursive notions of the prostitute constructed in the regulation and its implementation. In fact, they make these extreme notions, bound up in the duality of the mother and the whore, come to life. They strengthen the assumed logic that it is necessary to control prostitution and at the same time find ways to help the women 'rehabilitate'. Hence, the schism which positions the prostitute and prostitution at odds is reflected in the fragments which constitute the hegemonic image of the prostitute in the written press.

## THE COUNTER-DISCOURSE: FEMINISM AND SEXUAL SLAVERY

In the previous pages, brief references have been made to the feminist standpoint towards prostitution. The newspapers often include an interview with a member of the activist feminist group which works with clandestine prostitutes, or their literature is quoted extensively. As stated earlier, the feminists' position on prostitution is the only accepted alternative to the hegemonic discourse. Feminist non-governmental organizations (NGOs), to a greater or lesser extent, have appropriated their standpoint. Their counter-discourse debunks the myths of prostitution and proposes different political strategies which overtly oppose the strategies engendered by regulation.

The organization's dedication to improving the women's situation, and their expertise, has made them the only effective group with the objective of empowering clandestine prostitutes as individuals. The relationship they have constructed with this group of women in the last 20 years is based on mutual respect. Their protective stance, guarding the anonymity of the prostitutes, has led to their adamant refusal of every request made by the international and national media for contacts with prostitutes. Their methodology merits a great deal of respect. The points under discussion here are related to elements within their discourse which contribute to the construction of imagery which entraps women-who-prostitute within a gendered enclosure.

To begin with, the sexual slavery theory is a variation of the women's oppression theory which characterized feminist theory and activism for the previous two decades. It would be mistaken to conclude that, because feminist theory has moved on, the sexual slavery theory is outdated and no longer relevant. As recently as June 1995, at an international meeting organized by UNESCO called Violence, Sexual Exploitation of Human Beings and International Action, their closing statements and recommendations echo the notions of prostitution found in the sexual slavery theory. Hence, this theory is alive and highly visible in political views and strategies upheld by international agencies and local NGOs.

In a document written by the organization, prostitution is defined as a: 'sexual slavery of women desperately trying to survive, women with little or no education or workplace skills, women with a limited amount of self-esteem due to the status of women in our patriarchical society, a condition which has existed for centuries. It is not possible to call that which is slavery a profession' (unpublished, 10 March 1990). Prostitution is the most extreme expression of women's subordination in a patriarchal society. Further on they state: 'As long as society instrumentalizes women as a sexual object, as long as men consider sex as merchandise acquired by force, by money or conquest, prostitution will be perennial in our society. And as long as women are negated in their right to be a person, as long as they are conditioned to consider themselves as objects of pleasure for men, they will be candidates for sexual exploitation in marriage, at work and, finally, in the commercialized sex industry.' Thus, prostitution's existence is intrinsically related to male domination. The prostitute is positioned in society as a victim, whose possibilities in life have been determined beforehand by patriarchal society.

The conceptualization of prostitution as sexual slavery is simultaneously an assertion that it cannot be considered work. This standpoint implies that any initiative or measure which results in the legalization or recognition of prostitution as a profession will be contested. Consequently, the literature launches a frontal attack on the system of regulation. Moreover, the adherents of the sexual slavery theory will not oppose collective protests or the unionization of registered prostitutes but they will not offer their assistance. More importantly, they choose to work with the women who are most adversely effected by the existence of the regulation system. 'This prostitution is "clandestine" not because it escapes the possibilities of control. It is "clandestine" precisely because it is illegal and permits the police, and municipal authorities to collect bribes and quotas ... Regulated and clandestine prostitution equally result in the exploitation of women. Both systems are controlled by pimps, procurers, administrators of hotels and members of the police and the state' (EL POZO, n.d.).

The organization denounces the regulation and calls for its abolition. Their argument can be summarized as follows: 'We oppose regulation because it converts the State into an accomplice in the exploitation of women and promotes clandestine prostitution which functions on the basis of bribes. We denounce the ineffective "sanitary control" which justifies the regulation of prostitution. Said control is discriminatory (it is only applied to the prostitute) and does not protect their health nor avoid contagious diseases' (EL POZO, n.d.).

The organization considers the abolition of the system of regulation: 'as the first preliminary necessary step in any programme of action to combat prostitution. However, the repeal of regulation is a preparatory step and is insufficient in itself; it must be accompanied by measures directed at the prevention of prostitution, the re-adaptation of the persons who practise it, the repression of the traders and exploiters and the prevention and treatment of venereal diseases' (Creatividad y Cambio 1984). Included among the preventive measures are equal pay for women, sexual education, the organization of services to help young people find a job, establishment of day care centres for single, abandoned or divorced mothers (Creatividad y Cambio 1984).

The feminists' counter-discourse offers several points which shake the foundation of the hegemonic discourse. Like the abolitionist doctrine, it exposes how regulating prostitution serves to uphold the myth that prostitution is a 'necessary evil' and pinpoints aspects of the system of regulation which contribute to strengthening the prostitute's vulnerable position. Nonetheless, it continually ignores women's agency in favour of images of the exploited victim. The sexual slavery theory fights against the existence of prostitution and attempts to attack its existence from its origins: 'women's oppression'. This point of departure impedes the development of tools aimed to improve prostitutes' actual working situation. The feminist discourse on prostitution constructs a discontinuity between long-term objectives and the practical situation of all women-who-prostitute. In an attempt to empower women, it negates a necessary, indispensable terrain to accomplish this objective, namely, the empowerment of women-who-prostitute as prostitutes, so that they can ultimately decide for themselves what are the best alternatives in their own lives.

## FIXED IMAGES WITH NO WAY OUT

Few changes have taken place in the discourses of prostitution since the earliest publications. The old images and assumptions have not been discarded, but have been modernized to confront and tackle new problems such as Aids, ineffective regulation, the chronic economic crisis and new actors, such as homosexuals and transvestites, who have entered the scene. One of the most outstanding characteristics of these discourses is that they are unresponsive to their context. They are resilient in the face of change to whatever is going on in the context.

The contemporary situation manifests the results of more than 80 years of the functioning of the regulation system. First of all, there is a collectively shared assumption that a prostitute is inherently different from any other woman. This pervasive premise underpins the series of events surrounding the death of Marita Alpaca. It successfully provided the elements needed to gloss over the facts involved in her death, changing the issue to what the implications of being a prostitute had for her identity and to what extent this determined whether she was murdered or Reaño was innocent.

The alternatives for women-who-prostitute remain the same but have solidified into a no-way-out situation. Time and again a call is made to reha-bilitate the women-who-prostitute and in the same breath suggestions are given for improving the regulation system. In their work, they are expected to please the client but if they feign or really show pleasure they are con-sidered immoral. However, if they treat it like any other job and are indifferent then they are criticized for being a bad whore. Any attempts they make to improve their working situation are generally disempowered by the media and public opinion. The only role left opened to them is that of the victim.

The control/danger dyad has grown in significance and so has the number of clandestine prostitutes. Years of regulation have caused clandestine prostitutes to be pushed further outside the boundaries of accepted reasons for prostitution, and their media image has deteriorated even more. The presence of Aids in the population of prostitutes has caused them to be automatically associated with Aids reinforcing the dyad of control and danger.

Finally, and profoundly related to the former are the gender meanings used to construct the identity of the woman-who-prostitutes. Her identity is split between the prostitute and that of the mother. This split in the prostitute's subject position is welded together by the fact that the majority of the women-who-prostitute are single mothers who do it to support their children. This creates an unresolvable dilemma: how can a woman who is typified as a 'seller of love', a vector of illness and/or a decadent, sordid whore bring this imagery home to her children? What she does bring home and who she is at home is rarely written about. Further dualities exist between different types of whores – those who whore out of necessity and those who do it to earn luxuries – and also concerning the prostitute's sexuality with its multi-sided notion of promiscuity contained in the hypersexual image – all of which echo the images of the historical past but have been refined.

The counter-discourse is no longer the abolitionist discourse but is represented by a feminist strand of the women's oppression theory – prostitution as sexual slavery. In many aspects, this theory shares similar points of departure and strategies with the doctrine of the abolitionists. It fervently attacks the workings of the system of regulation, exposing the injustice concealed in its discursive notions and the implications for women-who-prostitute, particularly for clandestine prostitutes who make up approximately 70 per cent of all women-who-prostitute. One of its outstanding differences from the mainstream regulatory discourse is the role it attributes to men in relation to the existence and propagation of prostitution. As representatives of the patriarchal society, all men are oppressors and to blame for prostitution's perpetuation. Women-who-prostitute are exploited victims who will only be free when they leave the trade or when prostitution disappears. They have very few alternatives as prostitutes. Improvements in their work situations are out of the question because this would contribute to the perpetuation of women's oppression. Here, once again, one of the only viable roles open to them is that of the victim.

Contemporary solutions to the prostitution problem leave very little room for negotiation. The imagery created and reinforced by the media encapsulates women-who-prostitute within the boundaries of a gendered enclosure. Thus, the media actively contributes to constructing a no-way-out situation for prostitutes.

# 3 PROSTITUTION AND THE CONSTRUCTION OF MEN'S SEXUAL SELVES[1]

## FROM THE THEORETICAL PERSPECTIVE

Since the outset of this study it has been assumed that prostitution is a product of male sexuality. In Lima, going to the prostitutes is a commonly used sexual alternative which crosses class, age and ethnic boundaries. For generations, prostitution has served as a space for sexual initiation. The open, or in some cases, tacit acceptance that an adolescent or an adult will go to a prostitute, is perhaps a characteristic not solely belonging to the Limenean setting, but is, nonetheless, essential for its understanding. Therefore, to understand the cultural specificity of prostitution it is fundamental to unravel the construct of male sexuality.

It is easy to conjure up images of male sexuality just by mentioning 'the Latin lover' and the Latin American term *macho*. Latin American men are often depicted in continual pursuit of sexual satisfaction. This stereotypical image is founded on essentialist, instinctual notions of male sexuality. Nonetheless, they are reproduced in the regulationist discourse of prostitution and enacted by men daily. Yet, despite the importance ascribed to these characteristics in heterosexual men's sexual identity, the subject of male sexuality is almost entirely absent in prostitution studies and has only recently begun to be studied seriously in the Latin American context (e.g. Archetti 1992; Parker 1992; Gutmann 1996; Fuller 1997; Prieur 1998). Although these studies have unpacked the concept of *machismo* to show its diversity, it is still common to find it being used as a homogeneous category. Cornwall and Lindisfarne state, 'It is ironic that the logic of feminism as a political position has often required the notion of "men" as a single, opposi-tional category' (1994: 1). The positioning of men as an oppositional, homogeneous category obstructs the construction of knowledge concerning notions of sexuality, masculinity and power. It is within the realm of gender relations of power that male sexuality constructs another enclosure around women-who-prostitute, exacerbating their no-way-out situation.

In Latin America, the symbolic representation of masculinity and male sexuality merges in the concept of *machismo*. *Machismo* is an all-embracing concept determining women's subordination. It is often assumed to be synonymous with male dominance; the site where gender and sexual oppression conflate. Generally, it is defined by describing attributes of men's attitudes or behaviour that make them *macho*. Stevens considers *machismo* to be a cult of virility. 'The chief characteristics of this cult are exaggerated aggressiveness and intransigence in male-to-male interpersonal relationships and arrogance and sexual aggression in male-to-female relationships' (1973: 90).[2] The fact that gender and sexuality are intrinsically related in the concept of *machismo* need not be a theoretical obstruction. Ennew points out that 'the structure of gender differentiation in Peru [is] a structure which has a more explicitly sexual rationale than may be observed in many other societies' (1986: 58). Sexuality and gender may be far more entwined in Latin America than, for example, in Western Europe. Nevertheless, the concepts of sexuality and gender are not interchangeable; each possesses its own dynamics. But since few distinctions have been made between the two concepts, it is nearly impossible to capture how sexuality and masculinity feed into each other.

Very often the attitudes and behaviour of the *macho* man are assumed to be reflected in structural traits of society's institutions. Monzón states that: 'although violence is the most evident expression of *machismo*, there are a series of subtle attitudes which subordinate women and assign them a secondary status, which also originate from "male superiority" and have caused more harm to women than physical abuse' (1988: 148). She continues by showing how *machismo* is manifested in different institutions such as education, health, work and legislation. Lugo analyses how *machismo* affects women and minority groups in Mexico (1989: 219–30). In this perspective, *machismo* refers to all 'healthy' heterosexual men. They are assigned the entire chunk of power, and women and minorities have to do without. The analysis of power is straitjacketed into discovering the mechanisms of male dominance. Ethnic, class and sexual differences are barely recognizable. Moreover, there is no space allotted to explore how men's subjective experiences inform the construction of these concepts.

A similar tendency is observable in writings on prostitution. The position of Peruvian feminists towards prostitution and the implications for the sexual slavery theory for prostitutes was dealt with in detail in the previous chapter. Prostitution is placed on the same level as rape, abuse and sexual violence in general. This constructs an image that all men who go to prostitutes are sexually violent and capable of abusing women in other areas of their lives. One study exemplifying this tendency is encountered in the Dominican Republic. The authors devote a chapter to the client and label male sexuality as the *miseria sexual masculina* (masculine sexual misery). Men who go to prostitutes convert them: 'into one huge vulva which complacently opens in expectation of their penises. This helps them erase the faces, bodies and names ... Her function is to give pleasure (if you can call this sexual misery pleasure) and to reach this she only needs to have three instruments which can make him ejaculate: the vagina, hands and mouth' (Cavalcanti et al. 1985: 79–80).

Male sexuality unequivocally expresses the oppression/subordination relationship. The portrayal of male sexuality in this theoretical current as unchanging and predetermined echoes, albeit for different motives, the essentialist notion of male sexuality in the mainstream discourse of prostitution, which perceives prostitution as a necessary evil. How can this circle of reasoning, that continually reproduces its own assumptions, be broken? Edwards proposes a solution in her article after analysing different prostitution discourses. She concludes: 'It is men that we need to study, to understand their desire for power, for sexual mastery. We need to address and confront why it is that men are orgasming [*sic*] to visual images of women's subordination harm and abuse in pornography, and also to their use and subordination and insult in prostitution. We need to examine the social construction of male sexual arousal and the channelling of sexual arousal into a context of abuse and harm in which women are degraded' (1993: 102–3).

Although we are in agreement on the urgency for more research, our thinking diverges at the point when male sexuality is predefined as a complex, but nonetheless, fixed notion. Does the recognition that the use of prostitutes is a male prerogative, and thus a symbol for male dominance, allow us to presume that all men experience this relationship identically? Do these experiences figure uniformly in men's construction of their sexual selves and how they act out relations of power? Is it sufficient to assume that all men use prostitutes' services for the same reason? Perhaps questions such as why, when and why not are even more important. These are just a few of the innumerable questions which can be posed when the concepts of sexuality and gender are perceived as separate, plural, unfixed and changing. This chapter is founded on that premise. It intends to contribute to the growing body of anthropological literature that explores sexuality by questioning its meanings in a specific context. Ultimately this will enable a further analysis which positions prostitution within the constructs of masculinity and sexuality.

THE INTERVIEWS: THE PUBLIC PRESENTATION OF THE SEXUAL SELF[3]

Somehow the topics of sex and sexuality are difficult to talk about. Even though many Limenean men were eager to drop a few insinuating comments about their sexual escapades when I made reference to my research, when it comes down to discussing the subject seriously – as in an interview setting – the participants were not so eager to open up as one would expect. Obviously, talking with a stranger – or in the case of some of the respondents, an acquaintance – about intimate sexual experiences, can make the informant feel uncomfortable even if total anonymity is guaranteed. But it is not just a matter of shyness; there is more to this than meets the eye.

An interview about sexuality can be considered a public presentation of the subject's sexual self. Through relevant sexual anecdotes and stories he reveals a slice of his private intimate world, something he does not do every day. In this sense he publicly performs a representation of his sexuality.

The interview dynamics reflect an interesting dimension of knowledge production in relation to the subject of sexuality. The procedures taken to do the interviews, and the gender relations between the individuals involved, give insights into certain aspects of the construction of male sexuality. Although standard interview procedure considers what is actually said as the most important source of material, there are other clues to be found in the way things are told and what remains unspoken.

Twenty-one interviews with heterosexual men were conducted by my male assistant. The interviews were open-ended and traced the respondents' sexual trajectory from their childhood to the present. After a few questions concerning their family situation and social background they were asked to relate their first sexual experiences and their first relationships with women. This was not an arbitrary division but rather reflects the specificity of the Limenean context. As we will see below, men's first sexual experience was generally not in an affective relationship but with either a prostitute or framed as 'a fling'. Prostitution was focused on from three angles: personal experiences, imagery and the respondents' knowledge of the system of regulation. The objective of the interview was two-fold: first, to analyse what prostitution means in the lives of the respondents and what type of imagery they use in relation to the prostitute and prostitution and, second, to discover how their experiences of their sexuality creates meanings of femininity. This would assist in an analysis of male sexuality that problematizes the totalizing image of male sexuality and the position of prostitution in this intricate configuration.

At the start of the project it was our intention to choose the respondents randomly with only two criteria loosely structuring the selection process – age and class. Considering that the use of prostitutes' services amongst contemporary youth has significantly declined (Cáceres 1990: 40), it was decided the respondents should be over the age of 20. This would provide the opportunity to approach male sexuality from different moments of the men's life cycles and enhance the possibility that they would represent a group of men who considered prostitution a viable sexual choice. Class was considered an important criterion insofar as it was assumed to be a boundary marker of difference. It was hard to imagine these criteria would impede the selection process.

Although there are many convincing signs that men experience their sexuality along the lines of the image of 'the Latin lover', this assumption is questioned by problems which arose during the selection period. Many men were not willing to be interviewed and it was not easy to approach a stranger to ask him to participate. Despite their over-sexed verbal performance of their sexuality, it remained a sensitive subject. The details are not shared with just anybody. Consequently, the respondents were chosen for their approachability and generally encountered in my assistant's circle of friends and acquaintances. As a result, the majority of the interviews were conducted with (lower) middle-class men.

The difficulty of talking about sexual experiences was felt even more strongly when my assistant tried to rekindle old contacts in 'popular' neighbourhoods. His old friends were evasive or did not show up for the appointment. As Ugarteche states: 'The nature and view of sex and sexuality is completely distinct depending on the extent to which the person's vision is "westernized". The more westernized the vision the more the person talks and the less they do. A divorce emerges between the explicit and the executed ...' (1992: 62). Middle-class men felt freer to talk about their sexuality. When the respondents were asked their opinions about the interview, they generally commended my assistant. One of the only exceptions was a man from the 'popular' classes, who replied 'that you [the interviewer] wanted to meddle with things that you had no right to'. The change from random selection to approachability does not tell us what sexuality means, but gives some indication of certain areas which shape meanings in the interview process. Silence is a non-verbal expression and in this case suggests that class is a differentiating factor in men's experiences of their sexuality and brings into question the pervasive images in the discourse. Silence and lies are encoded; at times the messages they contain are an outcome of the motion between discourse and practice.

Another location where sexual meanings were created is found in the (gender) relationships between the interviewer and the respondent. I was convinced a man from Lima could use his experiential knowledge to delve deeper into the matter and conduct the interview better than myself. Although I cannot disprove this assumption, I am no longer totally convinced of its validity.[4] There were moments that the interviews reproduced conventional male gender relations. When certain words were used which would give more insight into the man's perception of his sexuality, these were frequently passed over without acknowledging and inquiring into their cultural significance. Often, the interview resembled more a conversation between friends. The respondent boisterously talked about his sexual experiences and the interviewer supported this by not inquiring further.

The respondents' uncritical stance towards their experiences produced a cumulative and forward-looking notion of sexuality. Rare were the moments of remorse, self-criticism or reflection on their earlier behaviour. Retrospectively, certain attitudes might have been considered childish, but the respondent or the interviewer never challenged them. It was a stage in the construction of their sexual selves.

The interviewer's difficulty in separating himself from the discourse was not confined to these moments. In one interview, my assistant could not hide his disapproval concerning the respondent's opinion of prostitution. The respondent never used the services of a prostitute. He felt it to be degrading for himself and the woman involved. Instead of capturing the uniqueness of the case, the interviewer probed the respondent, looking for moments in his personal background that might explain this 'abnormality'. These examples illustrate the reproduction of discursive sexual meanings in the interview dynamics.

A final clue can be read from the way the men told their stories. There was a difference between how they described their experiences in an affective relationship and in a sexual relationship with a woman with whom they had no emotional contact. They not only used different words to describe their relationships, but they were also more willing to show their vulnerability in their affective relationships. Pedro's account of his first experiences with a girlfriend and a prostitute illustrates this well. He recalls nostalgically his encounter with his girlfriend and has no problem demonstrating his insecurities. His experience with a prostitute shows his behaviour in a totally different world, and this is reflected in the changes in his speech.

*Do you remember your first girlfriend? What was this relationship like?*

My first true girlfriend ... was when I was finishing school. I was 17 years old. She was 13 and a relative of one of my neighbours. She lived in the neighbourhood ... I went to visit her, we started to fall in love, I don't know how. I invited her to my prom. When I entered university, we went to a carnival party. I declared myself [*declarar* – to declare oneself, to reveal one's intentions] and she accepted. She was 13 and still in school. And when she accepted I didn't know what to do with her. I never had the least experience of what you do with a girlfriend. So I bought her a Coca-cola. We continued to dance until the party was over and decided we would keep seeing each other. I usually saw her at her house. Finally, I got bored because her parents never gave her permission to go out. I called her up and told her I wanted to end our relationship.

*Tell me did your sexual life begin before this?*

Of course. I lost my virginity when I was 14, at one of the premises at Huatica. I went alone and paid 5 *soles*. The chauffeur who worked across the street was my friend and he brought me there. He assured me that with 5 *soles* I would be able to *culear* (to fuck). I entered Huatica, I had been there before without any money. I saw some women who were naked from the waist up. Without choosing I went into the first room so that nobody would see I doubted. The woman took my money, got undressed and I threw myself on top of her. I started to make love and at the same time started to bleed. The woman got upset because I stained her sheets and started to say horrible things to me. 'Get out of here you disgrace, you didn't tell me, you made everything dirty ... .' I left, rushed out of the room pulling up my pants. She picked up a pail of cunt water [*agua de chucha*] and followed me to the street and threw it at me. I was still pulling up my pants. The chauffeur was waiting for me. He took me to the public health centre. He was shocked and made them give me an injection of penicillin. My penis looked like a mummy and for one whole week every time I had an erection I hit the ceiling. (Pedro, 53 years old, divorced)

The interviews demonstrate the preponderant influence the discourse of male sexuality has in men's sexual selves. The most salient characteristics of this sexual discourse are the singular, essentialist concept of sexuality in which sexual desire is imagined to be virtually instinctual, and therefore uncontrollable, and the relational construct of gender which positions men and women oppositionally. Through the stories told, the way they were told and the interview dynamics, the respondents affirmed their sexual identities embodying discursive notions. However, they also disclose other alternatives.

## TALKING SEXUALITY

At a certain point in an adolescent's life, football, hanging around with the boys on the street corner and being mischievous are not the only meaningful things in life. Suddenly, or perhaps slowly but surely, the adolescent becomes aware of girls and sex. At this age, approximately 11 to 13 years old, sex takes on visual forms such as porno magazines or it is verbal. Conversations with their mates about breasts, legs, penises and masturbation are the topics of the day.

When a boy starts to like a girl and he gets enough courage to *declararse* (to declare oneself), if she accepts, they are boyfriend and girlfriend. They hold hands, kiss and perhaps there is an occasional caress. They go out together, but he will not make any bold sexual advances. If it turns into a lasting relationship, they may eventually make love. In the meantime, his sexual desire is growing and in many of the testimonies, the respondents told how they ended up at a brothel for their first sexual experience. It is as if their sexuality is on the fast lane while they are limited by all the boundaries which accompany having a proper girlfriend. Thus, sexual outlets are looked for outside the relationship and frequently found in encounters with other women. It is in this process that certain words, expressions or metaphors begin to take on sexual meanings. The Limenean lexicon of *jerga* (colloquialisms/slang) is rich with expressions and terms that construct sexual meanings that condition masculinity and femininity and gender relations. Men develop different attitudes, behaviours and ways of talking which make distinctions between women, and also between women and men.

The underlying essence of sexuality in Lima is expressed as a dualism. The words referring to sexual encounters and practices distinguish different sexualities for men and women. Men's descriptions of their sexual encounters have connotations of conquest, possession and sexual assertiveness. A verb such as *agarrar* (to seize, take or grab) was used to describe the act of touching a part of a woman's body, *me agarré su teta* (I grabbed her tit), or as a metaphor which implies sexual possession, *agarré a todas* (I grabbed all of them). *Meter* (to put) is also used to denote the action of touching, but carries the connotations of to shove or to push, *metí mi mano en su blusa* (I shoved my hand in her blouse). It was also used to describe penetration. Another word with subtler connotations is *chapar*. *Chapar* can be defined as to catch or be caught. In sexual language *chapar* means to kiss. Although it is sometimes used synonymously for *besar* a distinction is usually made. It refers to a kiss stolen in a situation like a party.

The words interchangeably used to mean sexual intercourse convert sexual intercourse into a male performance. The verbs *comer, dar, planchar, montar, tirar, cachar, culear* are expressions which signify making love. *Comer* (to eat), *dar* (to give), *planchar* (to iron or press), *montar* (to mount – generally used in reference to mounting a horse or a bicycle), *tirar* (to throw), are verbs which indicate an action which can be performed by both sexes. In sexual language, the man is the initiator of the action and what was the inanimate object has now been transformed into the woman. *Cachar* and *culear* are verbs which come closest to the English translation to fuck or to screw. They are used quite commonly to describe coitus. In rare occasions the term *hacer el amor* (to make love) was used, usually in relation to their partner.

The oppositional character of male and female sexuality is constructed by emphasizing men's actions. Women are the receiver, the direct object, implicitly conveying a notion of passivity. Underlying these expressions is a reified notion of sexuality implied in other expressions characterizing male and female sexuality.

Men's sexual desire is often described in terms of a functioning machine. A man can feel *cargado sexualmente* (sexually loaded) and in need to *descargar* (to unload). As one of the respondents stated, '*necesito estar descargado porque hace una presión psicológica*' ('I need to unload because it [*being loaded*] causes psychological pressure'). His desire can also be warmed up, implying sexual arousal without necessarily terminating in coitus – *calentar las pelotas* (to warm up the balls). Sexual desire is portrayed in terms that imply there is an impending danger awaiting if the man's sexual desires remain unsatisfied. What happens to a machine if it overloads or overheats? It is likely to explode. Thus, male sexuality can only be controlled with regular maintenance: frequent sexual intercourse.

Women appear in this configuration as a vehicle to obtain sexual satisfaction. Sexual encounters acquire an aura of premeditation aimed at achieving sexual satisfaction. To get to a woman's sexuality and obtain sexual satisfaction, she has to be worked – *trabajarla*. If she is worked successfully she can *caer fácilmente* (fall easily) or *aflojar* or *soltar* (loosen up or let go). These expressions evoke an image of men who manipulate women to get them to let go of what they want, namely their 'sexual favours'.

Many of the terms were used frequently in anecdotes about parties. In the adolescence stage of men's life cycle, a party is a metaphor for a sexual battlefield in which men, especially those in their teens, chalk up sexual experience. Women are sought out to see how far they will go. As one of the respondents related about parties in his early adolescence:

They were my field of experimentation. Sexually no ... I used them to *calentar las pelotas* (warm up my balls) ... *me las chapaba* (I kissed them) and ... didn't I tell you already that I wasn't looking for the occasion to *culear* (to fuck). I went out with them once or twice, *me las chapaba* (I kissed them), made my conquest and then I said so long. (Lucho, 31 years old, married)

In sexual language the verb *mandar*, which means command or order, takes on further connotations regarding men's sexual role. In this context, it means to seduce or conquer, making a man who is a successful seducer a *mandado*. If he does not exhibit behaviour which adheres to this image he runs the risk of being called a *quedado* (derived from the verb *quedar* signifying to remain or stay behind) – a man who has not mastered the art of seduction, and thus has not been able to conquer many women.

In a young man's early sexual experiences, when his own sexual satisfaction is his only objective, a woman who seduces becomes an object of pleasure. Since women's 'sexual favours' are seen as something which have to be won, a female seducer is seen as offering herself and therefore transgressing the appropriate behaviour outlined for women. In these situations the reaction of many of the respondents was to grab at the offer whether he was interested in the woman or not. One of the respondents recounted the first time he had sexual intercourse, at a party at the age of 14. He was asked:

*Who seduced who, you or her? (Quién se mandó, tú o ella?)*

I think it was simultaneous, but I believe that I began, because it was also the period of *la pendejada* (bullshitting around). Well, I mean if you are at a party and its like 'Okay what can I do to this girl', you put your hand in (*le metes la mano*), you kiss her neck and then you begin to kiss her (*chaparla*), and everything. Well I was playing around when I saw that she was responding and responding, so I picked her up. I felt scared. Scared because I did it at a party. She had more experience than I. How did I feel? On the one hand, it made me feel bad because they always told me that I should *mandar*. It's the man who should seduce. On the other hand it gave me a certain amount of confidence because in some way she helped me. It was satisfactory. I didn't take the relationship any further, during this period I was seeing another girl. (Hugo, 29 years old, single)

In retelling his story, Hugo reshaped the incident to portray himself as the one in control. The fact that the encounter began out of mutual interest becomes blurred in his retelling and loses significance because she agreed to go further, transforming her sexual desire into an offer. His discomfort subsided concerning his inability to live up to expectations and maintain control because he realized that going to bed with an experienced young woman was functional. She taught him the ins and outs of making love. This one-off experience was the commencement of his 'sexual career'. Although he rejected the idea of a relationship, this should not automatically be interpreted as being because the young woman was not a virgin. Going to bed with a virgin is considered delightful, but virginity is considered a scarce and prized possession, and it is not as decisive in selection criteria as the sexual discourse would lead us to believe. Asked his opinion of female virginity one respondent states:

It is one of the most beautiful things that can happen, that a woman comes to you as a virgin, but this is really difficult to accomplish. I do respect women who have had previous sexual experiences. (Eduardo, 22 years old, single)

Thus, if being sexually active is not a distinction which makes one woman different from another, than what is? It is whether they adhere to the expected behaviour associated with the label they are given. Whether a woman's sexual experience is perceived as something to be taken advantage of is greatly dependent on the man's intentions. His approach to the situation is different according to whether he is interested in the woman as a partner or just out for a good time. Hence, rather than reflect a woman's own perceptions of her gender identity and her expectations, the labels given to women are male projections.

## LABELLING WOMEN

In sexual language the over-simplified dichotomy of the mother/whore gives way to three different types of women: the potential partner or spouse, those who provide pleasure and are excluded *de facto* as a potential candidate for a relationship and the prostitute. There are different labels which designate women as belonging to a specific group.

A widely used term for a (potential) girlfriend is *chica de su casa* (a girl of her house). The term *chica de su casa* is a commonly agreed upon label, but other words are used that do not share this recognition. For example, one man called potential partners *amigas cariñosas* (affectionate friends).

Normally they are *chicas de su casa*, they work, study, they make something of their life, they are people who have a life, their world, their family. (Percy, 30 years old, single)

Another man called them *mujeres comunes* (ordinary women).

She is simply a girl leading the life of an adolescent. At a party she is looking to enjoy herself, dance, *planchar*, or maybe she is looking to find a possible boyfriend. (Lucho)

As mentioned earlier, the apparent contradiction that this woman is sexually active need not be assumed to be a problem. She belongs to the category of potential partners. Her sexual desires are placed in this context. Thus her behaviour does not take her outside the boundaries of the ascribed behaviour for her group of peers. No criteria were given by the respondents as to why a woman is considered a part of this group. Yet what makes a woman identifiable as a potential partner is a configuration of different subjective criteria: appearance, class, ethnicity, sensations and emotions. Accompanying this label is a code of proper behaviour which might not be spoken about openly but is tacitly recognized by all the individuals involved. Lucho continues and talks about his experiences with *mujeres comunes*:

I deceived them, I could deceive them because I could make them believe that we were going to have a relationship and that I loved them and that we were going to arrive at something firm, stable and coherent ... although you know deep down that the relationship isn't going to go anywhere.

Perhaps Lucho is an exception and other men would not think of manipulating the situation to such an extreme. In the interview, he reflects upon his behaviour as corresponding to a certain stage in his sexual development, implying that his behaviour has changed since then. Nevertheless, his strategic behaviour shows he was aware that certain expectations and behaviours belong to this category.

Most men talked about their relationship with their partners as an extremely positive experience. The relationship is the locus consolidating different needs and desires: intellectual, affective, emotional and sexual. Therefore, a man will act cautiously, protecting his partner's sexuality, making sure she is not threatened by his sexual desires until the appropriate moment is determined. For some men, having a serious relationship was a sufficient motive to stop going to prostitutes or stop looking around for sexual adventures. Others, however, still found it possible and enjoyable to *sacar la vuelta* (be unfaithful) or *tener plancitos* (this comes closest to having [little] plans, however the plan being referred to is a not-so-serious relationship with another woman). This proved possible because of the distinction they made between their partners and what they were looking for in a relationship with other women. Certain feelings, sensations and emotions are reserved for the first group of women. Sexual desire and satisfaction are enmeshed in a conglomeration of emotions. With the other group of women, sexual desire and satisfaction are broken off from the range of the man's emotions, and perceived as virtually instinctual, making it possible to have sexual adventures without putting their relationship in danger. This becomes explicit in their definition of faithfulness. When the respondents were asked whether they were faithful, several did not connect faithfulness with monogamy and initially answered affirmatively. Only after their answer was challenged did they reformulate it.

I never *sacaba la vuelta*, well let's not say never, but relatively no. Faithfulness does not mean you can't have other relationships with other women. (Hernan, 28 years old, single)

It is one thing to love someone and another thing to screw. You could screw with one person or another. This doesn't mean you stopped loving the third person. You can screw, simply speaking because you are horny. And if there is a woman who wants to screw you, why not screw her. (Percy)

For some of the respondents being faithful is a normative value with a logical rationale. It is not synonymous with monogamy because what they experience with the other woman is not intended to replace their relationship, but rather expresses another part of their sexuality. This constructs different notions of sexuality which are enacted with different women and is one of the underlying forces behind labelling women.

*Pacharaca* (*pacha, pachita*), *pampita, ruca* are different names for women who serve as sexual outlets. Some men use these terms interchangeably, but usually there is a distinction made between the *pacharaca* and the *ruca*. The *pacharaca* or *pampita* (the terms are synonymous but *pampita* was more often used by men growing up in the 1960s) is characterized as a woman looking for a good time with an enormous number of sexual contacts. She is normally found in bars, restaurants and discos, making it known by the way she dresses and her behaviour that she wants to be picked up. Often a group of men will go out to pick up *pacharacas*. Although some men admitted that a *pacharaca* is not only interested in sex but is looking for affection, or that some women were *pacharacas* because they were trying to find a potential partner to climb the social ladder, their attitudes and behaviour remained unchanged. The man is quick to make sexual advances, an unlikely occurrence if he considered the woman a *chica de su casa*. He is out for a one-night stand. There is no monetary transaction involved but a material exchange is expected. If a man wants to pick up a *pacharaca* then he is aware he has to offer her a good time. Food, drinks and maybe drugs are expected items on the menu. The essence of a relationship with a *pacharaca* is given by one of the respondents who could never get into being a *pacharaquero* (a man who frequently picks up *pacharacas*):

I couldn't get into it, you know bringing your girl home and then going off to look for *pacharacas*. It just isn't me. Sexuality is something more than just the physical, you know? Not necessarily a greater commitment, but something more, sympathy, I don't know, enjoyment, empathy, some type of human relationship which goes further than the physical. (Álvaro, 34 years old, single)

The *ruca*, which is closest to the English slut or tramp, is a woman who goes off with a lot of men. She could be known in the neighbourhood for being 'easy'. She comes closest to being a prostitute without needing to be paid for sex, and is usually an acquaintance, while the *pacharaca* is normally a stranger.

The *ruca* and the *pacharaca* are distinguished from the *chica de su casa* by boundaries that restrain or let men's sexual desires loose. The *pacharaca* and her ilk are sought out by men to satisfy their sexual needs. To a large degree, they are disassociated with their social identity and perceived in purely sexual terms. Men transform them into sexual actors, negating the significance that the women's social world has for themselves. This enhances the notion of male sexual desire as being virtually instinctual and uncontrollable. Men are able to let their sexual desire loose in these sexual encounters. The more a woman gains entrance into a man's emotional world, the more she is perceived as a social actor and other elements become decisive in determining the appropriate moment to have a sexual relationship. In this sense, a relationship with a *chica de su casa* restrains men's sexual desire. Nonetheless, having sex with a *chica de su casa* (one's partner) was often seen as the most gratifying.

The three categories of women are constructed through men's sexual intentions. A woman regarded as a *pacharaca* in a disco is most probably a potential partner at work or school. That labelling is a male projection is voiced by Hugo when he recalled his first girlfriend at the age of 12:

It was very platonic, platonic in the sense that it carried a lot of illusion and fantasy with very little eroticism.

*You didn't desire her?*

Of course not. At that time, the girls you desired had to be *rucas*.

Labelling women illustrates how the meanings of men's sexual desire shifts in different moments and simultaneously constructs meanings of femininity.

The prostitute, or *la puta*, is the third category of women. It would be inappropriate to conceptualize prostitutes as a label constructed in the same way as those of above, since prostitution is an officially recognized institution. Needless to say, prostitutes are sexual outlets for men. In sexual encounters, prostitutes are perceived as the furthest removed from their social world. They are the supreme example of the sexual actor. This image is buttressed by prostitutes who filter out many of the details of their personal lives and consciously perform the identity of the sexual actor. Sexual encounters with prostitutes stand for paid sex. This was described as a clear-cut relationship without emotional involvement. Paying for sex enables men to demand that their sexual desires are satisfied according to their fancy. This is not always guaranteed with the other groups of women. At first glance, the prostitute appears to be the least ambivalent category of all three. However, going to prostitutes is experienced differently by the men who were interviewed.

## GOING TO PROSTITUTES

It is difficult to generalize about men's experiences with prostitutes. Some never went to a prostitute and others frequented them regularly. Nevertheless, for all men, even those who never used a prostitute's services, going to a prostitute is a male prerogative. In other words, there comes a point in a man's life when he will choose whether he should go to a prostitute. Among the interviewed men, 15 had some kind of experience with a prostitute, six never used their services and only three of them had never been inside a brothel.

What all the men have in common who used prostitutes' services is they started at a young age. The majority were sexually initiated (*debutar* – to debut) in a brothel. In general, whether it was a brothel in Lima or one of the provinces, they referred to the regulated brothels, characterized by their anonymity, with huge factory-like corridors lined with small rooms and women posed in the doorways trying to entice a client to enter. This first experience was usually described as disastrous. Between being nervous and trying to conceal the fact that they were a novice and the prostitutes who were quoted as saying things like 'Hurry up', 'Have you finished yet?' or 'First-timers aren't good fucks', it was considered a memorable experience, though one they would rather not remember.[5] Entangled in the men's accounts is a layer of disillusionment which expresses a conflict between the actual situation and their emotional expectations.

It was disastrous. It wasn't the scheme that I had in my head nor the idea that I had in my life concerning sex. At no moment did I feel fulfilled as a man, which I suppose you should feel with your first sexual experience. (Percy)

After we finished I asked the whore, 'What do we do now?', was it possible to start making love because what we did was not making love? (Carlos, 31 years old, single)

What the men wanted and what they received clashed tremendously. They were looking for a sexual relationship comparable to having sex in an affective relationship. They imagined that that was what they had bought. However, what they got was paid sex. After the first experience, many went back on a regular basis. Although it took time to internalize the differences, they eventually found satisfaction in this sexual relationship. Only one man stopped going after his first experience.

Three patterns can be discerned concerning the use of prostitutes' services. First, there are those who never went to prostitutes. The second is found in the group of men who regularly used their services but eventually stopped. This coincides with the majority of the interviewed men. Finally, there are the men who continue to find occasion to go to an establishment where prostitution is practised.

Two highly related factors play an essential role for understanding why certain men never used prostitutes' services. These respondents had the hardest time accepting and acting out a fragmented notion of sexual desire. Words such as disgust, rejection, degradation and incompatibility were used to explain why they never ventured pass the threshold of a prostitute's room. With the exception of one informant, who said he never went to the prostitutes because he feared he would contract a venereal disease, they could not accept this purely commercial enterprise. Having sexual intercourse meant more than having an orgasm. This does not imply they withheld from having sex until they met the 'right woman', even though one man was still a virgin and did not feel the need to have sexual intercourse until he had a serious relationship. On the contrary, this decision was made easier because there were women who were not prostitutes available for sexual relationships which allowed for a certain degree of feelings.

If you put a girl in front of me who works in a brothel, it bothers me. I don't like to see the girls who are standing there in a *tanga*, or something of the like. A sexual relation should be with feelings ... At least there should be pleasure and money shouldn't come into it. I feel it degrades me to pay to be with a woman. (Angel, 24 years old, single)

In my group we measured our conquests at parties not at a brothel or with a prostitute. Although there are many attractive prostitutes, in essence it is a commercial contact, that's how I always considered it. It is incompatible with pleasure. (Carlos, 27 years old, single)

The men's motives for not going to prostitutes resemble the disappointment the majority of the men felt after their first experience with a prostitute. Their thoughts on this subject contrast most strikingly with men who continue to use prostitutes' services occasionally. The difference is found in how they give meaning to sexual desire. In the latter group, sexual desire, satisfaction and emotion need not go together, and thus they have no problem going to a prostitute. Despite the fact there must be many men who never stopped using prostitutes' services, only three respondents continued to go. One of the men had severe problems making social contacts. His last relationship with a non-prostitute was when he was a teenager. He found it much easier to relate to prostitutes and had a serious relationship with one of them. Even though he never stopped paying for sex, he wanted to marry her. The other two used their services occasionally. One of them claimed his eleven-year-old marriage is stable because he has frequent extra-marital relationships. He preferred to seek sexual satisfaction among the group of *pacharacas*. However, going to a prostitute was a last resort which he used on occasion.

I still go to the prostitutes sometimes. Where are you going to find a woman at one o'clock in the morning after you've had a few drinks? (Juan Carlos, 33 years old, married)

Finally we come to the group of men who stopped using prostitutes' services. The frequency with which they went to prostitutes varied. How they felt about their experiences cannot be generalized. Some of them enjoyed it; others never stopped seeing it as a last resort. What they do share is a change in their perception of their sexual selves. At some point, sex for the sake of sex becomes unsatisfactory, and they realized that their sexual relationship with their partners goes beyond the physical. Álvaro reflects on the change which occurred:

My experiences with prostitutes can be compared with a cold shower in the winter. You have to shower, you suffer, and when you finish you say that was that. I stopped going to prostitutes at the age of 24 when I started to have a sexual relationship with my partner. That was the age when my sexuality, partner and affection consolidated into one thing. (Álvaro)

In conclusion, men's experiences with prostitution are linked together with their sexual experiences in other areas of their lives. For the majority of the respondents, using prostitutes' services informs the construction of their sexual selves. Their different positions towards prostitution and their different experiences with prostitutes affirm the idea that male sexuality is neither homogeneous nor fixed.

The significance of going to prostitutes is best symbolized as a tug of war between sexual desire as virtually instinctual and sexual desire as one of many emotions. This mirrors the distinctions made between women as sexual and social actors. For men who never used prostitutes' services the cutting off of sexual desire from other emotions is less pronounced than in the other groups. These men look to satisfy their sexual needs, either with their partner or in the group of women who are conceived of as social actors. The men who continue to go to prostitutes can easily separate sexual desire from other emotions, pulling them to the prostitutes with one simple tug. The largest group of men is situated between these two extremes and is in a continual tug of war. They are pulled back and forth, with shifting outcomes at different moments of their lives. There are moments when the fragmented notion of sexual desire appears to be more unified. At other moments they have less difficulty in separating sexual desire from other emotions. The decision to stop going to prostitutes is a moment in their life cycles when the meaning of sexual desire changes and their perception of their sexual selves becomes less fragmented. It is impossible to predict whether it will shift again in the future. Since they have accepted prostitution as a sexual alternative, there might come a time when they decide to go back to prostitutes. If this is not the case, why was there a large group of men in their thirties and forties who frequented the establishments where I conducted my fieldwork? Do they all belong to the group who never stopped going to the prostitutes? Or does this group also include men who have returned?

The continual shifts in the meanings of sexual desire are most visible in the group of men who stopped using prostitutes' services; nevertheless, it is not a personal trait solely belonging to them. Men who continue to use prostitutes' services are just as unlikely always to perceive their sexual desire as virtually instinctual, just as it is also improbable that men who never go to prostitutes only identify their sexual desire in the emotional realm. Although many men wrestle with their position towards prostitution, the fact remains that prostitution contains the strongest essentialist images of male sexuality. How this essentialist notion is given form in men's sexual selves is highly dependent on their subjective experiences.

THE PROSTITUTE AS SEXUAL VERSUS SOCIAL ACTOR

In contrast to the elaborate descriptions given of their sexual encounters with prostitutes, when the time came to talk about prostitute imagery and the position of prostitution in society, or, in other words, prostitution as a social issue, the respondents' could scarcely respond. The answers given in reference to the system of regulation were based on personal experience or hearsay. They only had a vague idea that a sanitary control existed and what it entailed. Only when asked directly did they elaborate on related issues. For example, when asked their opinion of the sanitary control, they consider it necessary because of the increase in Aids and venereal diseases. Hypothetically they approved of control for men, but considered it impossible to accomplish. They had never thought about the significance of the state's role in the regulation of prostitution. In general they had absolutely no idea how it affected the women. Moreover, they had never contemplated whether improvements of the women's situation were necessary or what this might entail. When asked a direct question concerning improvements for the prostitute, they could not reply. Even my assistant frequently omitted the questions concerning this subject, showing he too had difficulty in seeing the importance when talking about prostitution in relation to sexuality. Only when the question was formulated as a leading question – 'Do you think other institutions should offer services to prostitutes to help and support them?' – did they reply.

When the respondents related their accounts of their experiences with prostitutes they situated them in the realm of sexuality. Once again, only when asked did they manage to look at prostitution in broader terms. Then, they visualized the prostitute as a socio-economic victim of society: a woman who is forced to enter prostitution for economic reasons and who is usually an unwed or abandoned mother. Her main motivation for continuing to work in the trade is survival. A distinction was made between prostitutes who work from necessity and those who do it because they like it. Thus the first group had virtuous motives while the second group's motives were dubious. However, very few men ventured to make any further projections. Although they recognized the social components of the women's decision to prostitute, they could not envision the social consequences nor what it entailed for women as individuals.

The interviews show the men's shortsightedness in relation to prostitution and women-who-prostitute. They are not exceptions. They duplicate rather well the media's representation and public opinion, including all their distortions. An enormous gap exists between the significance of the prostitute for the respondents' sexual selves and their knowledge of the position of prostitution in the Limenean social context. These interviews present yet another variation of the nineteenth-century duality in contemporary prostitution discourse – the divorce of the sexual from the social. This crack in society's collective awareness is so deeply ingrained that its logic is taken for granted. Yet, it is this division which significantly affects the situation of women-who-prostitute and contributes to the continual reproduction of the same scenarios.

CONSTRUCTING SEXUAL SELVES

The group of men who participated in this project could be considered mainly typical heterosexual middle-class Limenean men who are among the many being referred to in theories concerning *machismo*, oppression and male sexuality. These theories portray their lives as the reproduction of discourse in practice. I have departed from a perspective which used the concept of sexual selves to facilitate an analysis which includes the subjective dimension. This has shown that sexuality is not singular but contains various meanings in multiple configurations that shift their positions in different situations, at different moments in time and with different women. Some of these meanings embody the discursive notions of sexuality. Other meanings emphasize experiences that differ greatly from cultural expectations, or situate the discursive notions in a less prominent position, producing sexual meanings which re-work, reject or contradict, but nonetheless, coexist with the discursive notions.

The subjective dimension of men's experiences is often ignored in studies predominantly aimed at analysing women's subordination. There is a common unspoken belief that subjectivity is not very relevant for the study of male dominance because difference on a personal level does not change the gender order of society. The lack of analysis concerning how men construct their identities through daily lived experiences, and how these experiences filter through their subjective lens to create meanings, has contributed to the reductionist construct of power echoing through many feminist-oriented studies. The ethnographic analysis presented here gives glimpses into the complexities of how men enact power relations through the construction of their sexual selves. Labelling femininity is an aspect involved in the relations of power which constructs inequality. It also indicated areas where there is a potential for negotiating less constricting relations of power, for example in men's relationship with their partners, and it suggests moments when men appear to resist the appropriation of discursive notions into their sexual selves. This could be a possible interpretation for the position of men who (eventually) reject prostitution as a sexual alternative.

The stories the men told of their sexual lives illustrate the pervasive influence of the discursive notions in affirming their sexual selves. Men's sexuality as essentialist, virtually instinctual, is embodied in the metaphors they use to describe sexual desire and sex. The oppositional constructs of male and female sexuality are produced by emphasizing men's performance in sexual encounters. Women's presence and pleasure is mediated through these expressions.

Yet notions of women's sexuality are far more ambiguous than is supposed in the sexual language. It is not whether a woman is sexually active that constructs difference, but rather, if she sexually conforms to the label she is given. Underlying the labels of femininity is a fragmented notion of sexual desire which, in some situations, appears and is believed to be virtually instinctual, while in others it is enacted as one of many emotions enmeshed in the actor's emotional world. This is expressed in sexual encounters which seem predetermined as aimed at pure sexual satisfaction, constructing women who serve as sexual outlets such as the *pacharacas* and *rucas* as opposed to those with whom they can experience their sexuality within a realm of emotions that include sexual desire. Women's gender identity is split into those who are recognized as social actors and those who are recognized as sexual actors. The representation of the prostitute is the most powerful expression of the woman as sexual actor.

The significance of the partner for a man's sexual and emotional world illustrates how discourse and subjectivity continually interact. The relationship with the *chica de su casa* is the locus where different emotions are enmeshed in a social world. The woman's sexuality is perceived by men positively. The sexual relationship with the partner is considered the most gratifying. This meaning of the *chica de su casa* conflicts with the discursive gender notions which portrays her as the good, asexual woman. Yet, at the same time, the relationship reflects the workings of the discourse. The partner remains the woman who is protected, treated with respect and for whom certain feelings are reserved. In this sense, men continue to place their adult partner on a pedestal, as they did their girlfriends in their teenage years. There is little difference in behaviour between the adolescent who would not push his girlfriend to go too far and a man's adult relationship, in which he continues to make a distinction between his partner and other women. The different meanings embedded in the label *chica de su casa* simultaneously express difference and conform to the discursive image. Discourse and subjectivity conflate in this symbol of femininity.

The continual motion between discourse and subjectivity produces difference between men. Some men could not envision themselves as *pacharaqueros*. They had trouble experiencing sex as purely sexual. Other men are able to have a relationship and maintain a sexual life outside their relationship *sacando la vuelta*. The most transparent expression of difference is found in men's experiences with prostitutes. Despite the social acceptance of prostitution as a sexual alternative, and the frequency with which men turn to the prostitute for sexual satisfaction, many of the men's experiences reshape the idea that prostitution is a pleasurable way to obtain sexual satisfaction. They considered it a last resort rather than an erotic haven of pleasure, as it is often portrayed. Additionally, their experiences challenge the fixed representation of the client which is often found in prostitution studies. The difficulty of envisaging sex as the sole objective was decisive for the men who chose not to go to prostitutes. The initial experience with a prostitute for some men was such a disillusionment that it made it harder for them to find pleasure in their encounters. Other men eventually appropriated the sexual discourse concerning prostitution as their own and began to find their encounters with prostitutes gratifying. For those men who decided to stop going to the prostitutes, the decision was influenced by the gratification they obtained from their relationships with a partner on more egalitarian terms. Although going to prostitutes may not be considered a sexual outlet for all men, it still remains a male prerogative. Their rejection of prostitution is not a rejection of the essentialist notion of male sexuality. What they are rejecting, for various reasons, is its most extreme expression. Their accounts have shown that even if they did not use prostitution as a sexual alternative, the notion of sexual desire they uphold, is nonetheless, fragmented into two.

Male projections of their sexual desire and intentions are at the foundation of the sexual relations of power. Consequently, they perceive themselves as virtually always maintaining control in their sexual experiences. Through labelling, intricate relations of power are constructed with every kiss or caress given. Metaphorically speaking, these relations function as gendered enclosures. In this intricate configuration of male sexuality a specific place is allotted for prostitutes. Second, the separation between the sexual and social in men's experiences of their sexuality closes around the women-who-prostitute, disregarding them as social agents. Men's experiences with prostitutes is one of the strongest enactments of the divorce between the sexual and social. Improvements in the situation of prostitutes will be eternally postponed if the prostitute as a sexual actor remains conceptually opposed to the prostitute as social actor in men's experiences.

**PART II**

DAY AND NIGHT

# 4    WRITING UP THE RHYTHM OF FIELDWORK
An Introduction to Part II

## THE RHYTHM OF FIELDWORK

In my view social analysis should look beyond the dichotomy of order versus chaos toward the less explored realm of 'nonorder'. (Rosaldo 1989: 102)

Fieldwork is a space of interaction which heavily depends on constructing close social relations for its success. Paradoxically, it is defined by a determinate amount of time and predetermined objectives which could be interpreted as obstacles in reaching the research goals. When fieldwork gets into motion, a certain rhythm develops which is an outcome of a degree of repetition the anthropologist acquires in her daily practices. A certain energy level is reached – partially a consequence of being overly aware that fieldwork is not an endless process. It is produced by the relationships in the field, generated from the (un)events and the rhythms of daily life in the research setting. Fieldwork zooms.

This fieldwork experience was complicated. In this chapter, several of its aspects are mapped out. It is intended to serve as a prelude to the ethnographic narrative from three different perspectives. First, following this short introduction, a description of the two fieldwork localities are given to present their particularities and show the significance night and day work had for the main actors of the narrative: the prostitutes and myself. The positioning of myself in the narrative is based on certain epistemological principles contained in the notions of reflexivity and intersubjectivity, and brings me to the second perspective addressed in this chapter.[1] Reflexivity can be defined as:

... a possibility that loosens us from habit and custom and turns us back to contemplate ourselves just as we may be beginning to realize that we have no clear idea of what we are doing. The experience may be exhilarating or frightening or both, but it is generally irreversible ... subject and object fuse ... Reflexive knowledge, then, contains not only messages, but also information as to how it came into being, the process by which it was obtained. (Meyerhoff and Ruby, quoted in Schrijvers 1991: 168)

Taking a reflexive stance into the field implies a complete overhaul of the relationship between researchers and research subjects. This relationship is anchored on epistemological and ethical assumptions that inform a reflexive stance. Moments arose during fieldwork which brought into question these assumptions. These instances of epistemological and ethical dissonance were a valuable source of knowledge.

Finally, the chapter elucidates the decisions made during the writing process, which orchestrate and structure the movements of the research participants on paper and slowly transform the fieldwork into ethnography. These decisions contain certain (political) implications regarding the power of the anthropologist in this last phase of the project. Making these decisions explicit is one of the responsibilities of practising a reflexive anthropology.

*The Daytime Beat*

The neighbourhood which is the material of our study has a grand historical tradition which is intimately related to the total urbanization process of the city of Lima. Its streets carry tradition. They are the only ones which remain from Lima's past; each one offers a particular history that makes us relive the height of the colonial era, full of romanticism with its old viceregal mansions, surrounded by their fields where parties were held. Although these days it is almost in ruins, it remains a splendid memorial of this past era. (Verlarde Vargas 1957: 38)

This quote was not chosen for its romantic ode to the colonial era but rather because it still is an accurate description of Barrios Altos even today. Barrios Altos is one of the oldest districts of Lima. The colonial architecture which reminds Lima of its past has further deteriorated, in some cases to the point of dilapidation. It is a *tugurio* (slum) characterized by:

... dwellings in a state of near-demolition, multi-family units living in cramped space and paying high rents, or old houses divided over and over again, [this] and the range of social and legal problems, are discriminating factors which cause construction companies to prefer and turn to fast and easy expansion in places where these problems do not exist. (Milliones 1978: 13)

The majority of the prostitutes who work during the day do not live in this neighbourhood. They come to the street in the morning and leave at the end of the afternoon. Regardless of their place of residence, Barrios Altos plays a significant role in their lives and the construction of their identities. First of all, they work on one particular street for an indeterminate number of years and have become a part of the street picture. Often, their overt presence leads to accusations regarding their contribution to the neighbourhood's downfall. In any event, through their work they participate daily in the goings-on on this street. Moreover, they know everyone who lives there and are always up to date on the neighbourhood crises and 'scandals'. Whether the neighbourhood disapproves of their presence or not, they are a part of it. Second, and extremely relevant for this study, the women come from comparable districts – maybe not as infamous as Barrios Altos – and they are more than familiar with the daily problems in this type of urban setting and share many of the cultural values and norms with the surrounding neighbours. In many ways they are no different from the majority of women who live in urban impoverishment.

Many prejudices exist concerning the *tugurios* of Lima. These are not only commonly accepted by average Limeneans, but they are also subtly expressed in the academic literature and in the field of development. All of these contribute to maintaining the marginal position of this urban population.

Barrios Altos, or any slum in Lima for that matter, differs from the *pueblo jóven* or *barriada* (squatter settlement) in the significance given to the state of the housing in each area. Whereas a half-constructed or unfinished house in a *barriada* stands for progress and hope, in Barrios Altos it is a sign of dilapidation. Further distinctions can be made between these two types of urban settlements. The populations of *barriadas* generally consist of recently arrived migrants from the Andean regions, or people who are trying to escape Lima's overcrowded inner city, while many Barrio Altos inhabitants can trace their origins as far back as the colonial period. These *criollos* take pride in their cultural traditions, the most widely known of which are its music, parties (*jaranas*) and food.[2] Another group of inhabitants living in the district arrived during the first migration wave in the 1930s from the Andean regions (Milliones 1978). The *barriada* is characterized by its high visibility in the social science literature and its inhabitants are designated as target groups for non-governmental organizations (NGOs), while Barrios Altos and its residents are nearly invisible in both domains.[3]

Very few studies have dealt with the *tugurios* of Lima. Patch is one of the exceptions. He states:

There has been so much research and writing about the *barriadas* of Lima and the *favelas* of Rio de Janeiro that some people believe that the *barriadas* are the lower-class neighbourhoods of Lima. On the contrary, the lower-class neighbourhoods, where the poorest classes and criminals live, are found in Lima's centre. These lower-class neighbourhoods in the inner city are the places where the majority of individuals do not wish to establish themselves and are anxious to leave. The lower-class neighbourhoods are closed societies, impenetrable to the outsider, and it is not possible to study them through ordinary sociological and anthropological techniques. The studious stranger, if he is lucky to leave without being harmed, would have only received idealized and superficial answers to his questions. For this reason the lower-class neighbourhoods of the inner city have hardly been studied and rarely described. (1974: 230)

It is debatable whether the infrequency of research in slum neighbourhoods can be attributed to the characteristics described by Patch. It is certainly more difficult, and even more dangerous, to do research in such neighbourhoods, but it is not entirely impossible. His reluctance to enter these neighbourhoods did not impede him from studying them. It did, however, determine his methodology. In his article 'La Parada, el mercado en Lima: un estudio de clase y assimilación' (1974) he pays informants to interview inhabitants of Lima's infamous neighbourhood, La Parada. Situated close to Lima's centre it is not only one of the most dangerous neighbourhoods but also contains the wholesale market which feeds the majority of Lima's population. Still, Patch is guilty of basing his methodological decision on commonly accepted prejudices circulating about these urban settings. These prejudices not only put people off coming to these neighbourhoods but also have direct repercussions for their residents in their daily lives. Milliones relates an incident which occurred in 1975 when Lima was left without police control for several days. Businesses were ransacked and, when control was re-established, the police raided many of the houses of the residents in a neighbourhood of Barrios Altos, confiscating any electrical appliance, clothes or furniture that looked new and whose owners could not clearly explain its origins (1978: 57).

Living in a neighbourhood such as Barrios Altos is, nonetheless, different from living in a *barriada* or any other popular neighbourhood in the city. Milliones describes Huerta Perdida, the neighbourhood rumoured to be the most dangerous of the district, as follows:

> At 6 o'clock in the evening the doors are being locked all over the neighbourhood and comments are made about the juvenile bands who have terrorized the neighbourhood. Whether or not this is certain (our team never observed any type of vandalism), it demonstrates the general climate of mistrust that reigns throughout the neighbourhood. Huerta Perdida lives in fear of its own reputation. (1978: 60)

With few exceptions (e.g. Milliones 1978; Taller de Testimonio 1986) the image of the *tugurio* presented in the literature accentuates its negative qualities (e.g. Collier 1978; Champa and Acha 1986). Life in a *tugurio* is far more complex than the sketch which emerges from the literature. This picture excludes the moments of solidarity, the attempts to organize, how people have incorporated and manage the negative elements in their lives and, finally, how relationships are constructed in a perpetual condition of extreme poverty. Without insight into these issues it is extremely difficult to understand people's choices, their motivations, how they manage and why they stay.

The lives of individuals living in a slum and in a continual state of poverty are conditioned by the circumstances of this context. The problems they deal with daily – unemployment, the living conditions, violence – inform their world-view and how they relate to it. In criticizing the representation of Barrios Altos, I do not deny the existence of crime and drug addiction in the neighbourhood. Nor am I suggesting that a high level of solidarity is discernible in neighbourhoods like Barrios Altos. The point is that so few studies have seriously dealt with the *tugurios* of Lima that it is still hard to envision what it means to live or work there. The surface has scarcely been scratched.

The women working on this particular street in Barrios Altos have a very good idea what it means to be part of this neighbourhood. The majority have been prostituting there for many years, although I could never determine with any certainty exactly how many. They were equally evasive when the subject of age was mentioned. It slowly became clear the majority were either close to 40 or older. At least three were nearly 50. Age and prostitution is a very touchy subject. Although getting older is inevitable, it is nonetheless problematic. It appears that 40 is tacitly accepted as the cut-off line – the time to retire. Many women stay 38 for years to avoid being considered too old and less desirable.

On average, the women earn approximately US $2.50 for each client, a part of which goes to pay for the room they rent in a nearby *callejon*. This extremely cheap price designates them as the'lowest' class of prostitutes. Nevertheless, some managed to earn at least three times the official minimum wage (US $90 a month);[4] a feat unlikely to be achievable working elsewhere because none of them had completed secondary school and several had not gone further than the first years of primary school. The nature of their work is comparable to brothel work. It is the quantity of clients and not the quality of the encounter which counts. They terminate each encounter as quickly as possible.

Day-time prostitution has many advantages. The women leave the neighbourhood before nightfall and are not confronted with the nocturnal events that become more dangerous and illegal as the night progresses. Furthermore, if necessary, they can disguise their work for outsiders and members of their family. They uphold the appearance of having a day-time job. Finally, it permits them to complete their domestic responsibilities before they leave and be home in the evening to attend to their families' needs.

I visited this group of women twice a week at the house of Clara, who earns a part of her income preparing *almuerzo* (hot midday meal) for the women. I never accompanied them while they worked. When we met on the street we usually greeted each other in passing but I would wait until they came to Clara's house to converse. The topics of our conversations depended greatly on what was going on in the house at that moment. Neighbours frequently came in and out to borrow things, relatives who lived in the vicinity came by, and Clara always shared her house with someone else on a temporary or more permanent basis. Sometimes the women would not show up, sometimes they would eat hastily and return to work. A day of fieldwork in Barrio Altos was totally unpredictable. The acceptance of this rhythm of fieldwork caused radical changes to occur in the methodology and brought certain epistemological issues to the forefront.

## The Night-time Swing

The profile of the women who work at night contrasts sharply with that of the day-time prostitutes. They are considerably younger; the majority are in their early or mid-twenties. Many of them claim they finished some type of vocational training, but could not find suitable employment and had no other possibility than to start prostituting. They work in a middle-class section known for its entertainment and leisure establishments. The street prostitutes blend in with the nightlife. Most of them do not dress outlandishly or in any way that calls attention to themselves. It takes a trained eye to distinguish them from other women strolling the streets. Nonetheless, the women working at night belong to a sub-group. Their contacts are limited to the other people recognized as belonging to this group.

I became acquainted with a group of women who work on the street during the night and congregated at a restaurant. I visited them twice a week, accompanied by my male assistant Roberto. After several hours at the restaurant, we proceeded to a club in the vicinity where another group of prostitutes work.[5] We stayed several hours talking to the employees, the customers and the women. All the women who work in this area expect to be paid US $50 per client. Thus, they regarded the quality of the encounter as more important than the quantity. The encounter could take all night.

Working at night is physically and emotionally strenuous. As in any type of continuous nightwork, the person's biological rhythm becomes distorted. In addition, this type of work usually includes regular use of alcohol. Moreover, it is more difficult to think up a pretext for being absent during the night. Different strategies are employed to cover up their way of making money. Some women tell their families they work for a rich Japanese family as a live-in maid, renting a room and only returning home on their day off. Still others leave their families and children in their place of birth, only returning for holidays or a vacation. Finally, their nocturnal schedule limits their participation in day-time activities. Several women are completely estranged from a diurnal routine, while others – those who live with their children – make every effort they could to keep participating.

My life was also structured along the distinction between day and night. If I visited the day group, I returned home and continued normal daily activities. If I worked at night, I would go home at about four in the morning, hoping to sleep until late. There was little left of the day when I started to regain my energy, probably at the same time the women started to prepare themselves to go to work. It goes without saying that the comparison stops here. Our work, its gratification, the psychological or emotional pressures share no similarities whatsoever.

There are other aspects in relation to the two settings which ingrained the division of night and day even deeper. During the day, I met the women in the space they used when they took a break. I did not have to blend into their work environment. When I left the neighbourhood, I vanished until the following visit. At night, we were a part of the rhythm of the nightlife, with its loud music, alcohol and groups of people out for a good time. We visited the prostitutes while they worked. Consequently, more often than not, our conversation came to a close when a client showed interest in the woman I was talking to. No one expected me to act 'like a prostitute'; nonetheless, this setting placed some unspoken demands on my behaviour, different from those I felt during the day. In contrast to the day setting, I visited this middle-class neighbourhood frequently during the day. It was not I who did the disappearing act, rather the women vanished from the neighbourhood until the streetlights came on and the night began.

One totally distinct feature of the night-time fieldwork was working with a male assistant. My entrance into the nightlife was prepared beforehand by my male assistant and a friend of his who knew the ins and outs of the nightlife. From the moment I sat down at the restaurant, I entered directly into relationships with a certain degree of fluidity. Nonetheless, this did not erase the problems which characterized the research in both areas nor did it change the rhythm of the research process which was determined by the circumstances, the people who were present, the conversation and its unpredictability.

Working with an assistant had many advantages and also several problems and challenges. Although it is not always made explicit, our relationship cannot be removed from the material collected. It influenced the events and contributed to the construction of meanings. In addition, conflicts which arose between us brought on momentary changes in the fieldwork.

The first series of conflicts resulted in the dismissal of my first research assistant. One of the tasks of the research assistant was to serve as a type of protection if necessary. For example, if a client paid too much attention to me, I could always point to my assistant and claim I was accompanied. Another task was to help make new contacts and participate directly in the dynamics of the night. However, my assistant was having severe personal problems which made it difficult for him to manage the nightlife. I could not trust his judgements in regard to my safety and I questioned his approach to the women. I never envisioned I would be put in the position of the employer who eventually fires her employee because he does not live up to expectations. The decision was made even more difficult because I knew I was letting him go at the peak of the economic crisis. However, after much deliberation and various attempts to try alternative scenarios to lessen his burden without leaving him jobless, I had to let him go. The moments leading up to this decision did not cause any permanent damage, but they did not contribute positively to the research process.

In spite of our parting, we maintained an amicable relationship. He still appeared on the scene and kept his contacts. This was not very pleasant but it was unproblematic until the following unforeseen event occurred.

After a quiet conversation with my ex-assistant who told me he was going to leave the topic of sexuality and prostitution behind him, I ran into one of the women a few days later who explained she had been approached for a photographic interview by a journalist and photographer from the magazine *Caretas* whom my ex-assistant had brought there. Naturally, she refused. Nonetheless, I not only felt betrayed because our conversations concerning the ethics of fieldwork and the importance of anonymity had been to no avail, I worried about the consequences this might have for the women and for the research. *Caretas'* treatment of prostitution was no better than that of many of the sensationalist newspapers. Moreover, I could not predict the consequences, if any, this would have for my relationship with the women. For example, since I had promised them anonymity, did they still consider it a credible promise or would they begin to mistrust me? Thus, the only feasible solution was to try to have the publication of this article stopped. I spent several days, using all my contacts, to arrange a meeting with the editor. He could offer no guarantees that he would stop the article's publication, but to my relief it was not published.

Through my ex-assistant's actions a slice of fieldwork ethics was disclosed. I was outraged by his actions and could not forgive him. I terminated our friendship, but, to my dismay, he continued to come to the Plaza, looking for empathy amongst our mutual friends and stressing that he did not understand why I would not talk to him anymore. Interestingly enough, while I was wrapped up in this ethical dilemma, our mutual women friends did not dwell on the subject. They were more concerned with saving our friendship. Different women tried to get me to talk to him on several occasions. They could not understand my behaviour and, even after I explained in detail why I took this drastic step, they still were more concerned with patching up our friendship than the fact that he had helped the journalist or how I felt it affected my work. Apparently, my ethical questions about misusing contacts, anonymity, how an article of this genre could affect the women's lives, were exactly that – my own. The women refused to collaborate, shrugged it off after it happened and did not give it any more thought. This also says something about the conceptualization of power. A good anthropologist always tries to protect the group participating in her project. It is extremely important to maintain this ethical principle in the field and during the writing up process. However, because the research group is envisioned as vulnerable, it is often assumed they find it difficult to protect themselves, overlooking the fact that most vulnerable people are continuously protecting themselves and usually more experienced in this area than the anthropologist.

After the dismissal of my first assistant, I worked with his friend Roberto, who had originally introduced us into the nightlife. Our relationship puzzled many people. Whenever I appeared at the Plaza, he always accompanied me. Everyone knew we came there to work, but the idea of work was very vague. We sat, chatted and drank. When the women sat down at our table, they were generally taking a break and rarely made any explicit overtures to attract a client. They used the time to check out the scene, be with their boyfriends or talk to us. If one of our friends passed by, they joined us for a while without disturbing the research process. So what was this thing we called work?

For a very long time people thought we had an amorous relationship. I would explain repeatedly that they were mistaken, but this was met with a sigh of disbelief. Eventually, they accepted we did not have a relationship, but they did not rule out the possibility that we might be having an affair.

The same disbelief existed at the club, even more so. What else would a woman, always accompanied by the same man, be doing there if she did not prostitute? Here, once again the people eventually realized we were not an 'item', but they did not find it easy to describe our relationship. For a few of the women who aspired to have an affective relationship with Roberto, our working relationship was an obstacle. Once he got into a terrible fight with a woman after I left, because he had to leave her to accompany me to a taxi. Accompanying me to a taxi or seeing me to my door was a customary part of fieldwork. It would have been too risky to go home alone during the early hours of the morning. Normally, a ritual-like exchange evolved between Roberto and the taxi-driver. He said good-bye to me and exchanged some well chosen words with the driver conveying that he relied on him to look after my well-being. I would symbolically be given from one man to another. At other times, when I felt less safe, he accompanied me to my door. The women accepted that I was at the club to work but often became annoyed when they were reminded that Roberto was also working.

These examples show that during fieldwork the dyad of the researcher and assistant is one site where gendered relations of power both come into play and are taken for granted. Yet, this topic is rarely visible in ethnographic accounts. The recognition of the problems involved in working with a male research assistant led to a fruitful analysis of the construction of our gender identities, which will be presented further on.

## EPISTEMOLOGICAL AND ETHICAL DISSONANCE

Aware of the necessity of an investigation of prostitution which would represent prostitutes not only in relation to their work, but also as female individuals living in a broader community, I set out to the field with a research plan designed to investigate the 'meanings of gender' in the lives of women-who-prostitute. Assuming I would be unable to accompany women while they worked, I chose life stories as the most adequate means of representation for the research objectives. How was I to know I would easily gain entrance into the areas where prostitutes worked and I would be seeing the same women on a regular basis? I perceived this as a positive change and proceeded to remake the mental script of the fieldwork that was to follow. I was certain this change would make it easier to ask questions, to understand how things worked, and to perceive non-verbal, sensual aspects nearly impossible to reach in an interview setting. Ultimately, the relationships between myself and the women would flourish because they would be based on mutual trust and respect. In retrospect, I am still convinced of my good intentions, even though the fieldwork reflected little of this progressive, cumulative scenario. What ensued was a continuous confrontation between the reality of fieldwork and the ethical and epistemological principles I took to the field – some of a more feminist nature and others covering a broader social science terrain. What emerged from its centre determined the rhythm of fieldwork.

To put it mildly, doing fieldwork on prostitution in Lima was tough. It was physically exhausting, emotionally trying and the women-who-prostituted were not always cooperative. What was our relationship like? How can our communication be characterized? From my perspective our relationship can be classified as difficult and taxing. Curiosity, an excellent attribute for an anthropologist, is not considered a virtue in this urban setting. When I brought up topics relevant to my research, a silence would fall or curt answers would be given, lies would be told. Getting to know more about the women's lives outside work also proved difficult. Interpreting our relationship from their perspective, it was probably very similar to other relationships with strangers or outsiders. Very little is talked about, much is concealed or avoided and distrust reigns. They showed little interest in what I was doing and their lack of interest made it impossible to explain in detail how my research could (indirectly) make a difference – a *sine qua non* of achieving successful feminist research.[6]

One of the epistemological principles which defines feminist research is that it must contribute to the improvement of the research subjects' situation and give something back to the research group. The subjects should be aware of the research's potential to provoke change. Subsequently, it is assumed they willingly work towards this goal (for example, Schrijvers 1991). A quick evaluation of our relationship shows my research was failing on this count. My gesture of reciprocity was confined to distributing condoms, making a material difference for some women.[7] Still, I did not consider this sufficient. The closest I came to reaching this target was receiving several women's recognition of the project's importance, but more often than not they just saw me as a writer.

There is a tacit recognition in feminist anthropology that the research group will willingly work towards the research goals. Should I have looked for a group of prostitutes who wanted me to do research? This search would have been futile. There are neither organized groups of prostitutes nor prostitutes who have demonstrated an interest in participating in a research project beforehand. Instead of perceiving this as a failure, this made me reconsider the value of the assumption.

Holding on to the assumption that our research must benefit the group directly could ultimately lead to a process of exclusion of a large group of women whose unwillingness to cooperate is, for example, attributable to their desire to avoid confrontation with their pain. They will not try to sabotage the project, but they will not be as eager to help as the researcher would wish. If the only subjects deemed researchable are those that grow out of the research group's interests or structure to directly contribute to the research group's improvements, feminist research will be restricted to particular groups of women who are somehow involved in a process of change. Research topics will be chosen for their degree of compatibility with feminist assumptions. Should research be abandoned because the women-who-prostitute did not offer 100 per cent collaboration? Should I have given up my research because of the resistance I felt and because I knew it was unlikely my research would benefit them directly? My reply to both questions is no.

There is an urgent need for good feminist research on the subject of prostitution in Lima. I am not suggesting this project fulfils all the requirements, but it has the capacity to contribute to changing ideational notions concerning prostitution among the NGOs working with women and cause a commotion in other areas. This can serve as a first step to propelling change.[8]

Strongly related to this assumption is another of even greater significance, the intersubjective fieldwork relationship. An attempt is made to create a relationship of dialogue which minimizes power differences: 'both are assumed to be individuals who reflect upon their experience and who communicate those reflections' (Acker et al. 1991: 140) and produce knowledge together. In other words, both the Other and the Self are present in the fieldwork process and in the ethnography which follows.

Holding on to this ideal assures ethically proper research, but it does not necessarily minimize the power differences between the researcher and the researched. The decision to combat asymmetrical relationships has been taken by the researcher. The anthropologist assumes beforehand that both parties desire an egalitarian, harmonious relationship. It is not a joint decision or one necessarily reflecting the subject's yearning. Although such a relationship is less harmful than one based on asymmetry, the anthropologist once again is the person who orchestrates the setting. She does not relinquish the bandleader's baton and, above all, she still has the power to decide whether she will release it at all.

This premise makes too many presumptions about the concept of power. In the first place, the anthropologist assumes she is in the position of power. What is this notion of power based on? The power to define the research project? The power obtained from class, culture or ethnic differences? If the anthropologist finds herself in a position of power because she is defining the terms of research, is it not a bit audacious to assume she also defines the terms of power in the relationship in other areas? Why does the projection of power relations in the field reflect a nearly binary opposition between the powerful and the powerless instead of departing, as in other areas, from a notion of difference and the multi-positioned subject?

In the second place, what happens in situations where the research subjects are not interested in an egalitarian relationship? For example, either they have no problems accepting the difference which exists between themselves and the researcher and are not interested or do not feel comfortable in an egalitarian relationship, or, conversely, which happens to be the case in my research, the people being researched are not interested in sharing power. The women gave me no more than a minimal amount of room for manoeuvre, and control of the situation remained in their hands. They decided when, about what and whether we would talk. Of course I made efforts to negotiate alternative configurations of power relations. I attempted to build trusting relationships, in which they would eventually feel comfortable enough to relate their life story. There is no denying our relationships were founded on respect and a certain amount of trust, but this impasse in dialogue was never completely resolved. The women who participated in this study did not desire a relationship which minimized asymmetry. They seemed content to hold on to the reins throughout the duration of fieldwork.

Thus, it is necessary at times to rethink this golden rule and expose the ethnocentric assumptions on which it is based. One way to accomplish this is to analyse the relations of power in each fieldwork context individually and release the researcher and the researched from the fixed position given to them, to 'work the hyphens' between the Self and Other (Fine 1994, quoted in Lal 1996: 207). Accordingly, we will gain more insight into the notion of power and related issues relevant for the research project.

Intermeshed within these previously discussed assumptions is a third one. Woman should do research with women because all women are in the position of the Other. This will not only contribute to optimizing the potential for an intersubjective relationship but will also contribute positively to the construction of knowledge. Differences encountered between the subjects are acknowledged and used to enrich the relationship. This prevailing assumption is exactly that: an assumption which guides many of us in our explorations but does not hold up in all situations.

It did not take long to become aware that the nature of the relationships differed between the women and myself and with my male assistant. They seemed to be at ease talking to him, they let their guard down and confided in him, while I felt they often kept their distance and held up a certain image to me.

In retrospect, I accept certain things which felt like serious dilemmas in the field. I realize we received different messages and information. During fieldwork I assumed, as all good social scientists would, that if Roberto had received different information than myself, he had received the truth and myself the false information. I was inclined to think he received the truth more often than I did. After all, he had a more fluid, less problematic relationship with the women and was born in Lima, making it easier for him to read between the lines. After reading over my notebooks several time, I realized that Roberto was able to appeal to the women using male–female gender relations to his advantage. He was flirtatious and charming and the women enjoyed his attention. In the aftermath, I am no longer convinced there is a true and a false version, rather we received different versions of the truth, one more appropriate for a female listener and the other for a man. During fieldwork, this dilemma caused several reflexive moments which exposed certain features of femininity and masculinity in the world of prostitution.

There are various positions belonging to men in the nightlife. They are clients, husbands (*maridos*), pimps, managers, bouncers or waiters. Before the women got to know my assistant he was a potential client. When they became aware of his intentions, they continued to talk to him because he showed them respect, was interested in what they had to say and gave them affection. Many of the women trusted him and perhaps some wished they had a man like him in their daily lives and aspired to obtain him. Some of them fell in love with him, others appreciated his friendship.

There is no existing role for a woman who does not prostitute and her role is even harder to conceptualize if she is a foreigner. Gradually, I realized they regarded me as the *buena mujer* (good woman). *Buena mujer* has a double connotation. The first shows their acceptance of a non-prostitute in their setting. The friend who does not think badly of us, who helps us, who does not compete, a different person than other women who do not prostitute.

The second connotation overshadows the first by highlighting the differences between them and the woman who has a profession, a love life, a gratifying life. This second interpretation constructed barriers between us. For some I represented the type of woman they would like to be. Therefore my presence was a reminder of their dreams and desires, which they experienced as nearly impossible to obtain, making them feel too uncomfortable to tell me their stories. Perhaps they did not consciously compare me to themselves, nonetheless the result was the same. Either I was an exception to the run-of-the-mill good woman or, on another level, I reflected this very same good woman they maintained that I was not. They upheld gender dichotomies between us.

Sustaining the assumption that female anthropologists are better equipped and find it easier to do research with women led to a dilemma. Certainly the reflexive analysis which grew out of this dilemma was fruitful. Nevertheless, working with this premise blinded me to other conceivable relationships which were not necessarily the epistemological ideal, but would not necessarily exclude a relationship between the researcher and the research subject based on mutual respect and other elements that form the foundation of feminist methodology. If I had abandoned this assumption from the start, I would probably have experienced less frustration and this point would not have given rise to a conflict between my assistant and myself. I could have started from the point where I eventually ended. Who knows where that might have taken me. Because of my epistemological stubbornness, it took longer to find a solution to this dilemma. We decided to transform this conflict into an advantage. Roberto would keep a diary and, upon completing his fieldwork, would present a final report on his nocturnal experiences. This would not only permit the two versions to be woven together but would also facilitate an analysis of gender relations and identity in fieldwork. Unfortunately, his diary and final report never materialized. Thus, in the process of writing up, I am forced to reconstruct parts of his story relying on my memory.

A last issue which closes the subject of the intersubjective relationship concerns the methodological use of life stories to complete feminist objectives. In her discussion of feminist ethnography, D. Bell states, 'Feminist ethnography opens a discursive space for the "subjects" of the ethnography and as such is simultaneously empowering and destabilizing' (1993: 31). One of the ways of creating this discursive space for the research subject is through life stories. For these and other reasons, for example, the rich and subtle details which flow out of a life story, I was determined to use life stories as my primary source of material. Little did I know this would prove almost impossible. During fieldwork I conducted five interviews. Two of them resembled interrogations. The first was with a woman who worked at the club during the whole period when I was doing fieldwork. She gave me the interview at the beginning. The other was with a prostitute who lives in Barrios Altos. The three other interviews bear a strong resemblance to life stories, particularly the two interviews conducted with women with whom I was less acquainted. What does this imply about intersubjectivity and research aimed at empowering those being researched and at reducing asymmetrical relationships?[9] Suzanna eloquently answers these questions in a few simple sentences. 'I have left the past behind me. I don't want to think about it, I don't want to think about the future, I just live for today. I don't want to think about it because I don't want to recognize how I earn my money, I earn my money in an ugly way.' Doing a life story would force the women to recognize what they are doing and accept it as something more permanent. A life story is a reminder of what they do, it can work as a catalyst, that forces them to come to terms with the way they earn a living, which the majority of the women would rather avoid doing. And, as we will see below, a life story creates a dimension of permanence, which in their enactments as prostitutes they try to avoid at all costs.

Considering all of the above, it should come as no surprise that the majority of the women were not interested in doing life stories. The clearest statement made was when they did not show up for an appointment. Even one of the women whom I got to know more intimately, who promised and kept reminding me we had an appointment to make (referring to an interview), when it came down to it she did not show up and had a feeble excuse for why she could not make it. Life stories may be a way of sharing power with the research subjects, but for the majority of the women it was a threat to their identity and it put pressure on them to accept, recognize and incorporate the fact they were prostituting. This questions whether the use of life stories as a method of empowerment is appropriate in all situations. It suggests the need to evaluate the possibility not only beforehand but also during the fieldwork process.

The final aspect which influenced the rhythm of fieldwork is directly related to the nature of fieldwork. No matter what anthropological current one adheres to, one of the ultimate goals of fieldwork is to understand and make sense of what is going on. Even though non-order (Rosaldo 1989) may reign and need not be a hindrance, there is still a need to discover logical patterns or to search for continuity. This search constructs a dimension of permanence which is juxtaposed to the women-who-prostitute's objectives.

Many prostitutes dream of getting out as soon as possible. They experience prostitution as a temporary choice and they live within an illusion of continual temporariness by planning the moment of retirement either in material terms – 'When I have saved enough money ...', 'When I am able to start my own business ...', 'When I am able to finish my house ...' – or in temporal expressions –'Four more years then I'll quit', 'When I turn 30 I'll leave.' This belief is acted out in their evasiveness and in their lies. Perhaps the desire to get out does not match their actual situation but it is nonetheless what keeps them going. Thus, women-who-prostitute create a situation in which permanence is avoided, creating the sensation they can slip away without many questions being asked or without being noticed. An anthropologist who is prepared to ask questions, to delve deeper and try to make sense of things is creating permanence. In this fieldwork setting, the notions of temporariness and permanence were continually at odds.

Lying goes beyond creating an ambience of temporariness. It is a way of managing information. In most cases it is not meant to be a personal affront, nor should each lie be looked at as if it were something that could be unravelled to reveal the truth. Sometimes lies are never discovered. Being lied to during fieldwork drove me crazy; still, I did not always set out to find the truth. I listened to what was being said and tried to interpret the message being transmitted.[10]

I was told on several occasions that lying soothes, makes one immune in this hard world, it kills curiosity. Thus, lying glosses over what the women are doing and makes it easier to sustain a stance of non-acceptance concerning their work. At the same time it offers protection.

Lying symbolizes the burden of a double life and the energy needed to manage it successfully. In part, they are willing to conceal parts of their lives and carry this burden because of the shame they feel working as prostitutes, and would be made to feel if it became known to others. A protective coating intended to keep strangers out surrounds the personal lives of the women. Lying is a pragmatic decision. The truth can ultimately be used against them and could have severe repercussions in their private lives. Many of the women working at night concealed their work from their families. As mentioned earlier, they have found ways to avoid telling their families what they really do. Some women have hinted that they are involved in an illegal activity such as drugs or counterfeit money (this would account for their having so much money). One young women expressed it as follows: 'I would rather they think I am involved in something illegal than that they find out how I really earn my money.' Even when the family suspects, the women continue to lie at work, to protect their private lives and to make a distinction between the two worlds.

Another more refined tactic of lying is what I came to call a 'grand narrative': a believable account about some aspect of a person's life is only brought into doubt after hearing more or less the same believable story from several people. An example of this is how many women said they had been working at a nine-to-five office job but their bosses started to sexually harass them, coupling promotions or pay-rises with sex. This was considered the impulse to start to prostitute, 'If I am going to do it then why not be paid for it and make good money.' I am not underestimating the degree of sexual harassment that takes place in Peru. On the contrary, more and more complaints are being aired in the newspapers concerning this problem. However, its credibility is brought into question when each time almost the exact same words were used, in approximately the same place in the conversation, and the subject was never brought up or referred to again. This type of plausible lie justifies why they entered into the trade.

Many women who work as prostitutes are aware of the accepted parameters for being a prostitute. In other words the difference between the 'good' and 'bad' prostitute. They give people what they want to hear. Thus childless prostitutes are made into instant mothers, they always work with condoms and have regular check-ups. Lying serves as protection, negation, fantasy and a means of being accepted. A simple lie conceals messages concerning identity. It is a means to shape one's identity. Lal interprets silences and misinformation in the interviews as a form in which: 'research subjects shape their own presentations ... The fact is that our subjects are often not just responding to our agendas and to our questions, but they are also always engaged in actively shaping their presentations to suit their own agendas of how they wish to be represented' (1996: 204). In conclusion, lying is the most intentional performance of the prostitute.

These moments of dissonance not only expose the rhythm of fieldwork, they also bring into question many of the epistemological and ethical principles of our Western scientific tradition that we bring into the field. Furthermore, this analysis is meant to serve the reader as a frame for the following chapters. It gives significance to the fragmented nature of the encounters described, explains why the dialogues at times appear more to be interrogations than conversations and, finally, they explain the silences which can be read between the lines.

AN ETHNOGRAPHY OF FIELDWORK

The dissonance experienced in the field provoked gradual changes during fieldwork which were reflected in the type and contents of the material collected. The 'meanings of gender', which was meant to be a conceptual key in this project, was forced to play a less significant role because of the resistance encountered and expressed through silences, evasiveness and lies. Moreover, the representation of the women who prostitute was restricted to what was told, seen and felt in the working environment and not, as I had hoped, by sharing time outside their work. Unable to rely on life histories, I was restricted to the five handwritten notebooks of conversations, observations and details which epitomized the particularities of non-order; the date serving as the sole ordering principle. Conversations, interwoven with relevant and less relevant sidetracks, were re-read on returning home, causing disturbing moments because it appeared that the sidetracks outweighed the 'genuine' material.[11] I was not expecting to be able to make cultural generalizations, but I had no clue as to how I would construct a coherent whole. In the aftermath, what I felt in my fieldwork and what I came home with on paper were the workings of the gendered enclosures. Paradoxically, but not surprisingly, my movements were highly determined by the same enclosures which restrict the women. This was a logical consequence of our interactions. The women continually embodied versions of the prostitute by reacting to, negating or appropriating the meanings entangled in the gendered enclosures. Why would our relationship be different?

The next question is how to represent all of the above on paper without driving the reader crazy? Without unreeling the whole debate concerning the crisis of representation, textual practice and ethnographic authority, it is necessary to explain certain quandaries and decisions concerning the process of writing up.[12] These basically involve issues of representation (and) of Otherness, ethnographic authority and how both in turn are reflected in textual and stylistic decisions.

The written representation of women-who-prostitute clandestinely is a tricky and delicate endeavour. In the first place, as elucidated in Part I, clandestine prostitutes have been made scapegoats and demeaned throughout history. Second, Chapter 2 has shown that within this cultural setting the generalized image of the prostitute perpetually magnifies Otherness. How do you counterbalance these representations without tipping the scale to the other side, converting them into super-heroines or victims? Finally, and this is the trickiest point, the environment where many of the women work and the neighbourhoods where they live are harsh and in varying degrees violent. Their relationships are not always amicable and I witnessed and unfortunately was pushed into participating in several unpleasant episodes. In other words, how can difference be portrayed without doing more harm than has already been done? The solution lies in looking for an adequate style of representation which strikes a balance between expressing the negativity experienced in their daily lives as prostitutes with portrayals of the women as ordinary poor women living an unsteady existence.

   In the anthropological literature many literary experiments have been undertaken, concentrating on ways to minimize the tension between the ethnographer and the research subject. Emphasis is placed on literary forms which enable Others to speak for themselves, to keep the interference of the Western scientific tradition to a minimum. A turn to the postmodern minimizes the anthropologist's interpretative interventions and encourages polyvocality/polyphony (Clifford 1986: 15). In two feminist ethnographic narratives, the authors recognize their ethnographic authority and stipulate the textual and editorial decisions in the introduction. In the subsequent chapters, both make conscious attempts to minimize their interventions. Abu-Lughod (1993) writes up the Bedouin women's stories clustering them loosely around scientific concepts of anthropological interest. Her detailed and elaborate stories are a result of the use of a tape-recorder and the long-standing relationship with the group of Bedouins whom she writes about. After so many years of friendship, using a tape-recorder without either party being made to feel uncomfortable becomes a viable possibility. In my fieldwork this would be inconceivable. All conversations during the day and night were reconstructed after leaving the location. I never used a tape-recorder or notebook. Upon leaving, I would jot down key words and phrases trying to maintain the sequence of the conversation. These would be worked out at home. Behar (1993) co-produces the book with her research subject. It was not Behar but Esperanza, the protagonist of the narrative, who initiated the relationship with the author and had contemplated the story of her life before the author ever came to the setting. Behar and Esperanza's relationship and the telling of her story developed over a four-year period. In both cases the enduring relationships were an essential factor that permitted these ethnographic narratives to work and let the words speak for themselves, minimizing the anthropologists' interventions. Although currently this textual practice is considered the ideal for many anthropologists, it is not appropriate for writing up all fieldwork material and specifically not for this one. Neither traditional ethnography nor the more seemingly politically correct minimalist approach are the only solution. As Van Maanen states, 'We need to shop around more and encourage narrative ingenuity and novel interpretation ...' (1988: 140). Alternative forms must be able to exist side by side. The trick lies in examining each fieldwork experience individually and allowing it to determine textual practices, instead of shaping fieldwork to fit into existing moulds. 'The value and place of different discursive styles have to be decided by the situation we find ourselves in and the problems we address' (Jackson quoted in Abu-Lughod 1993: 7). Several decisions were made in reference to writing up this fieldwork situation which are elaborated below.

   The chapters that follow are an ethnographic narrative of fieldwork and not an ethnography arising out of fieldwork. The difference lies in that I do not attempt to represent the women's lives outside of the space of interaction constructed by fieldwork. The structure and content of my material does not lend itself to this objective. I construct the narrative by centring on the every-dayness and particularities of the experiences, incidents and events that occurred during fieldwork.

> ... insistently focusing on individuals and the particularities of their lives ... suggest[s] that others live as we perceive ourselves living – not as automatons programmed according to 'cultural' rules or acting out social roles, but as people going through life wondering what they should do, making mistakes, being opinionated, vacillating, trying to make themselves look good, enduring tragic personal losses, enjoying others and finding moments of laughter. (Abu-Lughod 1993: 27)

An ethnography of fieldwork also entails my almost continual presence in the narrative as a co-protagonist and narrator. I was told the anecdotes, dug at information and received non-verbal messages which had to be made sense of. The troubles which arose out of the conflicts of identity, interests and objectives were a result of my presence. If I erased myself from the fieldwork, it would be incomprehensible how my original research plans led to the enactment of another scenario, an unprogrammed different story, but nonetheless a story I am attempting to tell.

As stated previously, none of the alternatives discussed above are suitable literary forms for this ethnography of fieldwork. Although I have attempted to record the words of my informants exactly, and to a certain extent let their words speak for themselves, I have deliberately conferred the role of interpreter on myself. This was a gradual process, which made me feel very uncomfortable at first, because it goes against the grain of ethnographic experiments and assumes a more traditional role for the anthropologist. However, when I finally admitted to myself that I had to appropriate this role, I had less trouble writing up the difficult passages or what I have come to call the unattractive dimensions of daily life. During fieldwork I became highly aware of the intolerant ideas circulating about women-who-prostitute. After completing the first part of the book, I experienced the same sensation but this time on paper. Upon commencing the ethnography, I encountered actions, deeds and statements made by the women which might contribute to strengthening the existing stereotypes and the media-constructed bad reputation of these women. How could I let these words speak for themselves? Considering the Peruvian context and the conserva-tive stance taken towards prostitution, an interpretative frame is required. If I did not make an attempt to interpret and construct the lens through which the reader reads the narrative and chose to minimize my interventions, if I were to let the words lead a life of their own, I would potentially do more harm than good. Abu-Lughod suggests that new forms of writing require the reader to:

> ... adopt sophisticated reading strategies along with social critique. Does this make sense for anthropologists writing in a world still full of prejudice against those about whom they write? (1993: 28–9)

Thus, if the 'act of interpretation requires us to choose among the multiple identities and associations shaping a life' (Personal Narrative Group 1989: 19), then I have definitely chosen the subject matter treated in the following pages. Although, through reading my field notes several times, I was left with the sensation that the subjects made their presence known to me by surfacing and distinguishing themselves from the body of choppy, unpredictable conversations. The analysis of the material and the outline of the narrative was not predetermined, rather it was stipulated along the way. The following chapters are written in a narrative style, enlaced with my analytical interpretations.

Recapturing the distinction between day and night, the ethnographic narratives are structured to tell different stories by accentuating different contextual aspects. Chapters 5 and 6 retell the partial stories of the women who work on one particular street in Barrios Altos. The events and conversations that took place, their relationships with each other and with me are set against a backdrop intended to portray the intricate balance between the women as prostitutes and the prostitute as ordinary woman. Perhaps because they worked during the day and were surrounded by, and blended in with, the diurnal activities, when they were in Clara's house they normally made space for themselves to assume other subject positions. However, they could not entirely erase their prostituting identity when they shut the door behind them and then pick it up again when they returned to the street. It was ingrained in their relationships and informed their views and ways of communicating. In addition, my presence was a constant reminder of their work. The choice of focusing on these aspects in the representation of the day-time women is an attempt to counterbalance existing pervasive prejudices. In the first place they are the lowest category of prostitute, and are most often referred to in the articles concerning clandestine prostitution. Second, being associated with Barrios Altos adds to this stigma the dimension of slum-dweller, the consequences of which have already been discussed. Thus it was necessary to dismantle these prejudices by revealing the everydayness of their activities, their lives and their work. Chapter 6 situates the reader in Barrios Altos by recalling my entrance into the area. I have written up our conversations as dialogues because I presume that this expresses most adequately the mode of our communication and is exemplary for the other chapters in regard to the rhythm of fieldwork. To avoid repetition, I expect the sensations evoked by Chapter 5 to be taken with the reader on the rest of this ethnographic voyage. In addition, my entrance into Barrios Altos was more difficult than in the night, exposing the workings of the construction of identities between myself and several of the women. Chapter 6 goes on to highlight everydayness by clustering the conversations which took place around several events which either represented something significant during fieldwork or, for a fleeting instant, changed the course of the women's lives. These snapshot exposures construct a story based on the daily conversations. They address different issues, reveal values and meanings.

In contrast to the day-time setting, in which I try to create a broader context of everydayness where the women are, so to speak, no different from their female neighbours, in Chapters 7 and 8, which are dedicated to the nightlife, I try to bring to the reader the sensation of nocturnal enclosure, a sensation produced by always working at night. Night-time social life is fundamentally different than that of the day-time:

> There is a shared notion of danger ... when it can be determined that a fellow user of the urban night is trustworthy, feelings of unity and solidarity develop ... because those individuals who turn night into day are aware that they are part of a special situation, feel a common identity and a mutual force of attraction. (Brunt 1996: 75)

In this context, these nightly sensations are recognized and merge into the concept of the *ambiente*. Chapter 7 narrates the stories of fieldwork which took place on a plaza in the centre of this middle-class entertainment and leisure district. Chapter 8 moves us a few blocks further on, to a club called the Crazy Horse.

In its entirety, each locality contextualizes the embodiment and enactment of prostitution differently. Yet despite the diversity the performances share similar particularities – a result of the gendered enclosures which are always in motion.

# 5 SHAPING IDENTITIES IN FIRST ENCOUNTERS

## GETTING TO KNOW THE WOMEN AT CLARA'S

The first time I turned the corner, leaving the main avenue behind, it was unthinkable that this one long city block would eventually become a microcosmic world packed full of all the ingredients of daily life. At this moment, the street did not look any different from other streets of Barrios Altos. It was dusty, noisy and smelly with many houses in a state of deterioration. On this initial journey I was accompanied by one of the members of an NGO that worked with prostitutes, who had offered to show me a few areas where clandestine prostitutes worked. Barrios Altos had a long tradition of clandestine prostitution. When we passed the doorway where the women usually gathered, she indicated it inconspicuously. No one was there. Uncertain if the women still worked there, we went to visit a friend of hers, a nun who lived with a group of Sisters in a house on the corner, to enquire as to their whereabouts. We were in luck. Sister Marta was in. The contrast between the dirty, noisy, aggressive streets and her home – the essence of tranquillity – was heightened by the cup of tea and home-made apple pie we were invited to consume. Marta was certain my appearance was not a coincidence. For a long time she felt something needed to be done for the women who worked here. She agreed to introduce me to her friend Clara who cooked for the women. I would call her during the week to find out the exact time and day.

Between our first visit and the programmed phone call, out of sheer coincidence, I was introduced to a woman who was one of the founders and director of an NGO for the defence of children's rights, whose office was situated on that very same corner of this particular street. I told her of my plans and she was very enthusiastic. She offered me the use of their office facilities and their institution as a pretext for being in the neighbourhood.[1] In any case, I had made up my mind. This particular street in Barrios Altos would be my place of fieldwork. I only had to wait to hear if Clara would be willing to meet me.

Marta was detained the Thursday we had agreed upon for my introduction to Clara. Instead, she instructed one of the novices to accompany me who, unfortunately, was not well acquainted with Clara. We arrived at a door badly in need of repair. A woman answered and told us Clara was not home, 'You can wait if you want to.' She led us into a sparsely furnished front room where strangers are normally left to wait and visitors congregate on special occasions. It had a table and two red armchairs. Rays of light entered the darkened room through cracks in the wooden door. The neon light fixture attached to the high ceiling was in need of repair. Stretched out in one of the chairs with his feet across a new roll of *esteras* (reed mats used in constructing houses) was a man sleeping; he continued to sleep during my entire visit.

Clara, a strikingly tall, huge, white woman, arrived shortly after with a basket full of groceries.[2] The novice left after our introduction. Clara talked to me briefly, making no effort to conceal her indifference. I felt nervously uncomfortable. She abruptly asked me whether she should call the women in yet. I was taken aback, and replied 'Wouldn't it better if I come back after you have spoken to them?' It was not a part of my strategy to do interviews in such an early stage of fieldwork. She replied, 'Whatever.' Something made me change my mind, and I complied with what was expected of me. My anxiety increased while she called in a loud voice to one of the women from the doorway, 'Señora Pilar, Señora Pilar.' Señora Pilar came in accompanied by another woman called Señora Magda.

Señora Pilar was a heavy-set *mestiza* woman with reddish dyed hair. Except for her make-up and her knee-length skirt that was tighter than what is considered usual, her appearance did not differ from that of the women of a popular neighbourhood on a typical weekday. Señora Magda's well-preserved fairly white complexion could not conceal her age. She had to be at least 45. She wore ski pants and a sweater and when she smiled several of her teeth displayed gold caps. She carried a pack of cigarettes in her hand. This struck me as unusual, since the majority of the people who smoke cannot afford to buy a whole pack of cigarettes; they usually buy them one at a time from a neighbourhood store or street vendor. Señora Pilar hardly said a word. She stood there observing everything without changing the expression on her face. Señora Magda did most of the talking.

Clara introduced me as a Sister. I interrupted insisting I was not a nun, just a friend of Sister Marta. I told them of my plans, that I wanted to know more about their work and I purposely avoided the word prostitution for fear it might offend them. Señora Magda interrupted and said, 'You mean prostitution.' I laughed secretly at my own discretion.

*Lorraine*: I am not a journalist nor am I working for the government. Everything you say will remain anonymous. I feel it is important that people start to think differently about prostitution. But perhaps I have come at the wrong time. Have I interrupted your work? Would you prefer that I came back another day? *(I hoped they would ask me to come back another day.)*

*Magda and Pilar*: Ask us anything you want now.

*Lorraine*: *(I am totally unprepared and I keep stuttering. I will just ask them the first thing that comes into my mind.)* Do you work with other women?

*Magda*: We are a group of five or six.

*Lorraine*: Do you work here every day?

*Magda*: Almost every day except if someone is ill or we have to go to school for a meeting for one of our children.

*Lorraine*: Um, Um, um ... has there been a lot of work?

*Magda*: There has been a lot less lately, sometimes we go home and haven't made any money at all.

*Lorraine*: Where do you bring the clients?

*Magda*: We usually go to a hotel.

*Lorraine*: Are you registered?[3]

*Magda*: We go every 15 days to Chirimoyo [the popular name for the Anti-Venereal Clinic]. We even have an Aids certificate. They take us to Chirimoyo on the following morning after a police raid.

*Lorraine*: But if you are registered why do they pick you up?

*Magda*: They do it anyway, they bring us to the nearby precinct and they don't even allow you to receive any food. We have to check ourselves for our families and ourselves. We use condoms ...

*Lorraine*: All of you? Don't you have any problems with the clients?

*Magda*: Some of the clients bring them themselves, otherwise we use our own. They resist in the beginning, they say 'I never used one before.' I tell them I will put it on, they should keep their dirty hands off of it. They think we use them because we are sick. I show them my card and tell them it is better to protect us, so I don't catch anything from you and you from me. We buy the condoms by the box, it is cheaper, they are more expensive per piece. I keep a box at home. If they bring a condom I check the date, if it is too old, let's say from '85 or '86, I throw it away, it could break, and I use one of my own. If they ask why, I tell them. Every week, we also take an injection of 120 mm of penicillin, to prevent infection. *(I have heard this so often but is this really a preventative measure?)*
Before I worked here I used to work in Callao, in Trocadero [one of the officially recognized brothels].

*Lorraine*: Why did you stop working there?

*Magda*: *Madre* [Mother and Sister are interchangeable terms to denote a woman who is a nun] *(I mistakenly thought she was using it as comadre or mamita, both used to show affection)*, there was too much competition and it was difficult to find a room. I went to school but you can't find any work. Most women in the *pueblos jóvenes* work as street vendors. One time I was really sick of all this and went to look for other work. I went to an employment agency in Miraflores to find work as a servant. There were a lot of women there with long hair and dark skin. I sat there waiting and at the end of the day, all the other women were chosen; I wasn't chosen. They told me 'You don't have the face of a servant.' I had no other choice than to come back here.

What are you going to use this information for, for the university, for where you live?

*Lorraine*: In part, for the university in Holland and here, but I also work with a women's centre in Lima.

*Magda*: When I was working at Trocadero a group of students came to do a survey. They asked stupid questions.

*Lorraine*: What kind of questions?

*Magda*: They asked us if we liked 'it'. What do you mean do I like 'it'? It is my work, like any job, what do you think it's like to be with someone you don't love. I do it for the money.

*Lorraine: (Is she testing me?)* I agree with you totally *(searching Pilar's eyes for a reaction. She keeps staring in the direction of the door)*, part of my work is to study how people look at women-who-prostitute. Many people see them as if they are bad, like they are a problem. I hope my work will change the way people think that they will respect the women who work as prostitutes.

*Magda*: Mmm *(I could tell I was not impressing her)*. Did you ever see a movie about street prostitutes in the United States? There was a woman who kept visiting them and kept asking them questions. The women got annoyed until one day when they were picked up by the police, she helped them. At the end of the picture they realized she was trying to help *(I think she is comparing me to this woman, not bad for a first impression)*, but it is only a story, it has nothing to do with reality.

While laughing at this anecdote, I realized Señora Pilar was getting impatient since her eyes continually wandered to the door. I told them I would like to visit again. Señora Magda said, 'The best time to come is in the morning. Pilar comes at nine o'clock. She lives in Comas [a district situated approximately an hour's bus ride away from Barrios Altos] and arrives here after she brings her son to school.' I waved good-bye to Clara who was smiling and peeking out from the kitchen. I kissed them good-bye. As it is a normal occurrence in Limenean culture to kiss someone hello or good-bye even if you have just met, this came naturally. What I did not realize at that moment was that I was not only breaking class barriers but also that the women did not kiss each other. They greeted each other cordially and more often than not used the polite form *(Ud.)* to address each other and almost always used *Señora*. Señora Pilar stood at the doorpost and Señora Magda went strolling down the street with another woman.

Circumstances hindered a prompt return. In the week that followed, I came back to the neighbourhood for a meeting with members of the NGO. As I walked down the street with two of the members, we passed Señora Magda, who had just left a painted blue door accompanied by a man. We greeted each other and smiled, upon which one of the persons who accompanied me said 'She called you *madrecita*' (diminutive of *madre*). I did not take much notice of what he said. I was still convinced it was her way of showing affection. Suddenly, it dawned on me she still thought I was a nun. One of my companions confirmed my suspicion. 'But I told her at least twenty times I am not a nun.' He replied, 'The words of a nun weigh more than an anthropologist's.' I left in uncertainty, wondering whether it would be possible to shake off this new-found identity.

On my next visit I came to set a date with Pilar and Magda. I ran into Pilar, standing in front of Clara's door. She was obviously working so I intended to be as brief as possible. We kissed each other hello. I reminded her of our previous conversation and my interest in continuing our talk. 'I don't want to interrupt you while you work, what do you think if we meet for short conversations on a regular basis?' Our peaceful conversation was disturbed by a group of schoolboys passing by. One of the oldest boys murmured a sly remark to Pilar. Before I knew it I heard a hard clap. Pilar had smacked the boy in his face with her pocketbook. I must have looked surprised because she immediately justified her reaction. 'He is just a schoolboy, he could be my son, not only that, he should show some respect while we are talking.' Eager to show her I did not disapprove of her reaction, I nodded in agreement and did not dwell on it any further. I quickly changed the subject and inquired into Señora Magda's whereabouts. 'Magda hasn't arrived yet.' I told her I would return and went off to the NGO's office to wait for Señora Magda's arrival. When I came back to Clara's house Señora Magda had arrived and she was quick to tell me she had heard what had happened and added, 'Pilar is worried what you might think, she thought you wouldn't understand.' I explained, 'It took me by surprise, it happened so fast. There we were talking quietly amongst ourselves and then wham!, and we continued our conversation.' We all laughed at this incident and decided to continue our conversation the following week.

Despite my awareness that I was the initiator of all our conversations, that except for a bit of curiosity Pilar and Magda were not really interested, I arrived at Clara's house looking forward to our appointment. Clara opened the door still in pyjamas. I followed her back to an adjoining room where she returned to the mattress on the floor, lying next to her baby. On the wall were several pictures of naked women which looked as if they had been hanging there for years. There was another mattress rolled up and a bed. The small television was situated on a table which also functioned as an altar displaying several religious statues and pictures, among them San Martin de Porras and the Virgin Mary. The remaining space contained two large cabinets filled to their capacity. The bedroom opened up into another room used as the kitchen. Clara told me that Magda had not arrived. She usually came at about ten. It was nine o'clock and Señora Pilar was not there either. Once again, I returned to the office to await their arrival.

Entering the house the second time, I saw Señora Magda sitting in the kitchen smoking a cigarette. I approached and sat down across from her. She told me we would have to wait to continue our conversation, pointing to a woman who was sweeping the front room. While waiting, my eyes roamed around the room. The makeshift kitchen was partially covered with the recently bought *esteras*. The extensive use of the kerosene stove had changed the colour of the adjacent wall from green to sooty black. In the corner of the room was a walled-off cubicle where the toilet and a shower-head were located, a possession few houses in this neighbourhood could boast of. Laundry was hanging up to dry on cords way above our heads which could only be reached with a ladder. In comparison to many of the houses in the neighbourhood, Clara's was spacious and had the luxury of running water. In spite of the house's fatigued appearance, it was tidy, clean and well taken care of.

We moved ourselves to the front room. Clara kept walking in and out. The conversation, or rather what felt like an interrogation, officially began.

*Magda*: When are you going back to the United States?

*Lorraine*: From Lima, before going back to Holland. I always go for a visit. How did you know?

*Magda*: I figured you had to visit your family. My husband comes from the United States. Well, 20 years ago I married him, before I had my son. My husband sent us money so that we could come to live with him there. I wanted to live there, for the sake of my son, for school because we are very backward here in Peru. We got married here and he sent me money regularly but many times I never received it. The postman stole the letters and in the end I had to work. I didn't work in this before but I needed work. *(She told me a confusing story about tickets to Miami. It was not clear if she had been to visit or there had been a mix up with the tickets or her papers. She is giving me the feeling she is editing the story while talking.)*

*Lorraine*: How did you meet him?

*Magda*: We met at a party, he was working here and we got to know each other.

*Lorraine*: You never saw him again?

*Magda*: He came back five years ago and went to the house I used to live in but I had moved.

*Lorraine*: How did you find out?

*Magda*: My *comadre* [the political kinship term used to denote the relationship between the mother and godmother of her child] told me. That is why I never got married again or had another relationship. I thought he would come back to take me with him *(her voice cracked as if she was going to cry)*.

*Lorraine*: You don't want to see him again?

*Magda*: What for?

*Lorraine*: For the sake of your son.

*Magda*: My son thinks his father doesn't love him because he never came to get us and he never answered my letters. He isn't interested in him.

*Lorraine*: Is he going to school?

*Magda*: He is 23 years old. He got married, I hardly see him.

*Lorraine*: Do you have grandchildren?

*Magda*: I want to, but his wife has a child from another relationship. I taught my son to be good to children, animals and to every living creature. So he treats him like his own.

There was a knock on the door. Clara opened and a man entered. Magda handed him some money and he gave her a receipt. When the door closed behind him, she mentioned something about a funeral. Curiously I asked, 'Who died?' Clara and Magda laughed. 'No one died, its for when you die.' 'Oh, it is a kind of insurance.' 'That's right.' The question and answer period resumed.

*Lorraine*: You told me the other day that you had worked at Trocadero. Why did you stop working there?

*Magda*: Because they changed my hours. I only work during the day and the afternoon. I don't like *malas noches* [this literally means 'bad nights' but refers to too much drink, and staying up to the early hours of the morning].

*Lorraine*: Why did you come here?

*Magda*: Because I didn't know any other place to go. Since I live close to this neighbourhood, I came to work here. Also, I am able to work during the day. There are two groups: those who work from 10:30 a.m. until 6:30 p.m. and those who work from 7:00 p.m. until 11:00 at night.

*Lorraine*: But if you wanted to, you could work at night here?

*Magda*: Yes *(sounding annoyed)*, but like I told you I don't like *malas noches*, besides I want to be at home with my son.

*Lorraine*: How long have you worked here?

*Magda*: Six years.

*Lorraine*: What is the difference between working here and at Trocadero?

*Magda*: At Trocadero, nobody looks at you. You are inside and the men come to you. Here everyone looks at you, there is more shame. There I had to work quickly and have a lot of clients so I could pay for the room.

*Lorraine*: How do you choose the client?

*Magda*: I don't choose them, they choose me.

*Lorraine*: So you accept everyone?

*Magda*: No. If he is dirty, or his hair is dirty or he has scabs on his skin, I won't go with him.

*Lorraine*: Are there other things, for example the other day we spoke about children ...

*Magda*: *(She raised her voice indignantly.)* We never go with children, we would rather hide, come in here so they don't see us. *(She misunderstood me. As soon as she heard the word children she jumped to conclusions and assumed I was insinuating that the women accepted children as clients. Before she had interrupted me, I tried to use children as an example of the criteria they used to refuse a client. I had to talk a lot to clear up the confusion, but I think she finally understood.)* I also don't accept men who are sick. I throw out men who take too much time. I don't give either of them back their money.

*Lorraine*: What happens then?

*Magda*: Sometimes they become vulgar, but I throw them out with their clothes and tell them they can call the police if they want but nobody is going to force me to be with you. Not only that, I have already taken my pants off, they are paying to look at me.

*Lorraine*: Do you only work on this street or are there others?

*Magda*: I used to work on another street, but we had to leave the area because some of the women working there were crooks. The police raided the street looking for them. Since they all hid, the police took us in instead. That is why we left and came here, it is a lot closer to where we bring the men. *(She still will not tell me that the room they rent is nearby.)*

*Lorraine*: How do the police treat you when they pick you up?

*Magda*: They throw us in jail, we sleep on the floor without anything to cover us. The cell stinks. In the morning they bring us to Chirimoyo, even if you are registered, they pick you up. We would all be registered if it meant that they wouldn't pick us up, but that is not the case.

*Lorraine*: What do the neighbours do?

*Magda*: Some of them tell the police where we are hiding. Very few help. One time I was hiding, they found me and took me in. That is why I haven't renewed my licence, it is a waste of time, since they take you in no matter what. I have an Aids test every six months.

*Lorraine*: So this is a problem?

*Magda*: Yes, write it down, write it down. *(I was not writing anything down, I always wrote the conversations after I left Clara's.)* For the last mayor's election, I decided to vote for the APRA [a political party], because I saw Belmont [independent candidate, who won the election] on television and you could see the hate he had in his eyes for women.

*Lorraine*: All women?

*Magda*: No. The women who work [among prostitutes, a prostitute is often referred to as a woman who works – *la mujer que trabaja*]. He isn't going to solve the problem of prostitution by making more raids.

*Lorraine*: I agree. Not only that, it is not the right way to solve the problem either.

*Lorraine*: Are there other problems?

*Magda*: I am thinking, I can't remember.

*Lorraine*: What kind of risks are there?

*Magda*: Venereal diseases.

*Lorraine*: Do the men want to use condoms, aren't they a bit stubborn?

*Magda*: Yes, that is true, but we use them here. I put one on immediately.

*Lorraine*: All the women use them?

*Magda*: Yes.

*Lorraine*: I would think that at times it would be hard to say no because the client might leave and look for another woman and that means less money?

*Magda*: Yes. There are women who don't use them, but I am tired of telling them. It goes in one ear and out the other.

*Lorraine*: But it is not something that only all of you have to use, I have to use them too. We all have to protect ourselves. *(She looked a bit surprised at my admission.)* Do you think it would be any different if they received them for free?

*Magda*: No, things wouldn't change.

*Lorraine*: You know I want my work to let people hear the voice of women-who-prostitute. But I need your help and support. Do you think you could introduce me to your colleagues?

*Magda*: Yes, I could do that.

*Lorraine*: What do you think is important for people to know about prostitution?

*Magda*: There should be more information about condoms. They should create more work, if there was more work there wouldn't be so many women working like this. Bring more factories, more industries so that women can work.

Magda had a habit of reliving the emotion she felt at the time when she retold the story. Because she was a very temperamental woman, her stories were always filled with passages of ear-splitting volume. Perhaps for this reason, and the repetitive demonstration of how she always had control of her situation, and finally her frequent use of the word 'we' as if she were the collective voice for all the women, I endowed her temporarily with the rumoured title of the *jefa* (the boss, the chief) of the women. It would take some time before I would be able to reconfigure Magda's position in Clara's house.


CRAFTING EVERYDAYNESS

The presidential election had just taken place. Lima was in a state of shock because the *chino* (Chinese) – a relatively unknown political figure – had triumphed over Mario Vargas Llosa, the internationally recognized author who had promised Peru economic development by enforcing a strict programme of austerity. The public's fear of the consequences pushed them to vote for his unknown opponent, Alberto Fujimori, a Peruvian of Japanese descent who won the election by claiming that there was no need for such drastic measures to save Peru.[4] The awkwardness of having an Asian-Peruvian as Chief of State – the Asian community was characteristically known for its role in commerce, not politics – was stated eloquently by Señora Magda who mistakenly called Fujimori *ajinomoto* – a Chinese seasoning used in cooking – while explaining her decision. She expressed her fear when she saw him standing with his family, 'he was standing with all those *chinitos* (diminutive of *chino*) at his side. For a moment I thought this was Japan not Peru.' Clara had also voted for Fujimori, and Pilar, who had just arrived, did not differ from the others. 'My whole neighbourhood voted for Fujimori, even though FREDEMO [Vargas Llosa's party] distributed food provisions to the neighbourhood committees and mothers' clubs. I also received provisions, but I didn't vote for him.' 'You're a member of a club?', I asked. 'No, I do not belong to any club, I am only a member of the neighbourhood committee.'

Another woman I saw regularly, Señora Maria, was getting ready for work. She took off her street clothes and put on her work clothes which she kept in a cupboard. The only observable difference between the two was that her work clothes clung more tightly to her body, but this did not stop her looking modestly dressed. 'Señora Maria, who did you vote for?' 'I voted for Vargas Llosa', she replied. 'What about the rest of your neighbourhood?' 'I don't know, I don't talk to my neighbours, we just say hello when we meet on the street.' As she was standing in the doorway, I offered her my seat. She declined. 'I was just about to light my candle for the saints.' This was a ritual she completed at the commencement of each day. She lit the candle, murmured a prayer, crossed herself and, upon finishing, she touched the flame with two fingers and kissed her fingertips.

In this initial stage, it was almost a game to try to figure out who was who at Clara's house. Who lived there, who came to visit and what their relationship was to Clara – were they prostitutes, neighbours or relatives? At least Clara's living arrangements were finally becoming clearer. She lived with her six-month-old daughter Petra and Señora Rosa who had been living there for the last eight years. Every time I came to visit, Señora Rosa was lying on the bed looking very depressed. Gabriela and her two-year-old son Daniel had moved in recently. Gabriela was giving her son some medicine to cure his case of worms. A discussion evolved around the most effective medicine. The names of different medicines filled the air, up-to-date prices were quoted. I was astonished by the women's pharmaceutical knowledge. However, taking into consideration that all medicinal products are sold without prescriptions, and pharmacists often fulfil the prescribing role of the doctor, the women were accustomed to self-doctoring. A trip to the pharmacy, after all, is cheaper than a visit to the doctor.

There was a knock at the door. A neighbour came in and asked Clara to watch her baby while she went to the doctor. She was pregnant and was in danger of miscarrying. Another woman who prostituted, named Señora Myrta, came in.

The scene shifted all the women went out to work and I was left alone with the occupants of the house. The women came in and out frequently, always having enough time to stop and play with one of the babies lying on the bed. Clara told me a little about herself. 'I cook for the women and I wash clothes. I can really wash clothes well. There are some people, for example Señora Magda, who won't trust their clothes to anyone else. That's how I survive. My mother was a *morena* [literally "brown", but it is used to denote a person who is part black. *Morenas* are known to be excellent cooks. Clara was indirectly suggesting she had inherited her mother's cooking skills]. My father was German. My sisters are blonde and have green eyes, I am the darkest. I have three children. They are from three different fathers. My oldest son is in a drug rehabilitation centre, my eleven-year-old daughter is living with my sister and then there is Petra.' Repeatedly she emphasized how she had no problem being alone (read: without a man). 'I am used to it, I don't need anyone. You know, you have to forget the past.' I replied, 'You also have to learn from it.' She agreed without conviction.

The door opened and in walked a stylishly dressed young woman, Gabriela, who was washing clothes throughout our conversation, turned to Clara and jokingly said, 'Remember Chavela, she stopped visiting us since she has money and lives in San Miguel' (a (lower) middle-class neighbourhood). They gossiped about different friends; men's names kept zooming passed my ears. Chavela kept talking about the likes and dislikes of her *novio* (fiancé). Demonstratively, she gave Gabriela some money to buy milk for Daniel. Gabriela accepted timidly, her eyes searching for my reaction. Chavela went out and returned with two cold beers, which we consumed upon her return.

What the three of them had in common was that their *maridos* were in the same prison. Chavela had met her *marido* (whom she previously called her *novio*) while visiting the prison with a friend. He was in the same block with Gabriela's *marido*, but Chavela's had finished his sentence. Clara's *marido* was sentenced to 20 years. I asked, 'What is he in for?' 'He is in for being such a good person.' Laughing, she corrected herself. 'Actually, he was a policeman and is in for drugs. He will be coming out next year for good behaviour.' The conversation went in all directions, from the colour of nail polish to their experiences with abortion. The woman who had gone to the doctor came back to pick up her baby and told Clara she had miscarried. I was getting ready to leave, when Clara said, 'You are welcome to come whenever you want, even when you don't want to come to talk to the Señoras. If there is any way I can help you in my humble manner, don't be afraid to ask.' 'Thank you', I said, 'the same holds true for you.' 'No, it is better that I don't get used to relying on anyone.'

Clara would become a very significant person for me. She not only opened up her house to me, but she regularly functioned as my eyes, my mouth and my guardian angel. I took her up on her offer and returned the following day.

The door was open and I proceeded to the kitchen. Upon passing the bedroom I saw some new faces. I suspected that the two women who were joking and conversing on the bed were prostitutes. However, they were different from the other women I had met before. They were younger, provocatively dressed and had reddish-blonde hair. They were bolder and more aggressive. The scars on one of the women's faces, obviously made with a sharp object, reinforced my suspicions. Another woman who was taking a break was sitting at the edge of the bed watching a soap opera. She was oohing and aahing at the tragedies occurring on the screen. She left when her programme finished. In search of Señora Pilar, I almost bumped into Señora Maria, who was bent over a neighbour holding an ignited cone of paper to her ear. The treatment was almost finished. I could not contain my curiosity and burst out, 'What are you doing?' Señora Maria replied 'This woman has an earache, many times earaches are caused by air, when you make a cone of paper, light it and place the smallest part in the ear the heat of the fire causes the air to be released.' We heard a swooshing sound coming from the woman's ear. Clara was examining my reaction, I could tell she expected me to find it a superstitious practice. 'We have everything in house here, even a doctor', she said. From the other room a voice called out 'Who is that?' Clara's accurate description of me made my day. 'She is a friend of Sister Marta who was born in America and lives in Holland, she is an anthropologist.' I stuck my head around the doorpost and said, 'Hello, how are you? My name is Lorena.'

A neighbour came in, a boisterous black woman named Charo. She often came by to visit Clara. A day would not go by, during one of her visits when her back was turned or upon leaving, without someone insinuating that she was a lesbian. Whether it was because of her boisterous manner or because she was 31 and single without children or because 'Rumour had it ...', she was branded a lesbian. In this first encounter, her vivaciousness and curiosity would contribute to making the day special. Clara introduced us, once again describing me better than I could do it. We sat with the other women in the bedroom. 'What are you doing?', she enquired. 'Do you really want to know?', I answered her in a loud voice so the other women would take notice. 'I am doing a study on female prostitutes and do you want to know why? Because I believe that people who are not prostitutes have to become aware of what it is really like.' 'Yes, I know what you mean, the only people I speak to in this neighbourhood are the Señoras.' Before I knew it a conversation developed and Charo transformed from a curious neighbour to an efficient research assistant. Even Señora Rosa, who was always as quiet as a mouse, started to participate. It was then that I realized she was also a prostitute. They started to talk about the difference between working on the street and in a brothel. Carmen and Yalu took turns answering questions. If they liked the answer given, they made a 'give me five' motion, slapping one hand in the palm of the other's.

*Rosa*: In brothels, the women are exploited. They have to give their tickets to the administrator and also a part of what they earn. They even have to do unnatural things.

*Carmen*: Yes, they have to do everything the client wants. On the streets, we choose and decide what we want to do.

*Lorraine*: When do you work?

*Yalu*: Whenever I feel like it, whatever time of the day. Other women have men who depend on them.

*Lorraine*: *Cafiches* [pimps].

*Yalu and Carmen*: *(Laughing that I would know such a word)* Yeah, *cafiches*. We don't have them here.

*Charo*: The women here are their own boss.

*Yalu*: I work around the corner, I just stopped by to visit my friend.

*Charo*: Where do you take the men?

*Yalu*: We go to a hotel or a room, I won't go to their house because they can rape me or kill me. I knew a girl who went to one of their houses, when she got there, there were five of them. She was raped and beaten, they were *masochistas (masochists, but she means sadists).*

*(I want to talk about how the regulation works and what they think are the problems. Yalu does not seem familiar with the word reglamentación [regulation]. The only thing she said on the subject was that it doesn't pay to be registered.)*

*Charo*: Aren't you scared of getting Aids?

*Carmen*: That's why we use condoms.

*Lorraine*: When did you start to use them?

*Carmen*: Since the disease made its entrance.

*Lorraine*: Always?

*Yalu*: Not always. *(She repeats the symptoms of the disease that she had read in a pamphlet given to her by a 'Señora'.)*

*Lorraine*: Where do you get the condoms?

*Carmen*: At the Centre [meaning the Anti-Venereal Clinic].

*Lorraine*: How can you go there if you are working illegally?

*Carmen*: We pay. It doesn't cost that much. 50,000 *Intis*; maybe now it is 100,000. They give us a check-up, take blood and do a vaginal examination.

*Lorraine*: Do you think men should be checked too?

*Yalu*: They aren't going to go for a check-up.

*Lorraine*: What do you do if they don't want to use a condom?

*Carmen*: We throw them out. We get a check-up for Aids every three months.

*Charo*: Are condoms effective?

*Yalu and Carmen*: Yes, they are.

*Lorraine*: Not always, but everyone has to use condoms nowadays.

*Charo*: Why aren't they always effective?

*Yalu*: Because they might have a hole. You should come back to talk to us again.

*Lorraine*: When?

*Carmen*: Friday, the same time.

*Charo*: Does your family know what you are doing?

*Carmen*: No, they don't. I never bring them here.

*Charo*: Where do you live, how many children do you have?

*Carmen*: I have one child. I live in Comas with my mother and child, I don't see them much.

*Lorraine*: Yalu?

*Yalu*: I have three children.

*Charo*: *(Turns to me)* Did you speak to the *pituca* [a term used to describe people who have money or attitudes like people who have money].

*Lorraine*: Who is that?

*Charo*: *Pituca* is a word.

*Lorraine*: I know what the word means. Who do you mean?

*Charo*: Magda. The woman getting on in age.

*Lorraine*: I know Magda but why do you call her a *pituca*?

*Yalu and Carmen*: Because she dresses like one.

*Lorraine*: Well, I don't want to take up any more of your time. I will come back on Friday.

*Carmen and Yalu*: We aren't going to work today.

*Carmen*: I feel lazy.

*Yalu*: Me too.

The conversation died down as quickly as it started. This was the first time I left in the late afternoon. There were at least five women standing outside, among them Magda. We said hello when I passed by. I realized I had been coming at the wrong time of day. The afternoons would be better.

My possibilities in fieldwork increased enormously with Clara's generous show of hospitality. Nonetheless, there was too much going on in Clara's house and too little space for conversations with the women individually. I was convinced of the necessity to keep making attempts to take some time with each woman separately. This was proving more difficult than I had expected and I sensed it would not get any better.

When I returned on Friday to talk to Yalu and Carmen, Yalu did not show up for our appointment and Carmen did not feel like talking either. Señora Pilar finally reappeared. Pointing an incriminating finger at her, I reminded her she did not turn up for our appointment. She told me she had been to the hospital to visit her father who was having a prostate operation. 'That is a problem often related to old age', I said. Pilar replied, 'And also when a man is very *mujeriego* [a womanizer]. He is not old, he is 65, he is a real *mujeriego*, he has had a lot of women.' We made an appointment for the coming Tuesday which, however, never materialized. The idea of making appointments began to seem ludicrous. With few exceptions, nobody makes appointments in Lima. If appointments are made they are usually in the *hora peruana* style (Peruvian hour, an appointment is kept if the person arrives between the designated hour and an hour later), why should these women be any different? Yet, at the same time I realized that if I only relied on informal group conversations I would get caught up in the everydayness of the relationships that were not very revealing. Perhaps they confided in one or two of the other women, but they rarely spilt a word about their private lives when they were in a group. Their way of communication expressed their wariness in trusting each other, let alone a stranger. I feared I would be unable to break this pattern. Thus, I decided to change my procedure. I would take my midday meal at Clara's house to allow me more time to participate in daily activities and to be able to subtly remind the women why I was there.

With my new mental plan, I returned to Clara's. It was morning and Señora Magda was sitting alone at the kitchen table in her favourite chair eating her breakfast which consisted of a few rolls and some cheese she had brought with her. There was a tacit acceptance that when Magda was there no one else sat in that chair. If she came in and her seat was occupied, the person would normally stand up, except on those occasions when someone was deliberately trying to annoy her. There was still so much more I wanted to know about her life. It had been a while since I had had a conversation with Magda and I thought this would be an appropriate moment to resume our talk. When she finished breakfast I asked her if we could continue our conversation.

*Magda*: I already told you everything. *(Her answer takes me aback.)*

*Lorraine*: I still have other questions, or don't you trust me?

*Magda*: OK. Ask away.

*Lorraine*: I have been coming here for a while and I hardly ever see any men.

*Magda*: There aren't many men. There has been less work, sometimes at the end of the day you only have one or maybe none.

*Lorraine*: What do the women do then?

*Magda*: Some of them have other ways of making money, some have a *marido* who helps them.

*Lorraine*: They have *maridos*?

*Magda*: Some, but those who don't have a *marido* have nothing. Sometimes, my earnings from one day are spent on *almuerzo*, no money for anything else.

*Lorraine*: How is your day organized? I know you start working at eleven o'clock but what else do you do during a day?

*(Somehow the subject quickly changed to condoms which I am beginning to realize is her favourite subject).*

*Magda*: I use condoms with every client, I don't want to get sick.

*Lorraine*: What do you do if they don't want to use a condom?

*Magda*: They always accept but the next time they look for another woman and I have lost a friend.

*Lorraine*: Where did you receive your information concerning Aids?

*Magda*: Pamphlets, television, the health centre.

*Lorraine*: Are you afraid that something could happen to you?

*Magda*: Yes, I always think they are all sick.

*Lorraine*: Are you afraid of anything else?

*Magda*: No, not with Peruvian men, they are not sadists but foreigners are.

*Lorraine*: Who controls the relationship? You or him?

*Magda*: I do.

*Lorraine*: You know why I am asking this question, because there are many people who think that prostitutes do not have control.

*Magda*: No, I have to guess what the man wants and do it as quickly as possible. For example, I never lie down on the bed because it takes longer.

*Lorraine*: So, what do you do?

*Magda*: *Filo de Catre.*

*Lorraine*: What is that?

*Magda*: It is a position. This is a *filo (she points to the edge of the table)*. I sit on the edge of the bed with my legs raised *(she raises her legs to her chest)*.

*Lorraine*: Are there things that you refuse to do?

*Magda*: Anal sex.

*Lorraine*: How do you avoid it?

*Magda*: For example I say it will cost 300 *Intis* but I know they can't pay it, they try to bargain, and I convince them to do something else. That is why I work here because I have the control.

*Lorraine*: How do you treat them? *(She looks a bit confused, I help her along.)* Do you treat them affectionately?

*Magda*: I can treat them affectionately, but I do not feel anything. It doesn't bother me if I have to argue. For example, I say it costs 130 *Intis* and 30 is to pay for the room, other women have to argue when they enter the room, I don't. I don't like to argue.

*Lorraine*: Is the room nearby?

*Magda*: It is a few doors away. *(Finally she told me the location of the room.)*

*Lorraine*: If business has been slow and a client offers you less, will you accept it?

*Magda*: No.

*Lorraine*: Do you come here at ten in the morning?

*Magda*: I begin to work at 11:00 a.m. and I finish at 6:00 or 6:30 p.m.

*Lorraine*: What do you do afterwards?

*Magda*: I go home.

*Lorraine*: Do you live alone?

*Magda*: Yes, I live alone, I bathe and take off my make-up.

*Lorraine*: Do your neighbours know what you do?

*Magda*: Yes they know, I don't have contact with them, I don't feel like talking to them.

*Lorraine*: Although you like to talk a lot.

*Magda*: We talk together here.

*Lorraine*: It seems as if you all have good contact?

*Magda*: With some of them I have good contact but there are fights.

*Lorraine*: About what?

*Magda*: For example, I change the sheet on the mattress. One of them makes it dirty and when I make a remark she starts cursing, I can't accept that someone talks to me like that, I won't talk to her anymore.

*Lorraine*: Does your son know what you do?

*Magda*: Yes, he does.

*Lorraine*: What does he think about it?

*Magda*: He says I shouldn't do it, he doesn't come that often.

Señora Magda went out to work and Señora Maria entered. We were no longer strangers but we had never spoken about our respective work. I decided I would approach her today. 'Señora Maria, have you heard anything about what I am trying to do?' She gave a vague reply but affirmed she had an idea. 'Could you find some time to talk with me?' She immediately made it clear she was going out to work. When I enquired as to a suitable hour she told me between 1:00 p.m. and 3:00 p.m. While changing she told me a little about herself.

'I come here after I have cooked, washed the clothes. I leave the house tidy and then I go to work. It is work like any other work, like office work. Other women who work here get drunk and stay in the neighbourhood. I come to work and go home just like it is an office. Except when there is a raid. I don't get back to my house for 24 hours, this can happen at any time of the day, any day of the week.' She had already said that she had three children, two who were married and no longer lived with her and a daughter of eleven years. I asked, 'What does your daughter say if you do not come home?' She misunderstood my question and interpreted this to mean what does her child think about her work. 'She doesn't know what I do, I tell her I was dropping off some merchandise for my office in this neighbourhood and I was picked up in the raid.' Neither of us used the word prostitute in our conversation.

Since there was still some time before *almuerzo* would be ready, I set off to the office to jot down some notes. On my way back to Clara's, I ran into Sister Marta who invited me in for a cup a coffee and immediately set a plate of cookies in front of me. Again she expressed her gratitude for my work and told me that she had a friend, who teaches macramé, 'Would that be an alternative for the women? They could sell their products on the market.' I explained those types of productive activities are doomed to fail because they could never replace the amount of money the women earn as prostitutes. I left shortly after.

'Hermana Marta sends her regards.' Clara thanked me while stirring the stew she was preparing for *almuerzo*. She made a sign, pointing to the pot she said, 'I am sick of all this, I want to leave this house, I want to find other work.' I kept her company while she was cooking and during our conversation I asked her what she thought the women thought of my work and whether they trusted me.

'Yes, they trust you but they only think of themselves. They think this [prostitution] is the only way to earn money. They only think of money.'

'All of them?'

'Yes, all of them. Everyone who comes here wants something from me. They only come when they need something. Do you think the Señoras appreciate my work? No they don't. I started working about nine years ago, cooking for one and little by little for the others. I don't trust anyone.'

'But I believe in you', I said.

'You shouldn't. I stopped believing in people a long time ago. It is better like that. I can't be disappointed. The same thing happened with my mother. She was a good woman. When I left my house 15 years ago, my whole family said I was a whore. My son doesn't have a name [meaning the surname of his father], but what do you think, they always come here when they need something.'

'What about Chavela?' I asked.

'I don't know her that well, she is Gabriela's friend. I have no problem living alone.'

Sitting at the kitchen table, I asked her about some of the women. 'Pilar only comes when she feels like it. Carmen is not coming any more because she has been fighting with one of the Señoras who never hurts a fly. I had to break them up, they were beating up each other. I am sick of all this.' She draws an imaginary line above her forehead.

I asked, 'Why are they fighting?'

'Carmen is an alcoholic.'

'What about Yalu?'

She made a gesture of smoking a joint. 'Keep away from them, they are no good.'

'What do you think the women think of me?' I asked.

'They are ignorant.'

'No they aren't.'

'Yes they are, some of them stopped school after the first grade and you are a professional.'

'Are they scared of me?'

'No. One of them told me she doesn't want to speak to you, "What for?" she said, "To be reminded of what I am and what I do?" I told her, do you think when you leave the trade you will forget what you were? You will always remember.'

'Who said that?', I asked.

'Julia. You know the one who is really close to Magda. You saw her once when she was sitting on the corner of the bed watching a soap opera and ruining it for everybody. Just give them time, they will start talking to you.'

Nothing had changed despite my new efforts. My conversations with Magda had the same interrogative lilt as the other times we had spoken. Her brief answers to questions intended to stimulate associative conversation still constructed silences which I felt obliged to undo – by jumping from one subject to another. Other women barely recognized my existence or it never was an appropriate moment to sit down and have a talk. Perhaps this was the moment I abandoned all attempts to have individual conversations, postponing the idea of life stories or interviews – if they were to materialize at all – to the future. I decided to work from the circumstances and the unpredictability of each situation I encountered.

## SHAPING IDENTITIES

The staccato nature of our question-and-answer style conversations did not inhibit the shaping of identities. In fact, much can be read into the simple phrases, the contradictions and the moments of perturbation. This was most apparent in my conversations with Magda.

My identity was shaped in a bit of confusion but eventually stabilized. In a short time it had undergone several changes, from nun, to insensitive university student, to potential saviour. These finally gave way to a simpler title, Señorita Lorena. It might not have been clear, as yet, who this woman was, but I no longer matched any of the identities that zigzagged through the first conversations. I was a foreigner from the United States or Holland who wanted to work, to write a book on prostitution.

Magda presented various versions of the prostitute. Initially, she presented a collective version of prostitutes as health-conscious (always using a condom for the sake of themselves and their family), law-abiding (all the women were registered) and with the correct justifications for prostituting (they never missed a day except when ill or to go to a meeting at their children's schools). Her individual account embellished this version. She made an effort to show me she had attempted to leave the trade; however this was not possible for her because all street vendors and servants – women with 'long hair and dark skin' – are *cholas*, a term with negative connotations denoting women of indigenous origins. Although she did not say it blatantly, her description of indigenous women showed the disdain she felt towards them. Thus, her skin colour was an unchangeable factor impeding her from leaving the trade. Her only alternative was to continue to work in this work which she detested. She did not want to work at night, because she did not want to be a part of the nightlife and wanted to be at home to care for her son. Finally, she indirectly made sure I captured the message concerning her marriage and the birth of her son. She did not meet her husband while working as a prostitute. Her marriage and her son were not products of a relationship of prostitution, they were legitimate. Her husband did not abandon her; instead circumstances caused her to lose contact with him (thus distinguishing herself from many prostitutes), which eventually drove her to prostitution.

However, the more we talked, the more these collective and individual representations fell apart. She talked passionately about the futility of registering, and admitted that no one registered. When I suggested the client's stubbornness could impede the use of condoms, she repeated the reprimands she gave to the women who did not use them. Without batting an eyelash she stated that she lived alone, recasting her first description of her family life into the realm of fiction.

There were several muddled moments in our conversation related to her past that confused me at first. I could not untangle the details into a transparent story. Magda's relationship with her American husband, her trip to Miami and other related matters were impenetrable accounts, resistant to my questions. This suggested she was only willing to share her past with others partially, that is, she would share the parts which contributed to the image she wanted to project. The conversations with Magda show the fluidity and unfixed nature of the construction of identities through relationships.

The incident with Pilar and the schoolboy illustrates that particular components of the women's identities have the illusory power of appearing permanent and unchanging, specifically the notions of shame and motherhood. Three readings could be given to this incident. In the first reading, her reaction was provoked by the shame she felt by being a prostitute, especially in my presence. In the second, she is driven by the pride she feels at being a mother and the respect she feels she deserves as an adult. Finally, the slap in the boy's face represents her attempt to manage both these perceptions in her own identity. For the majority of mothers who prostitute, the significance of motherhood is permanently embedded in their identity and is one of the few aspects which make their work gratifying. In the embodiment of the prostitute, the notion of shame continually comes to the foreground and appears to be unchanging and constant. It is braided into many realms of the women's lives, determining their views of themselves and of their work.

The majority of the women were not as outspoken as Magda, although Pilar's action with her pocketbook spoke far louder than words. Clara was the person who plaited together many of the bits and pieces. She had lived in the neighbourhood for many years and, looking back on her past, she situated herself among the 'bad elements' of the neighbourhood, but something had changed. She claimed she was determined to keep those elements out of her life. She was resigned with her situation but at the same time desperate to change it. Clara knew a lot about the neighbourhood, and especially about the women who ate at her house, although she never told me everything and I never asked. It did not surprise me, however, when she told me that Yalu and Carmen were addicts. Their presence in her house always felt different from that of the other women. It would take some time before I would realize how significant this difference was in the construction of the identity of the prostitute. Although the shape of identities is unfixed and in a continual process, within the enclosure of Clara's house they had a steadfast appearance which was informed by the gendered enclosures constructed in the community and society at large.

# 6    BETWEEN THE STOVE AND THE KITCHEN TABLE

*Almuerzo* was served. Clara served my soup first as if I was the guest of honour and then proceeded to serve the other women. 'The soup doesn't have enough potatoes', Magda proclaimed, annoyed. 'I like potatoes. Tomorrow I want more potatoes.'

Clara replied calmly, but obviously restraining her temper, 'I put the same amount in as always, they probably disintegrated.' During *almuerzo*, Clara, who usually said what was on her mind, would often adopt a servile attitude, complying with the women's culinary whims without losing her patience. Hastily, she would place the plate of salt, limes or hot peppers on the table, while answering *ahorita* (in a moment) to the next request. She was rarely given a compliment. When the rush was over, and the women had finished, she eased into a chair to eat her *almuerzo*.

It was in the time before, during and after *almuerzo* that the majority of our conversations took place. Between attending to the simmering pots, the neighbours, relatives and the women-who-prostitute who all came in for one thing or another, Clara and I talked about our lives and she would fill me in on the daily occurrences in my absence. When the women entered to eat, the action shifted to the kitchen table where we would partake of *almuerzo*, at times conversing and at times in overwhelming silence. While they relaxed or freshened their make-up there was still time to chat, until, one by one, they drifted back to the street and returned to work.

The conversations were unpredictable and shifted constantly from one subject to the next. Very often they produced a strong sensation, as if life was lived in the immediate present. As an outsider, it was an arduous task to decipher and abstract the meanings and grasp the dynamics of their relationships in these everyday conversations. The lack of continuity in the subjects from one day to another made it even more difficult to piece together the conversations to construct a coherent account. This chapter approaches the everydayness of daily life by expanding on five different subjects. As mentioned earlier in Chapter 4, one of its objectives is to illustrate the tricky balance which exists between the women as ordinary women who share and experience life like their female neighbours living in similar conditions of poverty, and women-who-prostitute who have more in common with each other than with other women. These two identities are intimately entwined.

The women's enactments of the prostitute are continually fed by the components by which they identify themselves as urban poor. The episodic narrative presented below, clustering the conversations around certain incidents, is meant to position their everyday experiences in the broader context of urban poverty without losing sight of the original purpose of this narrative: to portray the embodiment of the prostitute as a reaction to and in interaction with gendered enclosures which construct specific meanings in regard to prostitution and the prostitute.


EVERYDAY DYNAMICS OF EVERYDAY RELATIONSHIPS

*Scene One*

While sitting at the kitchen table talking about Magda's dislike of Italian films, Gabriela's son came in, stating that his mama was crying. Clara's voice could be heard in the background, but what she said was muffled by the conversation taking place in the kitchen. Señora Maria claimed Gabriela put herself in danger every time she went to visit her *marido*. Magda, who tried to make herself heard in the bedroom, shouted, 'Drop him, act like he is dead. My mother always told me if a man doesn't give you money forget him.'

Señora Myrta looked at me and before she began to talk she made me promise not to tell any of the women what she said. She whispered, 'Gabriela's husband only stays with her because she gives him money. She puts herself in danger every time she goes to visit.' The danger being referred to is related to prison conditions. The Peruvian prisons are like pressure cookers: overcrowded, violent and potentially explosive. When a visitor arrives, after waiting in long lines in the hot sun, they are allowed to proceed to their relative's block. There is no telling what may happen along the way. The women who frequented Clara's house were all familiar with the ins and outs of prison visits. If they had not experienced them first hand then they had gathered their knowledge from someone in their close proximity who had.

Gabriela was having problems with her *marido*. According to the women, she visited her husband and when she returned to the neighbourhood she heard he had received a visit from his girlfriend – 'a young little thing who lives in the neighbourhood'. She knew he had a girlfriend, but he had promised he would not accept a visit from her. According to the version Gabriela told me, she was upset because a girl had gone to visit him to badmouth her. 'How could she make someone worry like that who is stuck in prison? It will make him want to escape. I felt ashamed, not for myself, but for Daniel. He has to learn to respect his father.' Gabriela thought of ending the relationship, but she continued to make her usual twice-a-week visits to the prison. Her *marido* promised not to accept any more visits from his girlfriend. The women concluded that she loved him too much. Since Gabriela decided to continue her relationship and buried the incident in the past, the women also acted as if the incident had never taken place and the inquiries into her *marido's* well-being recommenced.

Clara's birthday approached. She would be 37. Chavela came by to celebrate the upcoming festivity and went out to buy a few bottles of beer. Magda could not hide her disapproval and commented to Clara that Chavela liked to drink just like Carmen, implying that Chavela was an alcoholic. Clara disagreed. 'She likes to drink but not like Carmen. She came by to celebrate because tomorrow is my birthday.'

Magda, who was sitting next to Señora Myrta, tried to cover up her mistake by telling a story about the times she went drinking with Miriam – a woman who used to work there. 'She was really beautiful and tall just like you Lorena.'

'Yes', Myrta added, 'she used to wear *pituca* boots ... ', then she realized what she had said and corrected herself, 'boots with high heels, like you Magda.' Myrta went on: 'There were days there was no business, and Miriam would say "Let's go for a drink Magda", we would go for a drink and when we returned there was still no business, so I would say let's go and have another drink. She was a real good person and very pretty. She stopped working because she went blind. They did all types of analysis but nobody knows why she went blind. I am sure someone put a curse on her [*hacer daño*: to do someone harm]. She had a boyfriend. She must have given him a picture. His wife probably took the picture and put a curse on her.'

'Yes', Magda said, 'Miriam's boyfriend came from the provinces, they use a lot of witchcraft there.'

Clara started to complain to Chavela about Gabriela. 'I have had enough. She comes in at all hours. Last night she came home at eleven, Daniel was crying. I called it to her attention because I am concerned, but she got angry and told me, "Just let him cry." I don't know why she lives here.'

Chavela responded to Clara, 'Well she can't live with her *marido*'s parents.'

The problems with Gabriela would escalate in the coming weeks. Clara was angry. Gabriela never paid for anything in the house, even when she had the money. Clara always made sure Daniel had enough to eat: 'I treat him as if he were my own. She borrows money and never pays me back.'

In the following month Clara and Gabriela's daily problems would come to an end. Gabriela moved out, but not without spreading rumours in the neighbourhood that she had been kicked out. This made Clara furious: 'I didn't kick her out. I only took her in as a favour to her husband. She made the same mistake as the last time she lived here. She is selling *pasta* [a derivative of cocaine]. She went to live with some friends. If she wants to bring her child up with that kind of people, that's her decision. All I know is in my house, nobody comes in here with *pasta*. I have had such horrible experiences with drugs – you know about my son and my brothers – no one enters here with drugs. And as you know, there are no men here, you won't find anyone screwing here. If she wants to bring her son up in that type of environment, then it is up to her.' Gabriela and Clara would eventually be on speaking terms again. As Clara described it, 'We are cordial, but that's all.' However, I never saw Gabriela in the house again.

Gabriela's brief stay at Clara's shows several aspects concerning relationships. There is a tacit recognition that the majority of relationships are not durable. It is not out of the ordinary for someone to participate intensely and then suddenly disappear from the scene, leaving few traces behind. After Gabriela left, following a short rumour and name-calling period, nobody mentioned her or displayed any curiosity about her. No one found it particularly strange.

The way people deal with other people's problems bears a strong relationship to the way they perceive relationships. Before Gabriela made her decision to stay with her *marido*, the women offered their opinions and supported her. When she decided to continue the relationship, they accepted it and behaved accordingly, erasing the implications of the previous conversations. In the everydayness of daily life, the women deal with the immediate situation they are presented with, always trying to conserve a certain amount of distance because becoming too involved can eventually backfire, turning words of advice into the cause of the problem.

Gabriela's story tells more. The women's opinions concerning her *marido*'s behaviour elucidate gender morals pertaining to relationships. Gabriela is described as a woman who puts herself in danger to maintain her relationship with her husband and thus complies with the expected behaviour of a good spouse. However, her husband makes her suffer. Regardless of his living arrangements, he should treat his wife with respect and fulfil his obligations. Her husband fails on both counts. He does not contribute economically to the household and he treats his wife disrespectfully by allowing his girlfriend to visit.

Although male infidelity is not condoned, there is a certain degree of acceptance that men are not monogamous. This is intrinsically related to notions of masculinity which portray male unfaithfulness as an outcome of their uncontrollable sexual desire. In Gabriela's case, her husband's unfaithfulness was not under discussion, but rather his treatment of his wife and the consequences of his behaviour for her. Magda and Myrta showed no disapproval of their friend Miriam for being 'the other woman'. On the contrary, they pitied her for being the victim of her boyfriend's wife's rage. Señora Flor, one of Clara's neighbours, has a long-established relationship with a married man. Her children were born out of this relationship. He visits her every day but never stays over. He gives her money for the *olla* (literally meaning pot, but used to signify money used for daily food consumption). If he has troubles at home he stays away. She would never ask her *marido* to leave his wife and family.

In the configuration of gender relationships, men's fidelity is generally not negotiable. If a woman decides she wants to stay with her husband, her room for manoeuvre is extremely restricted. Witchcraft may be resorted to, to try and make her husband stop. If that fails and he does not see the urgency in her request, there is little she can do to change the situation. She could cause problems and hope he will give up the other woman, but she runs the risk he will choose the other woman instead. Señora Sylvia, another woman working on this particular street, was abandoned by her *marido* who married another women. After several years he came back to her. She told me how much he makes her suffer. Her fear of losing him again makes her endure his abusive behaviour.

Only three of the women who frequent Clara's house live with their *maridos*. However, all of the women have children and, in all likelihood, at some point of their life, they lived with their *maridos*. Although these relationships are systematically written off by outsiders as relationships between prostitutes and pimps, the women consider themselves married. The complexities of these relationship are never talked about. Subjects such as the influence of their work in their relationship and vice versa were hermetically sealed off. Señora Myrta gave only a few glimpses into her relationship with her *marido*, with whom she had been together for 16 years. She described him as a loving man who earned his own money. Smiling, she told me about the plans he had made to celebrate Valentine's day. Once I commented to Clara that Myrta appeared to have a good relationship with her husband. Clara clucked in disagreement, 'If he really loved her he would do everything possible to get her out of this world.' A high degree of scepticism exists concerning men's capacities to love a prostitute. Can a man really love a prostitute, and, if he does, why doesn't he make her stop? The underlying assumption is that prostitution and love are incompatible. Thus, other motives must exist to justify a relationship with a prostitute.

*Scene Two*

Right before Gabriela left, Clara's house had a new addition. Señora Rosa's daughter Juanita came to live with them. Rosa is 48 years old and has nine children from three different husbands. Juanita was brought up by her aunt and later by a sister who lives in Chiclayo, a large city in the northern coastal region of Peru. She returned to Lima a while ago. Juanita, who is 19 years old, visits her mother frequently. Her recent move to Clara's house was a consequence of being unemployed. She quit her job working in a store because she had suffered a temporary partial paralysis on the right half of her face. The doctor gave her some exercises and a makeshift brace to stimulate the muscles to return to their original place. However, she paid no heed to the doctor's orders. This infuriated her mother because her condition did not improve. On a return visit, the doctor suggested she should be hospitalized. Rosa tried to earn more money in order send Juanita to the hospital. Perhaps because she was unable to save enough money – it was swallowed up successively by various (minor) emergencies – or because a slight improvement could be observed in Juanita's condition, she never did go to the hospital. Juanita stayed at home feeling awkward and depressed. Problems arose because she did not help her mother either economically or with the housework. Both are obligations of a dutiful daughter. Little by little, Juanita got over her awkwardness and started to help around the house. She joined her brother's business, selling tape cassettes and cigarettes on a street in the centre of Lima. She even began her own business which was abruptly terminated by a police raid in which they confiscated her merchandise and locked her up for a few days.

Juanita was changing. There was a twinkle in her eyes and she went to parties, staying out late, much to her mother's dismay. Although she insistently denied she had a *novio*, rumours were reaching Rosa's and Clara's ears of the opposite. Her *novio* (boyfriend/fiancé), according to Clara, was nothing but a 'no-good thief'. Juanita moved out to live with a girlfriend. She visited her mother regularly. On one of her visits Juanita told me she wanted to move back. Shortly after, she did. After a brief stay, she made plans to settle down with her *novio* turned *marido*. Her relationship was established. Subtle changes could be observed in Juanita's attitudes and behaviour. She began to behave more like a Señora and was treated like one, too. The women passed on information pertaining to renting suitable accommodation for a young couple. In spite of the fact that it was suspected her *marido* derived his earnings from dubious sources – Juanita maintained all along he was a watchman at a factory – her relationship was accepted and she was looked upon as a married woman.

Juanita's way of managing information in her relationship with her mother reflects one dynamic aspect in the parent–child relationship. By withholding certain information and complying at home to the behavioural expectations of a good daughter, a façade is created which resists her mother's questions and concerns until she is ready to share her outside world at home. Her strategy is shared by many adolescents of all economic strata of Lima because, if they revealed what was actually going on, their freedom would be taken away from them. This applies especially to young women, whose parents will do everything to protect their child from being (sexually) harmed. However, in Barrios Altos a parent's inclination to protect their children intensifies. This is attributable to the way people relate to the environment and the way they conceptualize human nature in this dangerous and violent neighbourhood.

Many residents of Barrios Altos share a philosophical vision of human nature in which the environment is perceived as an external world filled with impending dangers and temptations for children. Once a child is drawn into it, it is extremely difficult to pull her back. In this sense, children are envisaged as helpless and naive. Their well-being and their future balance on a razor's edge. It is a parent's obligation to make sure the child does not lose her balance.

Many conversations about children took place at Clara's house. They reflected the precarious nature of the notion of luck entangled in this environment. The women accepted the idea that their luck could change at any moment. Señora Rosa once asked me if I had ever visited a prison. I replied I did not know anyone in prison. She had never visited one either. 'None of my husbands were in jail, one of us had to stay healthy.' (She is implying her husband was healthy – without vices. She could not be healthy because she was a prostitute.) 'But you never know, I have children and grandchildren, maybe one day one of them will end up there.'

The dangers of this environment also threaten adults. However, in contrast to children, they can control it. The women tried to avoid coming in close contact with the bad influences, troubles or neighbourhood problems. Getting involved is dangerous. It could result in unexpected, adverse changes in the course of their lives. Although their lives were filled with hardship and struggle, nonetheless, they were doing their best to improve their situation. One of the ways they maintained control over their relationships was to maintain a relationship with the undesirable person. They created a friendly illusion, close enough to know what was going on but at the same time enabling them to keep their distance. Clara received regular visits from individuals who fitted the description of a 'bad element'. However, by letting them into her house she minimized their influence in her household.

Embedded in the women's protective stance are norms and values that contribute to their definitions of themselves by drawing a distinction between themselves and others who do not live up to these standards. Generally, these norms become visible when they are transgressed. On one occasion, one of the women came into the house very drunk and was causing problems during work. Señora Myrta disapproved of her coming to work drunk and when the woman left the house she said, 'I drink, too, and sometimes too much, but I drink at home. I would never come to work drunk.' If a woman made an *escandalo* (scandal) she would be avoided. A mask of indifference hid their opinions in her presence, but the comments which followed when she left showed their disapproval of such performances. 'This house is the place where we rest, I have my problems, too, but I leave them at home. At least she should leave them on the street', said Señora Maria.

Inasmuch as this environment is perceived as dangerous, these types of relationship are protective. They gloss over the true intentions and messages being transmitted. Other versions of this tactic – to make things appear differently from the way they are – are created continually. This mode of communication is not confined to the women-who-prostitute. It is a culturally used tactic encountered in all social domains in Lima. However, as we will see below, people frequently voice their emotions in this manner.

*Scene Three*

Magda was angry because it was the second time today that the police had come by asking for money. In the morning she paid but this second time she refused. 'It is no crime to stand in a doorway', she said to the two policemen who were new to the neighbourhood. 'At least the old cop only asks for money when he catches us in the room.'

'What!', I exclaimed. 'They enter the room while you are with a client and ask for money?'

'Yes', she replied, without changing the inflection of her voice. 'The old guy came by and I saw him reprimanding the new one because he asked for money when he didn't catch us in the room. He is not a bad cop, some of them are good.'

Magda was not angry because she had to pay a bribe, although she sarcastically remarked that she sometimes felt she worked to keep the police, but rather because the policeman disregarded the norms regarding bribery. After letting off steam, she went back to work to try to get some business before *almuerzo*.

In general, the women's nonchalant attitude towards bribes exemplifies their resigned and impotent position as clandestine prostitutes. Only in specific situations, when something out of the ordinary occurred, as Magda's story reveals, was the presence of the police in the neighbourhood mentioned. However, the police came by much more frequently than I realized, especially when near the end of the month or before a holiday. The women accepted that paying off the police was an occupational hazard.

Señora Rosa sat down at the table; she was worried. 'I am going to look for any other type of work, it doesn't matter what. Fujimori said in his inaugural speech he was going to combat drugs, delinquency and prostitution. That means he is going to reinforce the law to keep us in jail up to three months.'

I tried to calm her down, repeating what the commander of the Department of Licencias Especiales had told me in our interview. He claimed there were no short-term plans to change the Penal Code with regard to prostitution.[1] I added, 'Even if they would enforce the law again, they do not have enough equipment or personnel to guarantee its functioning.'

Rosa did not seem convinced, 'That's because they haven't started the changes yet, but Fujimori is going to put aside money for these goals.'

The women started to trickle in for *almuerzo*. Magda came in, followed by another woman called Sylvia, who had recently returned from one of her customary recesses. Different versions explained how she could permit herself this luxury. One explanation was that she had derived additional income from other sources, of an illegal nature, some added. Another version portrayed her as a prostitute who *jala mucho* (*jalar* is to pull or tug, implying that she pulled in a lot of clients). She did not need to work the whole year. Whatever the case may be, when she worked she did not miss a day. Sylvia, a tough woman with a sharp tongue, had no qualms in showing me what she felt about my presence. In lieu of responding to my greetings, she expressed sarcasm or grunted. This would be the first time we sat down to eat *almuerzo* together.

Rosa's concern for the future under Fujimori rubbed off on Magda who told us she was worried about the changes Fujimori would enforce concerning prostitution. Sylvia enthusiastically joined the conversation. 'What's the problem?' she said, 'Just look at it as a month's vacation.' I threw her a disconcerted look, upon which, keeping a straight face, she winked at me to let me know she was not serious.

Magda became indignant and replied, 'That's fine for you or the other women who have extra incomes, but I only earn my money from this.'

'It's a month vacation', Sylvia repeated. I looked at Sylvia again and this time I asked if she was serious. She kept a straight face and said yes, but when Magda was not looking she winked again. Thinking this was a joke, I joined in the joke and stated, 'Sure, you can send postcards "Greetings from the Women's Prison of Chorrillos".'

In the meanwhile, Sylvia, who always brought something extra for herself for *almuerzo*, divided a piece of steak in two and offered me a piece and gave one to the baby. She did not offer any to Magda. This action expressed my acceptance as well as Magda's exclusion. Other women took their place at the table and the conversation went in various directions. Magda finished her tea and went outside.

When the door closed behind her, Sylvia immediately told Myrta and Maria about our conversation and how upset it had made Magda. Only then did I realize I had not partaken in an innocent prank but in an intentional conversation. 'She is probably complaining to her girlfriend Julia outside', Sylvia said, and continued, 'I don't know why she worries, it would be different if she had children to look after but she has no one. Myrta and Maria have children, my children can take care of themselves but it would be different if Myrta or Maria were imprisoned.'

Myrta added, 'She never thinks of stopping, she is going to keep working even if she has to use a cane to walk.'

Sylvia again said, 'I don't know why she worries.'

'Well Sylvia, no one wants to go to prison for a month even if they don't have any children.' For a brief moment Myrta came to Magda's defence.

On another occasion, Magda complained throughout the day about stomach pains. When we sat down to eat, Sylvia told Maria about a radio programme she had heard about Aids. I perked up my ears thinking this was an illustration of how information was passed on to one another. Only after Sylvia repeatedly stated that the symptoms of Aids included stomach problems, did I realize she meant to scare Magda. Although these conversations often targeted Magda, Magda employed the same tactic to express her grievances. Once she told me a story in front of Yalu about a prostitute who stole from her clients, who never cleaned up the room and was dirty. I found the story a bit out of context, but being accustomed to Magda's way of jumping from one subject to another, I took no notice. When Magda went back to work, Yalu was very upset. Magda might have created a fictitious woman, but Yalu knew she was the intended recipient of this message. 'Why does she say those things? She knows I steal and have trouble keeping clean.'

These incidents demonstrate two tactical ways of conveying messages and expressing unkind feelings. In the first incident, Sylvia joined in a conversation in progress and used it to pass on a message. Her actions were deliberate and calculated. In the second series of conversations, uncharitable messages were passed on in casual conversations made up for the purpose. The underlying message is not verbalized, but it is easily read by the person to whom the conversation is directed and to the other listeners. It took me some time before I was proficient in managing and interpreting this 'culture of indirection' (Joseph 1996: 116).[2]

There are other circumstances that call for a more direct indirect approach. In these cases, actions speak louder than words. Clara described how Magda and herself expressed their anger or annoyance to one another. 'When Magda wants to annoy me [*frigar*] she eats somewhere else or doesn't tell me she won't be coming to work and I cook more than necessary. When I want to annoy her I put *yuca* [cassava] in the soup knowing she doesn't like it.' These mundane actions indirectly pass on clear messages.

One of the most salient characteristics of this culture of indirection is that it is nearly impossible to accuse the initiator of the action or conversation of deliberately trying to hurt the other person. For example, if Clara wanted to accuse Magda of intentionally going to another restaurant to annoy her, Magda could simply deny it. The same holds true for the conversations. If the person targeted defended herself, the storyteller could reply, 'What are you getting so upset about? I am just telling a story, that's all.' Thus, the meanings remain buried under the everydayness of daily life.

Magda and Sylvia's conversations conceal strong notions concerning acceptable behaviour and honourable justifications for prostituting. Magda's reasons for prostituting are suspect. She lives alone and does not have any children to support. She continues to work even though, as rumour had it, she is able to save in dollars, a possibility denied to the majority of the women. In their totality, these are sufficient grounds for her to stop working. Moreover, she does not show any signs of trying to retire. On the contrary, the woman think she will never stop. Magda and Sylvia are approximately the same age, yet these comments were never made about Sylvia, probably because people could see she planned to get out. Sylvia points to Myrta and Marta as two women who exhibit the acceptable reasons to prostitute because they do it for their families.

However, Magda's reaction shows the other side of the story. She is the one in a disadvantaged position because she is a woman alone who has no family to take care of her when she grows old and no additional income. According to her, her motivations for prostituting are more righteous than those of the other women, because they are surrounded by their families, have additional sources of income and less to worry about.

The notions underlying the conversations explain, in part, the tension between the women. It also made certain things clear concerning the women's positions in the configurations of relationships. As stated earlier, I was under the impression Magda was the leader of the group. Therefore, I could not figure out why I had so much trouble approaching the other women. These conversations made me realize that my association with Magda did not work in my favour. She may have been boisterous and even cantankerous, but in no way did she represent the other women. The way she embodied the prostitute conflicted with several of the other women's perceptions. Nonetheless, in spite of the lack of empathy the other women displayed towards Magda, she was not considered a 'bad element'. As will be shown, much more is required to receive the label of a 'bad element'.

Thus, the moment I mistakenly joined in conveying an indirect message to Magda, and Sylvia offered me a piece of her steak and I accepted, I symbolically severed my association with Magda. This did not bring forth any dramatic changes but it did make my presence more acceptable.

*Scene Four*

The majority of the women who frequent Clara's house work as prostitutes to improve their (families') situations. The neighbourhood calls them *zanahorias* (literally, 'carrot', but in this case it refers to a healthy person without vices). Unlike the prostitutes dependent on drugs or alcohol, they do their jobs, keep to themselves, try to keep out of trouble and return to their families at the end of the day. They share many of the norms and values of the residents of the neighbourhood who are trying to improve their situation without getting involved in criminal activities. Paradoxically, for these same neighbours, they are probably included in the list of 'bad elements'. Nonetheless, the women make a clear distinction between themselves and those whom they consider to be the real 'bad elements'.

The women shunned the prostitutes who were drug addicts and alcoholics. The methods used to avoid them were very subtle. If one of them was present at *almuerzo*, they would not be ignored but only included if the situation demanded. If word had gone around that one of them was aggressive, then the women would keep out of their way until they calmed down. These women represented their mirror image: they were known to make trouble continually, they rarely went home to see their children and they used a large part of their earnings to support their habit. They would often become physically aggressive.

One day, Señora Myrta was extremely quiet. She had been crying. She was standing in a corner conversing in a soft voice with Clara. Above her t-shirt her chest displayed three long deep scratches. She decided to go home early. When she left, the women told me she had been in a fight with Carmen. They were angry that Carmen had picked on her because Señora Myrta was a person who kept to herself and caused no troubles. They claimed Carmen often picked on Myrta because she knew she would not fight back.

Stealing in itself was not something that caused a woman to be labelled a 'bad element'. It depended on who was doing the stealing. In general, it was common knowledge among the prostitutes who included pickpocketing as an 'additional service' for their clients. It was even given as a reason why some prostitutes did not have to work as much as others. They calculated the additional income obtained by pickpocketing in their earnings. The fact that Yalu stole worked to reinforce her bad image. Señora Pilar approached the subject openly. Once at the kitchen table, she explained to me why she could hold out a little longer before she raised her prices. She had other ways of increasing her income. She made a gesture with her hand and accompanied this with a swooshing noise as if she made something disappear.

Through the everyday relationships on this particular street different versions of the prostitute are enacted and different locations are allotted to each of the women. Sylvia, Myrta and Maria usually formed a group together. Julia or Pilar often joined Magda but frequently she was alone. Rosa seemed to get along with everyone. Since she lived at Clara's house, she could distance herself from it all when she wanted to and dedicate herself to taking care of Petra and the household chores. Yalu and Carmen were outcasts who always stuck together. When it came to dealing with them, the women usually formed a united front. The construction of these relationships is anchored in the women's perceptions of the environment. They do not fight to change the environment, they accept it for what it is and arm themselves against the eventual harm the people in the environment can have in their personal lives. Underlying these relations are various perceptions, intentions and codes which shape the way the women deal with their problems and relate to one another. This develops into strong normative distinctions between good and bad and is reflected in their embodiment of the prostitute.

## EL PAQUETAZO

President Fujimori's promise to combat prostitution remained unfulfilled. He did not make any noticeable efforts to eradicate the 'prostitution problem'. Nonetheless, the women's concerns for their future under Fujimori's government were not unwarranted. The day was approaching when the government would announce its package of economic austerity measures – *el paquetazo* – claimed to be a necessary step to fight inflation and put Peru back on the road to development. Fujimori's electorial pledge to combat inflation without applying a shock treatment was an empty promise. *El paquetazo* would be the first group of drastic measures undertaken in what would gradually be known as the Fujishock. The contents of the *paquetazo* took Lima by surprise. The city was unnerved. Fujimori's proposed Emergency Plan, to soften the shock for those living at the most extreme level of poverty, was uncoordinated, chaotic and bureaucratic. Many Limeneans regretted ever having voted for him. It was said that Vargas Llosa's plan was carefully thought out and well organized, but Fujimori's was more severe and he appeared to be making it up along the way.

Barrig (1993) refers to this day – 8 August 1990 – as 'the day the country became mute' (*El día que el país enmudeció*). Her study captures the consequences of the *paquetazo* for six families who lived in poverty. The years before this *paquetazo* they had developed an elaborate net of survival strategies, enabling them to push on and gradually improve their economic situation. These strategies virtually disappeared after the announcement on this infamous day. Nearly all economic strata of the country felt the effect of the *paquetazo*. It increased the number of persons living in extreme poverty from 7 million to 12 million (Riofrío 1990: 33). In July, an average family of 5.5 individuals needed 5.5 monthly minimum wages to satisfy their daily basic nutritional requirements. At the end of August this had increased to 8 monthly minimum wages. Although the average salary rose after the *paquetazo*, its buying power declined from 70 to 32 per cent (Gamero 1990: 13).

The day after the official announcement almost all businesses were closed as a preventative measure against *saqueos* (looting of stores). It also served as a golden opportunity for merchants to readjust their prices to the new economic situation. It was in the middle of the Limenean winter, when the sun rarely breaks through the blanket of grey clouds permanently covering Lima's skies. Ironically, it was a beautiful sunny day, as if the sun paid no heed to the shock felt by the majority of the Limeneans. I mentally prepared myself to go back to Barrios Altos, wondering how the women were coping with this new situation. How did it affect their working and private lives?

After the announcement, a period characterized by uncertainties and insecurities commenced. The *paquetazo* had produced ruptures in the ongoing rhythm of daily life. Business had declined drastically. On the one hand, the clients had less money to spend. On the other hand, the women raised their prices to 400,000 *Intis*, of which 150,000 went to the rental of the room.[3] Clara raised her price for lunch to 550,000 *Intis*. The women complained about the price rise.

When I entered Clara's house, Señora Rosa was sweeping the floor and listening to a televised discussion about the *paquetazo*. The economist suggested the public should only buy essential products. He considered this a collective form of protest to force the prices down. Señora Rosa agreed with him and complained about the outrageous prices. Last week she had managed to find a new way to increase her income. She had bought toilet paper – an indispensable tool for the women's work – at wholesale prices, earning a bit of profit on each roll she sold. However, this new-found source of income disappeared as quickly as it came. Every bit of extra money had to be used for food. It was unthinkable that enough money would be left over at the end of the week to continue her new enterprise.

Magda came in. She had been speaking to Hermana Marta who told her that prostitutes in other countries have organized. Hermana Marta advised her to talk to me about it because I knew more about the subject. Magda followed her advice and asked me, 'Lorena, why can't we organize?' To say the least, I was taken aback. What should I say, 'Sure, let's start tomorrow'? At the same time I realized it was Magda talking and she was not the most representative of the group.

*Almuerzo* was ready. I called the women in to eat. The *paquetazo* was felt directly in their pocketbooks. Señora Maria turned to me, put her finger to her neck and made a knife-like motion meaning she had no money. Magda and I sat down to eat, joined a bit later by Myrta who only ate the entrée and Maria came in for a bowl of soup. During *almuerzo* Sylvia and Pilar came in and quickly shut the door behind them. A police jeep arrived looking for someone. The tension could be felt in the air. Suddenly, we heard a loud thump which sounded as if someone has pounded on the door. The women nearly fell off their chairs. It was only Clara who had closed the closet door. The police left. They had picked up the son of the man who rented the room to the women. Clara said that they picked him up for drugs. Sylvia and Pilar returned to the street.

During *almuerzo* the issues related to the *paquetazo* dominated the conversation. Politics, the possibility of a *golpe de estado* (a military take-over) and the outrage they felt about the increase of prices, were the women's primary concern. Myrta said that she had five people to feed. Maria had six. 'But what would happen if we had more children?'

Magda said, 'I bet they are going to loot all the Japanese stores.'

'That wouldn't be right', I replied.

Myrta said, 'How can you say that, you haven't been to the *pueblos jóvenes*. People are dying of hunger there.' She misunderstood my comment. She took my response to mean I could not understand why people looted.

'What I meant to say is, it would not be right to only loot the Japanese stores, it is not their fault.'

'Oh', she replied.

Maria disclosed one of her tactics to try to make ends meet. 'When I finish work at 6:30 I go to La Parada in search of the best buys. It is cheaper than the central market. The last time I went, I found a damaged pepper and I asked the woman how much she wanted for it, she only asked 10,000. At the central market they sold peppers for 50,000.'

Sylvia came in, took off her skirt and put on a pair of pants. This action normally meant the person had called it a day, but it was only one o'clock. I found it a bit odd. When she left I asked Clara if she had finished working. Clara replied, 'She is going to eat somewhere else. I laugh about it in front of the women, but it hurts inside. She is probably angry because I have raised my prices.'

A few days later things were still quite unsettled. Magda sat at the kitchen table. When I greeted her she said, 'The situation is really bad.'

'Did you ever think of starting a rotating fund among all of you? It could be very useful now, considering the situation.'

Her enthusiasm for organizing had definitely tapered off since Monday. She claimed it would be impossible. 'The women are different here than in other places. They only screw for their households. You know I used to work at Troca, if someone got sick they passed the hat around to contribute to the costs. This would be impossible here.' She began to get very angry and started to complain about the women. 'The majority are quiet, but they are always gossiping behind your back.' At that moment Señora Maria came in. This did not put an end to her complaints. On the contrary, she became more fervent. 'They are all ignorant. Hermana Marta gave me a book to read. You know you have to be intelligent to read, isn't that right Lorena?', making an attempt to pull me into the conversation. I replied with a simple 'Mmm.'

'They are ignorant, they are really ignorant.'

Timidly, I replied, 'Everyone can learn, nobody is ignorant.' Between her emotional outbursts, the conversation continued about the prices which appeared to be stabilizing. When Magda left, Clara and I were alone. She told me Magda had had a fight with the other women. Somehow, it did not surprise me. 'She is driving me crazy. She wants me to lower my prices. She said her electricity and water bills are going up. I told her so if I lower my prices it's better for you, but then I will have problems, my bills have gone up, too.'

'Clara', I asked, 'did you hear they want to organize a *comedor popular* [communal kitchen] with the *quintas* [used interchangeably with *callejon*] on this street?'[4] Clara's economic situation was worse than ever. Nonetheless, she did not change her standpoint with regard to getting involved with people in the neighbourhood. Myrta told us that Cambio 90 (Fujimori's party) was organizing *comedores populares* throughout the city. Her sister was participating in one. Señora Maria thought they were a good idea but she thought only women with small children should be eligible, the rest should go out to work. Julia admired the good intentions of the NGO but doubted the likelihood of success. Clara repeated, 'I don't want to get involved with the people in the neighbourhood. They are bad.' She named all the people in the nearby *quintas* who used drugs. 'I am sorry Lorena, but those people don't deserve any help. They use all their money for drugs. Let them clean themselves up first. That is what they really need.' Ultimately, the women were proved right. Whether it was the bureaucratic entanglements involved in the initiative causing its failure or the residents' lack of drive, the *comedor popular* never got off the ground.

Clara was washing clothes when I returned on my next visit. Whenever possible she increased her income by washing clothes for people in the neighbourhood. 'I washed 57 pieces of clothing this weekend. I'm not supposed to wash clothes. The doctor told me not to, but what am I supposed to do?'

The expression on her face changed, she began to smile. 'If my mother was alive, she would come here and help me, she would help wash the clothes.'

Nonetheless Clara was in a bad mood caused by her last visit to her *marido*. She had taken Petra along and her father had bitten her face, leaving a black and blue mark. 'I have had enough. I am not going back again. I brought him food and he threw it on the floor. The drugs make him that way. I am going to give Gabriela all his clothes. When she visits her husband she can bring them to him. But I am not going back.' This was not the first time she tried to convince me she had left her *marido*. On various occasions she briefly stopped visiting him, but she eventually started again.

Something was going on. The women were very upset. It turned out that the man who rented the room had decided to raise the price. The women had already raised their prices again to 600,000 *Intis*. They knew they could not ask the clients for any more. He insulted Señora Myrta, calling them *putas de mierda* (whores who are pieces of shit) and saying that they were the lowest of the low. The discussion re-ignited every time someone else entered the kitchen. They went on strike and would not return to the room until he lowered the price. They used another room in the neighbourhood. Magda and Sylvia gave a vivid description of him. 'He is such a horrible man. He sells *pasta*. It is no wonder his children are drug addicts. He doesn't deserve to be called a man. He left his wife for a woman who owns a restaurant. Every day, he sends his wife food and makes her pay for it. What kind of man is that? She is afraid of him. He beats her and beats her good.'

Sylvia jokingly said '*la huelga continuará*' (the strike will continue), taking the tone of a factory worker on strike. The women continued their strike for several days until they finally achieved what they wanted. The man did not raise his prices and they returned.

In between this discussion another conversation emerged concerning the recent problems they had with their rotating fund. My consternation was caused by Magda's previous comment. She gave me the impression the women did not organize such things. It was a ludicrous idea. However, she also participated in the initiative and it has been functioning for several years. Clara told me later this was typical of Magda. 'She blows off steam and does not listen to what the other person says.'

Señora Rosa is in charge and explained how it functioned. 'The women contribute 300,000 *Intis* daily. Every ten days, the fund is paid out on a rotating basis to one of them. However, there are always problems.' Julia was behind in her payments. She never paid on time. The women started to exchange stories about Julia, how she never returned what she borrowed. 'She asked me to loan her a condom and promised to give it back', Magda said, 'but she never gave it back. I am not going to lend her any more condoms. I work with condoms, I need them.'

Señora Myrta approached Julia standing at the door. She came back and reported to the women that Julia denied that she had missed a payment. No one believed her. Rosa exclaimed, 'I don't want to get involved.'

'Why don't you participate, Clara?', I asked.

Rosa answered for her. 'She doesn't want any problems. There are plenty of problems, especially when the day arrives to pay the person and someone is behind payments.' The women went back to work.

Life went on in this particular street in Barrios Altos as always. The *paquetazo*'s tumultuous effects subsided in a few weeks. Prices would stabilize, albeit higher than ever, but the guesswork was over. The new situation would enmesh in the rhythm of daily life and the women would be able to manage and face their situation in their familiar way with less uncertainty. Immediately after the first wave of panic, the clients slowly trickled back. It would not be long before all the women ate their lunch at Clara's house as usual, without skimping on one of the meal's courses.

The period directly following the *paquetazo*, as I mentioned earlier, profoundly shook the population's security. For the poor, especially, it uprooted all the ways they had constructed to survive and improve their lives. Perhaps for this reason, during the first period following the *paquetazo*, the moments of resistance and solidarity, the struggle for improvement and the daily negotiations were transparent. Yet these moments of resistance and solidarity are always present and should not be idealized. They do not contain a catalytic power which will eventually produce profound changes in the women's lives. On the contrary, the women do not recognize the power in these moments. In their approach to people and their treatment of issues, they frequently highlighted the negative aspects while the positive went unnoticed. Thus, the events which took place after the *paquetazo* illustrate that power and control exist entwined in the scepticism of the everydayness of daily life.

CONDOM(S) TALK(S)

I had been waiting for the appropriate moment to announce that I could obtain free condoms. I had arranged with an NGO which had an Aids prevention project to receive regular allotments of condoms, donated from the US. My decision to distribute condoms had some ulterior motives. I certainly considered it a possible point around which the women could organize – for example, they could eventually take control of the distribution – but I did not feel I should push things to reach this goal. Basically, there were other reasons for my decision. First, receiving free condoms lessened their economic burden in this time of economic crisis. It could eliminate the financial obstacles impeding their continual use. Second, it was a way to give something in return. Distributing condoms was a tangible demonstration of reciprocity.

I chose this moment because I felt my position was sufficiently established so that condom distribution would not be misinterpreted. They would not associate it with social work or charity or try to take advantage of me. Of course, there were women who saw me as one or the other, but they were not regulars at Clara's house. I gave out condoms to any woman who asked for them. I did not discriminate between one group and another. I attempted to create favourable circumstances required for more women to use condoms regularly in their work. I did not intend to use condoms as a means to negotiate my identity. This, however, does not imply that distributing condoms did not influence my fieldwork. It most certainly did. When I proposed doing this, I had no idea it would have such positive consequences for fieldwork. It opened doors to subjects never spoken about earlier and once again it demonstrated the complex dynamics of relationships.

To comply with the conditions of the NGO, I needed an estimation of the quantity required weekly. I set out to ask the women individually. Señora Magda sat at the kitchen table drinking a cup of tea and Carmen was eating *almuerzo*. When Magda got up to leave, I approached her with the news and asked how many she needed. She replied, 'I usually buy them by the box, it's cheaper. I need 70 a week.' She went back to work and I took a seat at the kitchen table. 'Carmen', I said, 'I have some good news. I will be able to give out condoms, but I need to know how many you need weekly.'

Carmen became pensive, it took awhile before she answered: 'It is difficult to say. Some days there is a lot of business, other days there is none. I need about five daily. Why should I lie? I only use them when a client brings them or if I have enough money to buy them, but I don't use them often. If I receive them regularly I will always use them.'

Señora Myrta came in. Carmen immediately told her about the offer. 'How many do you think you need daily, just give her an idea, what do you think?'

Myrta listened to Carmen but avoided giving an answer. When Carmen left Myrta changed her seat and kept a watchful eye on the door. I remarked, 'Maybe the offer does not interest you?'

'It's not that', she replied. 'I don't want her to know how many clients I have. She is a very jealous and mean person. I use 15 to 20 daily.'

Clara said, 'Myrta could have 50 a day if she wanted, but Carmen only needs five because she steals.'

I must admit, Myrta's answer surprised me. I never expected so much business went on beyond these four walls.

Maria came in. She complained about the *cochinita* (dirty, slob in diminutive). I had never heard anyone use this nickname before for any of the women working here and I asked Clara, 'Who are they talking about?'

Clara said, 'Julia, because she is dirty and never takes care of herself.'

They talked about Julia's son. She was such good friends with Magda, but she treated her son so badly. Myrta said, 'You should never treat your son badly. After all, he will stand by you all your life. He is your son, but how long will Magda be by her side?' This was followed by a flood of gossip about Magda. 'She is such a bad person. She is always shooting her mouth off. She has no consideration for anyone else.'

Maria said, 'She says she has been educated by nuns. She had a better education than many of us. You would think she would speak better than us, but she doesn't. She comes in here screaming on the top of her lungs telling all the details of what went on in the room.'

Myrta added, 'I used to care about her a lot. We used to talk a lot together, but now I can't stand her.'

When the conversation died down, I told Maria about the condoms. Maria replied, 'That is fine, I will use them when the client wants to.'

Clara said, 'That's not the idea. The idea is you always use them and grow accustomed to using them.'

At that moment, Maria produced a handful of condoms from her bag and showed them to me. 'Magda thinks we don't use them. She probably told you that but as you can see I do. We don't tell her because we want to keep her out of our business.'

Sylvia came in and joined the conversation. Both Maria and Sylvia had the same number of clients as Myrta, except that Sylvia worked seven days a week, while the other two worked six. Maria turned to Sylvia and reminded her of the radio programme on Aids they had listened to. 'It is good to use them.' Sylvia agreed.

They expanded on the client's thoughts on the subject of condom use. 'They think we are *quemada*' (literally, 'burnt', but refers to catching a venereal disease). Maria told a story about how she asked the client to put on a *poncho* (a cloak used in the Andes as a jacket, it is also slang for a condom). 'The client didn't understand, he asked me if I wanted him to put on his *poncho*? I replied, "Yes, put it on", and then he said "It is too warm to wear a poncho." Then I realized what was the confusion and I corrected myself and said I meant a condom, and I explained to him in this way I will be protected if you have anything and you won't run the risk of bringing anything home.'

We all laughed at her story. Before Sylvia continued, she excused herself beforehand for the language she would use (this was a usual occurrence among the women when I was present). 'Some think it's better to *pajear* [jerk off] than to be made to use a condom.' They talked about the disadvantages. The clients take more time if they use a condom. The rubber causes vaginal irritation and the nationally produced condoms are unreliable.

I excused myself and went over to Clara. I wanted to know if I should approach Rosa. Rosa's timidity made it difficult for me to approach her. I did not know if she still worked and whether she would be offended if she had stopped. Clara began to chuckle, because she knew Rosa all too well. 'She hasn't had any clients for a long time, and then all of a sudden she keeps pulling them in. Once in a while she gets it into her head that she has to go outside and work, she is outside right now. Yes, you should ask her if she needs any, she is too shy to ask you.' When Rosa came I approached her. She used five daily and bought them by the box and sold them to the other women. However, she still had some she bought before the *paquetazo*. We agreed she would let me know when she needed some more.

I returned to the kitchen table where Sylvia was eating her *almuerzo* alone. She asked me, 'How do you prevent Aids?'

I replied, 'The best way is by using condoms', and I explained why. Without realizing it, I fell into another one of her traps aimed at pestering Magda.

'Magda told you she always uses condoms.'

I nodded.

'But what is the use of using them if ... ' – she made a gesture as if she was putting a penis in her mouth – 'and you put it on afterwards. I never do that.'

I suddenly realized that Magda offered certain sexual services the other women did not and that was one of the reasons she had so many clients. If I momentarily doubted the truthfulness of Sylvia's story, I was convinced later after hearing the same thing from other women who were less aggressive towards Magda.

Sylvia continued her lunch and it was the first time I felt comfortable enough to ask her some questions.

'How long have you been working here?'

'For years, but I used to travel to the provinces a lot to work. It is about five years since I went to the *selva* [the jungle].'

'Did you ever work anywhere else in Lima?'

'No. I have always worked here, you get used to it.'

'I never see any new faces on the street.'

'That's because we don't let anyone else work here.'

Her answers were not elaborate, but they were not hostile either. 'Thank you, Señorita Lorena, for the conversation. It was nice to finally have some time to talk a bit together.'

Right before I left, Señora Pilar came in. She said she needed some condoms. 'I haven't been working regularly, but I will be coming here more often. I need about 25 a week.' Clara explained why Señora Pilar had changed her mind. 'She has a married daughter who gives her an allowance. I guess things have become tighter since the *paquetazo* and her daughter can't give her enough.'

The next visit, I brought the condoms. I could not supply the quantity each woman needed because the NGO would not supply so many condoms outside of their own project. Nonetheless, the amount given covered the greatest part of their needs.

I sat down at the table with Myrta, Maria and Sylvia. Señora Magda came in but she stayed in the bedroom. Something was going on between them. They had probably had a fight again. Even so, it was a very pleasant lunch. Maria told us the preparations she had made for her daughter's confirmation. We talked about a television programme about prostitution. Maria always told me when she saw or heard something on the subject. Myrta talked about her husband. She had told her husband all about me. Maria offered me a glass of juice she had brought from home and Sylvia invited me to try the food she had brought to eat. When the women left, Magda approached the table with a sad look on her face. She told me she had not worked yesterday. I replied, 'You look ill.' 'I am having stomach problems.'

When I left, I approached Magda outside to talk about the condoms. She stood alone leaning on a doorpost. I suggested, 'Why don't you give me a sign when you finish your supply and need some more? I made the same agreement with Señora Rosa.' The expression on her face changed immediately. She looked hurt and angrily said, 'If you want to give them condoms go ahead, I don't need any, don't worry about me.' She thought the other women had put me up to this. I tried patiently to explain, while following after her as she walked away. I repeated several times that I had made the same agreement with Rosa but she did not listen. This incident initiated a period of several weeks when Magda stopped talking to me. She ignored my presence entirely. I decided that, since she did not respond to my explanations, I would deal with this problem the way I was taught working in this environment. I ignored her, too, and waited until it all blew over. When she finally began to talk again, the disagreement was buried without spilling a word. We chatted and conversed as was our custom. Magda accepted the condoms without any problems.

Months passed and condom distribution was incorporated into the daily rhythm of my visits. Of course, this could not occur without one or two women trying to manipulate me to obtain them. But, in general, it went smoothly.

It was December and the women had raised the prices several times since the *paquetazo*.[5] They now charged 1 million *Intis*. Señora Pilar was there. Despite her intention to work more often, she came regularly but infrequently. She told me once again she was planning to come more often and then began to reminisce about her daughter's wedding. 'She got married when she was 19, *ella metía la pata* ['she made a mistake', but in this context it means she got pregnant before she was married]. I did everything in my power to make sure she got married in white and in the church. She had a civil and church ceremony', and she had some pictures to prove it. She showed me a picture of her daughter dressed in a white bridal gown, descending a rocky path leaving her home. Behind her stood a house built partially with *esteras* and partially with bricks. The contrast was not shocking, on the contrary it illustrated perfectly how impoverished people try to improve their situation by accomplishing things for their children they could not manage for themselves. Our conversation was interrupted by Hermana Marta. She came by once in a while to inquire into the women's well-being. She told us the Sisters would be moving to another neighbourhood. Their lease had terminated and the owners had raised the price drastically. We all decided this called for a *despedida* (farewell party) and we made plans to do it right after Christmas. Everyone would bring something to eat.

The day of the party arrived. Clara, Petra, Rosa and I went to the Sisters' house. The other women said they would follow shortly. We sat around talking and entered in a room converted into a chapel to sing 'Silent Night'. I went downstairs for a moment to see why the women were delayed. They replied '*ahorita*', which actually means 'in a moment', but in this situation it was a message which meant they would not be coming and they knew it all along. I returned in the middle of Clara's account of how the women came to the neighbourhood. 'They split up from a group of women who always got into trouble. Some of them worked in La Parada before coming here.'

Marta asked their ages and Clara replied that the majority were over 40, but they all lie. She told us a bit more. 'Myrta owns her house in Comas, she says she has five children, but they are actually her husband's children. Maria has just finished her house in Vitarte and will move there soon. Her husband uses it for storage for the business he recently started. She also makes aprons and sells them to the vendors on the market. She has one daughter, actually it is her niece but she treats her like a daughter.[6] Julia is finishing a beautician's course, she wants to get out of this and hopes to start her own business.'

We said farewell and went back to Clara's house. On the way I ran into the women. I teasingly told them about all the delicious food they had missed and how much I could eat because they had decided not to come. Julia said in a very serious tone, 'We didn't go because they don't treat us well. You are different.' Magda agreed. Julia continued, 'You give us condoms, you help us with our work. They don't treat us nicely.' I tried to explain the obvious differences between us. But it did not change her opinion. 'If anyone deserves a party, you do. Why don't you come and have a meal with us after New Year's?'

Julia's perceptions of the Sisters did not correspond with mine. As nuns, they had very progressive views with regard to prostitution. Nonetheless, whether Julia's impression is correct is of less importance than what her statement shows about the significance of condom distribution. It contributed to their work in a positive manner. She had voiced what I had been sensing from the women since I had started to distribute condoms. They realized I respected them. This in turn made them respect me.

The simple act of distributing condoms unintentionally made certain subjects concerning prostitution approachable and disclosed the complexity behind condom use. It gave a rough idea of the number of clients each women had daily. Subsequently, this revealed the income differences between the women. Moreover, it facilitated a calculation of the women's monthly earnings. The women who had more than ten clients daily earned far more than the monthly minimum wage of US $90. Those who worked less frequently and had an average of five clients daily and/or augmented their earnings with pickpocketing, still easily earned more than the minimum wage each month. Of course, these calculations say nothing about the uncertainties and risks, the fluctuation in the numbers of clients, or express the emotional stress involved in their occupation. However, against this backdrop, the women's continuing to work as prostitutes is very understandable. Although their earnings are not sufficient to maintain their households, it is unlikely they could earn the same amount on the labour market.

Second, it reveals that the discourse on condom use and Aids prevention is thoroughly internalized. They might have varying degrees of knowledge concerning the details, but all the women have received information concerning Aids prevention from various channels. They manage the proper answers and apply them accordingly. In my first encounter with Carmen (see Chapter 5), she asserted that she had always used condoms since the discovery of the illness. When she had the opportunity to receive condoms, she now admitted without remorse that she hardly used them. Magda's stories about condom use gave the impression she only had safe sex. However, she did not use condoms when giving oral sex – a risky sexual practice. This brings us into another domain. As an older prostitute, she found a way to maintain her income at a decent level. She offered a sexual service many of the other women refused to do.

The clients' image of a prostitute who uses condoms and the fact that clients can always choose another prostitute who does not, makes it even more difficult for the women to incorporate condom use in their sexual services. On several occasions, I suggested that if all the women who came to Clara's house refused a client if he refused to use a condom, the client would have no other choice than to oblige. However, the women did not believe this could be achieved in practice.

The conversations also disclosed that talking about condom use is even more difficult because of the relationships between the women. The number of clients each one had was kept a secret because of fears the other women would become jealous and make problems. I was surprised to discover that Myrta, Maria and Sylvia used condoms. Magda's convincing stories concerning the other women were printed in my memory. When the other women told me why they kept it a secret, I realized that condom talk cannot be separated from the dynamics of daily life.

Condom distribution definitely influenced my fieldwork favourably. However, the positive developments it produced during fieldwork cannot be equated with a successful condom distribution campaign. Did distributing condoms serve as an stimulus for the women to change their sex practices at work? Did they use condoms with every client? The answers to these questions remain a mystery. Because they accepted the condoms on a weekly basis and rarely went into detail about the quantity that remained from the week before, they gave the impression that they used them continually. However, retrospectively, I realize I received clues that using condoms remained a difficult point of negotiation with the client. Several of the women stored their supply of condoms in Clara's closet. Clara and Rosa would give an account of who still had a large supply. At the time, I did not automatically suspect this to mean they were not using condoms, I thought there were fewer clients or they had decided to work less. I am inclined to think the majority of the women used condoms more frequently than before they received them for free, but there were still many moments when they did not. Giving out free condoms does not guarantee they will always be used. There is much more involved in condom use than merely putting one on a man's penis.


## A FEW WORDS DEDICATED TO THE SUBJECT OF SEXUALITY

It was a few weeks before Christmas and the first thing I heard upon entering Clara's house were Pilar's and Magda's complaints about the lack of business. 'There is nothing, absolutely nothing', Magda said, 'business has dropped, no one has money.' 'Is it always so quiet around Christmas?', I inquired. 'Yes, but this is worse than ever.' 'Do you need some more condoms?', I asked. Pilar accepted and went back to work. Magda did not need any. 'Since there hasn't been any business, I still have some', and filled me in on her latest condom episode. Pilar returned half an hour later because there was nothing happening outside. Yalu came in and asked for some condoms. She told me she always uses them, 'There are even clients who ask for them.'

Almost all the regulars were present today except Sylvia. Carmen had heard from Yalu that I had condoms and reproached me for not giving her any. I tried to match the irritated tone in her voice and replied, 'I have not seen you for a while.' Myrta, Maria, Magda, Yalu and Carmen were waiting for their lunch. Julia entered, and left quickly to show she was annoyed that no one had told her *almuerzo* was ready. She returned shortly after and joined us at the kitchen table.

Yalu told us about the Christmas present she had bought for one of her children. She told me she had three children. Carmen talked about her two children. 'One is 15 years old and the other is 6. The oldest lives with his grandparents on his father's side. His father is in Italy. I had my children before I started to work in this.' Since I had finished *almuerzo*, I offered my seat to one of the women and squatted on the floor next to Yalu to drink my tea. Yalu asked me the symptoms of Aids. This was not the first time. She always consulted me on the subject and in reference to other sicknesses. In spite of her outwardly aggressive way of acting, underneath she was scared and insecure. She constantly feared getting sick, and she would search for ways for me to tell her how pretty she was. I asked her, 'Are you afraid you are sick?'

'No, I'm okay, but I am afraid.'

'Why don't you take an Aids test?'

'I just did. Carmen and I went to Chirimoyo to take the test. The results will come back in 15 days. I am going to work at the Nene [one of the official brothels in Lima].'

I replied, 'But you need your papers to work there.' Carmen joined in, 'That's why we took the test, we want to get our papers so we can work at the Nene.' Whether they actually took the test or their plan to enter an official brothel was more than just a desire, I cannot say. They continued to be a part of this street picture throughout my fieldwork.

Magda said, 'One of the preventative measures for Aids is to eat a lot of protein.'

'What kind of protein?', asked Yalu.

Magda could not hide her irritation, 'Protein! Eggs, milk, meat!'

Yalu sounded relieved, 'Oh you mean you have to eat well. That is no problem for me, I always eat a lot.' While drinking my tea, I noticed Yalu had a tattoo on her arm. She noticed I noticed and said, 'It's ugly, isn't it?'

'You can hardly see it.'

'You noticed it Lorena.'

'Yeah, but look at where I am sitting. I am squatting on the floor. If I stood next to you I would not have noticed it.' Señora Myrta described a movie she had seen a few nights ago called *American Nights* in which one of the men was completely covered with tattoos. From that moment on, the conversation took a surprising turn.

'The film also showed a striptease club where men stripped. The female clients put money in their underwear.' The women screeched with laughter. Myrta continued, 'One woman put the dollar bills between her teeth and approached the guy.' The laughter continued. I said, 'You know they say there is a club like that in Lima for old *pitucas*.' Myrta was surprised by my description, 'Lorena!' Clara added, 'They are all male prostitutes.'

'No, most of them just strip. The majority of male prostitutes are gay.' Yalu took the floor and told us the details of a porno film. 'There was a virgin who only wanted to be fucked in the ass. The man cut off her tits and started to eat them. I like to go to porno movies. They sometimes make me laugh.' The women could not stop laughing.

I said, 'No, stop. This is gross, ugh.' They laughed at me. Clara was at the stove and she called out, 'Look at Lorena, she is really enjoying this.' Then someone told the story of a porno film about dildos, provoking another uncontainable wave of laughter. Myrta said, in a serious tone, 'It's strange, when I watch porno films they kill my appetite for sex. I don't know why.'

I said, 'It's understandable, the films are made for men.' I turned to her and Maria and said, 'We need a different type of stimulation, don't you think?'

Myrta replied, 'Oh that's why, yes you are right.'

Maria told a story about dildos. One time after a police raid, a policeman entered the cell and screamed, 'I don't like women, so you don't have to beg or try anything to make me let you out.' When he left the cell he put on a dildo connected to a belt and went off to the other cell where they kept the men. 'That was the first time I ever saw a dildo.' Lunch was coming to an end and so did the conversation. They went back to work and I went home.

This excerpt is included because of what it shows about sexuality. This was the only conversation I participated in which came close to touching on the subject of sexuality. The women never talked about sexuality or sexual pleasure in relation to their private lives and a total taboo existed with regard to talking about sexual pleasure with clients. It can be assumed that letting business mix with pleasure undermines the image of the good prostitute, the one who works for the money, for her family. If pleasure is involved, she would be associated with the category of the prostitute who prostitutes because she enjoys it. Perhaps the silence concerning the subject was directly related to my presence and all the meanings constituted by my identity. This might be a feasible explanation for their reluctance. Notwithstanding, there are other reasons why sexuality is not a very popular subject. The women's silence must also be interpreted from within the cultural context.

Female sexuality is a subject not talked about frequently. Barrig's study (1982) concerning *convivencía* (living together) explores this specific type of relationship in the *barriadas*. In the first chapter she states that: 'In the *barriadas* it was difficult to talk openly about the sexual life in the relationships. The subject was hushed or it was touched with reserve. However, it can be deduced from several of the conversations that many women considered themselves "cold" or "indifferent" and did not have nice memories of their first sexual experiences ...' (1982: 43).

The women's conversation concerning sexuality was not about their experiences of their sexuality, rather, it was a conversation mediated through the discussion of male sexual symbols. Pornography, dildos and the striptease are different expressions of men's sexual excitement and are assumed to produce the same sensations for women. Myrta's remark contained some anxiety that she was abnormal because she did not feel what she thought was expected of her. The fact the conversation evolved around male sexual symbols is in itself a conversation concerning female sexuality. Cardich and Carrasco's (1993) study illustrates how the construction of female sexuality is mediated through men's desires. Women rarely spoke about their own sexuality without referring to the men's desires.

In conclusion, although the women as prostitutes represent another symbol of male sexuality, the woman behind this symbol upholds notions of sexuality which reflect broader meanings of femininity in society. Their silence concerning the subject of sexuality voices this persuasively.

THE FUNERAL

Christmas and New Year had passed and I returned to Barrios Altos ready to work. Walking down the street, I ran into several familiar faces with whom I exchanged New Year's wishes. Arriving at the front door, I could see Señora Magda sitting at the kitchen table at her usual place. When I sat down at the kitchen table she asked me if I could make some enquiries about a problem she had.

'The last two weeks, every time I use a condom, I feel a very annoying, itchy feeling on the outer part of my vagina. I am sure the lubrication is causing this problem. Years ago, I had the same problem when I used soap and only recently, it has come back.'

'Do you wear cotton underwear?' I inquired.

'Yes.'

'Do you think the inflammation could be caused by having many sexual relations?' She denied the possibility and kept saying she was fine, the lubrication caused the problem. She was unwilling to consider that it was not only the lubrication but the nature of her work which was causing health problems.

Yalu and Carmen came in drunk. Whenever Yalu drank too much she took exaggeratedly small steps as if she was afraid she would topple over if she walked at a normal pace. Myrta took a seat at the kitchen table. A conversation developed concerning Carmencita, a transvestite prostitute and drug addict who lived in the *callejon* at the beginning of the street. She was very sick and progressively getting worse. No one was sure if it was Aids or TB.[7] 'She doesn't want to take care of herself.' Señora Rosa suggested we take up a collection and get her into the hospital. 'She needs to be under medical care.' Everyone agreed this would be the best solution, except Carmencita did not want to go. I said, 'Maybe she doesn't want to live anymore.'

The subject shifted to other diseases. Meningitis was the next topic of conversation. They listed all the residents in the neighbourhood who had had it. Yalu became nervous, as she customarily did when the conversation concerned illnesses. She remarked, 'I am healthy. My ELISA test came back negative. The only thing I suffer from is nerves and the fact I like to drink too much.'

My return visit to Clara's house was delayed. I passed the *callejon* where Carmencita lived. Carmencita was sitting on a chair in what remained of a doorway. Her face showed she had got worse since my last visit two weeks ago. She just sat there staring out in front of her. This was the other *callejon* where a few prostitutes rented a room. The living conditions were dreadful. There was no running water and the fumes of *pasta* in the passageway were overwhelming. Parts of the walls had collapsed and other parts miraculously remained upright. It was populated by drug addicts, alcoholics and a few families. Some of the women living there had a stall at the market and two of them prostituted. I visited this *callejon* on various occasions to talk to Negra, one of the prostitutes who lived there and worked on this particular street during the evening.

At Clara's house my entrance was greeted with '*Que milagro*' (what a miracle) referring to the fact I had returned after being gone for so long. I told them my last adventures in my sick bed and waited with the others for *almuerzo* to be served. Clara brought me up to date. 'Julia is back, even though she claimed that this time she was leaving for good. Today is Myrta's first day back. She stayed a way for a while, she does that often. And Maria didn't come to work for a few days because her daughter was sick.'

Myrta and Magda were complaining about the lack of business. Yalu came in with her arm bandaged. When she left, Clara filled me in on what had happened. A drug addict who accused her of stealing had stabbed her. She asked Clara if she could have *almuerzo*. Clara lied and said she had not prepared enough. 'If I give her *almuerzo* she won't pay me until the next week. I need to be paid immediately. I don't need more problems than I already have.'

A conversation began about the son of the man from whom they rented the room. Maria said, 'He told Julia he doesn't live off the money of whores but from drug money, and Julia replied, "Just wait until your father is jailed for selling drugs, then we will see what money will you live off, the money from whores." That child has no respect.'

'How much is he charging now?' I inquired.

'Five hundred, and it is a pigsty.'

'That's a lot,' I replied, 'how much are you charging now?'

'One and a half million', was the reply. 'But look', she took a piece of toilet paper and divided it in two. 'Before we charged 1,300,000.' The smaller piece of toilet paper represented the 300,000 she gave to rent the room. The other piece of paper was the money she kept. 'Now we charge 200,000 more and what we earn remains the same.'

They calculated how much the man earned each day from renting the room. The names of the women passed by my ears with the number of clients they had a day. Maria said, 'Even on a day when business is slow he earns at least 40 million *Intis* [US $8].'

Maria asked Clara if she could borrow a lime, 'I will give it back tomorrow.' She took the lime and went into the bedroom and rolled it all over her body. I asked her what she was doing. She said, 'I have a headache and this helps.' Her knowledge on the subject of traditional medicinal practices never ceased to surprise me. I hoped at some point she would sit down and tell me how she came to know so much (wishful thinking). Julia arrived after *almuerzo*. She told us about the nightmares she was having. 'The last couple of days I have been dreaming about death and corpses. I awoke today in the early morning and turned over my pillow and finally discovered the cause of my nightmares. I was sleeping with a black t-shirt under my pillow, I threw it on the floor and went back to sleep. I found it so strange that I was having nightmares.' She left and went back to work, and I decided to leave, too.

One morning, shortly after my last visit, I received a call from the director of the NGO in Barrios Altos who told me Clara had come to ask the organization to contribute to the funeral costs of a neighbour who had died and had no family. 'Was the funeral for Carmencita, the transvestite who had TB?'

She confirmed my suspicion. When I got off the telephone I called another organization which often took up collections for homosexuals who had no financial means to pay for medicine or for the funeral. They promised to start a collection immediately. The NGO working in Barrios Altos would give $20.

When I arrived at Clara's, Rosa had just returned from accompanying Julia to the doctor's. The doctor advised Julia to stop working because she had an acute bladder infection. He wanted to do an ecogram but it would cost 6 million *Intis*.[8] Julia told the doctor she could not afford the test and could not stop working because she had to pay her children's school tuition. The doctor prescribed medicine to ease the inflammation.

Clara was taking care of the paperwork for the funeral. She went to many different places to get all the official papers, stamps and signatures required. She met many problems along the way. Rosa said, 'Carmencita doesn't want to go yet, she is setting traps to keep herself from leaving.'

'What do you mean?' I asked.

She smiled and said, 'Sometimes the dead do not want to go, so they cause problems.'

Sylvia, who had just come back from a three-month recess, entered the kitchen and discussed the price of coffins with Clara. Clara had found someone who would make a coffin for 35 million *Intis*. Sylvia told her the funeral agencies across the street from the morgue charged 45 million *Intis* for the coffin and transport. 'How many months ago?' Clara asked, knowing time to be an essential factor in determining prices during this chronic period of inflation.

'About one and a half.'

She decided to check it out. Sylvia explained that one of her neighbours needed her help because she could not get the corpse out of the morgue because she had a different surname than the deceased. Coincidentally, Sylvia had the same surname and the neighbour asked her to accompany her to get the body released from the morgue. Clara assured her she would not have the same problem because she had received official permission to take care of it.

Julia was eating her lunch and saved her soup for the toddler who lived in the other *callejon*. Every day his mother, an alcoholic, locked him out of the house when she went off to prostitute or drink, and there was no one who cooked for him. I saw him frequently, standing in front of the *callejon*, naked, with his stomach bloated (a symptom of malnutrition or parasites). Clara took the bowl and filled it to the brim and Julia left to take the soup to the boy. Ten minutes later she returned to finish her lunch with the empty bowl. Julia is a person who has a bittersweet character. On various occasions she demonstrated how she cared. Not only did she worry about this little boy, she regularly saved the leftovers from *almuerzo* to give to the dogs that lived in the *callejon*. At other times, she acted as if she was the only one who existed in the world.

Carmencita's burial would be the following day. When I arrived at Clara's she sat on the bed counting the money collected – 64,750,000 *Intis*, approximately US $120. According to her calculations, this covered all the expenses for the burial. She expected a bit more from the *comedor popular* situated at the corner, because they had also made a collection. Clara had ordered the coffin the day before and was occupied until late in the evening arranging all the paperwork. She gave the impression she did it on her own, but Julia accompanied her. At the last moment, they told her she needed to fill in another form because the deceased's name was spelt incorrectly on the death certificate. This required an additional visit to another office for a certificate that noted the error and corrected it. At one of the offices a clerk asked her for a bribe, but she managed to squirm her way out of it.

Off we went to the funeral parlour to get the body out of the morgue. On the way, we stopped at the *comedor popular* to pick up the money they had collected. Negra approached us and Clara arranged for someone to bring Carmencita's clothes to the morgue. While they were talking, Clara told her the price of the coffin and immediately showed her the receipt. When we continued on our way, she told me that Negra had been gossiping behind her back, accusing her of taking the responsibility for the collection in order to keep the money. Clara straightened out the gossip with this one gesture. Without saying anything, she made it clear the gossip was unfounded.

On numerous occasions during this day, Clara used the fact Carmencita had no family, and the community took it upon themselves to bury him to try to get things accomplished. It helped in many different circumstances. When we went to remove the body from the morgue, the owner of the funeral parlour accompanied us across the street because he understood the situation. He presented the papers to the official in charge and helped speed up the procedure.

While waiting outside for the body, Julia and Sonia showed up. Sonia worked around the corner. She had taken care of Carmencita in the last week before his death. They arrived out of breath, afraid we had already left for the cemetery. Sonia asked about Carmencita's clothes. Nobody had come to drop them off. Evidently, his clothes had been stolen. Clara had bought a robe from the funeral parlour so that Carmencita would not be buried naked.

Clara took the opportunity to tell the women about her encounter with Negra. This led to a brief moment of gossip questioning Negra's integrity. 'She never uses condoms. She used to tell the men who entered with Carmencita she had Aids. She said that to take away her business.'

Clara said, 'Carmencita did not die of Aids. She died of malnutrition caused by TB and bronchial pneumonia.'

Sonia said, 'I slept with her the last period, she was like a child. She would hardly eat anything and would awake in the middle of the night complaining she couldn't sleep because I am so fat, I was using up all the air. She weighed 28 kilos when she died.'

Clara recalled, smiling, the time Carmencita told her she was such a beautiful woman. 'He was tired of living.' Various complaints were made about Carmencita's 'good friends' who did not lift a finger to help him and did not show up to accompany him to the cemetery.

Sonia said, 'Negra said she couldn't go because she had to cook *almuerzo*. She planned to go to church afterwards and dedicate a mass to him. Yalu and Carmen said the burial was too early and asked if it could be postponed for a few hours.'

We got tired of waiting in the sun and entered the funeral parlour where the owner invited us to wait in his office. The coffin was brought in. The stench immediately reached our noses. The body was in a state of decomposition. I asked, 'Why is the body decomposing if it is kept in the morgue? Aren't they kept in refrigeration?'

Sonia replied, 'You probably have to pay extra for that.'

I was relieved to notice I was not the only one who could not bear the stench. We decided to wait outside and I invited them to have something to drink at the cafeteria next door. Clara stayed behind to make some last arrangements, only to join us shortly after requesting someone to identify the body. 'I am not going to do it. I did not do it for my mother, I won't do it for her.'

Sonia went and Julia immediately asked her when she came back how she looked. 'Her body was swollen but her face looked like this' – Sonia sucked in her cheeks.

The funeral agency charged an extra 5 million *Intis* to clothe Carmencita, because the body was in an advanced state of decomposition. We were ready to go to the cemetery. Sonia would ride with the coffin and we would follow in a taxi. Clara asked the funeral parlour owner the price of a cemetery plot. He thought about 35 million *Intis*. We knew it would be impossible to pay this amount. The collected money was nearly spent. Clara asked the owner to instruct the driver upon arriving at the cemetery to tell the employees that Carmencita had no family and we were doing it out of charity.

We got into a taxi which cost another 5 million *Intis*. The money was definitely running out. I told them that, if necessary, I could give some extra money to cover the remaining costs. Julia promised to pay me back when we got back. Although her remark showed her integrity, I knew I would never ask her for the money. Just the day before she had told me all the money she earned went to her children's tuition and the medicine for her bladder infection.

We arrived at the cemetery. It is one of the illegal cemeteries of Lima. The majority of poor living in Lima cannot afford to bury their dead at official cemeteries. Illegal cemeteries are the solution. The negotiations started. The cemetery employee said a plot cost 45 million *Intis*. Clara emphasized once again Carmencita's situation. 'Ask the Señor', indicating the driver. He corroborated what she had said. 'We can't afford that much money. Isn't there some place, it doesn't matter where, where you can bury him?' The employer asked how much could we afford. She turned to me looking for the answer. 'Ten million?' she said. 'Twelve', I replied. The employer said it would cost 15. Clara got him down to 14 million *Intis*.

We walked and walked through the sand. First we passed rows of miniature chapels covering the graves of the deceased. We went through a garbage dump. To the left and right sides, there were more graves with less elaborate monuments. As we went further, a makeshift cross or a pile of stones were the only objects that distinguished a grave from a barren piece of land. Finally, we climbed a small hill and came to the furthest end of the cemetery where two men awaited who would dig the grave. They could not begin to dig because they were waiting for the only shovel, which was in use. We stood there in the sun. The wind came up and brought the stench directly to our noses. Flies circled the coffin. We all lit up cigarettes in an effort to cover up the unpleasant odour. One of the men asked if we were in a hurry. Clara told him she had to get home because she had left her child alone. He asked if the deceased was family. 'Was he a terrorist?'

'No,' Clara replied, 'he wasn't a terrorist and they are not terrorists they are guerrillas.'

The man asked, 'You agree with them ... ?'

She continued, 'At least they have ideals, what we have is nothing. The state doesn't even let you die in dignity, look what we have to do to get her buried. Is this justice?'

The men agreed. The shovel finally came and it was decided Carmencita would be moved to another plot. The men asked us to buy a bottle of Coca-Cola, insinuating that a refusal could delay things even further. We complied with their wish, to avoid further delays. They dug a deep grave and finally the coffin was laid to rest. Quickly, they covered over the coffin with dirt causing a momentary sand storm. Sonia enquired how much a *capilla* (miniature chapel) of cement would cost. The women decided it would be a good idea to take up another collection. They were upset when they realized they did not even have a wooden cross to mark the spot of Carmencita's grave. Julia promised to come back soon and put one on top of the grave. They crossed themselves and we walked back to find a bus.

We got off the bus in the middle of the central market and walked back to Clara's house. Being tired and covered with sand did not stop us from making jokes. It was the time of the Persian Gulf War, and after this ordeal we remarked that we felt as if we had just come back from Operation Desert Storm. Shortly after we arrived Clara told me she had obtained a copy of the autopsy report. It was her proof that Carmencita did not die of Aids. Once again, when used at the appropriate moment, this action would speak louder than words.

Carmencita's death made a deep impression. Julia, Sonia and Clara's despair concerning Carmencita's grave reflected their own fear and anxiety that they will end up in the same way, with no money for a decent burial and nobody to make sure their graves will have some type of monument. Magda and Clara talked about funeral policies. I asked them to explain the details. 'You pay a weekly amount of money and this covers all the costs and the cemetery plot.' Clara continued, 'I have a policy for two of my children and my mother who passed away. Four years after someone dies you are able to replace the person's name with another. I am going to put Petra's name on the policy. I haven't paid for the last three years.

Magda said she has a policy for herself, her son, one of her sisters and a nephew. She pays 800 *Intis* on a weekly basis.

I got up to leave and when I walked down the street Sylvia, Maria and Myrta were standing together. Myrta put her arm snugly around my waist. I noticed Sylvia had a white mark on her behind and told her discreetly. She thanked me and brushed it off. Maria noticed that the back of my pants were covered with white powder and she brushed my behind off. Sylvia said, 'So you also had a trick who made you do it standing up against the wall.' We laughed at her joke, which made her repeat it several times. It was not the first joke she made implying that I worked as a prostitute. In fact, she loved making jokes like this and I enjoyed trying to find a smart answer to reply with.


INVENTING A MOMENT OF CLOSURE

Señora Magda and I walked down the street together to Clara's house. Something was obviously wrong. I asked her several times before she gave me an answer: 'I wanted to use the bathroom at my house and it was occupied. The landlord's son was showering and shaving. After a while I asked him to hurry up and he answered me rudely, we had a fight. I told his father and asked him to talk to his son. In the evening, when I asked his father to return the fan he borrowed, he told me he spoke to his son who denied ever saying the things I told him. He said he thought it would be better if I looked for another place to live, to avoid problems. I said, fine, but give me some time to find something else.' Magda had been living there for nine years and it obviously affected her that she would have to move.

As she finished telling me her story, we arrived at Clara's house. We talked a bit more about her bad luck and she went back to work. I entered and she returned to work. Clara told me she had had a fight with Magda the day before and told me the details: 'She is a very jealous person. For some inexplicable reason Rosa had three clients in a row yesterday. Magda came in ranting and raving. I didn't know who she was talking about. When Sylvia came in I figured she was referring to her. So, I asked Sylvia about it and Magda overheard me talking to her and began to scream at both of us.'

Our conversation was interrupted by Sylvia's entrance. She had changed into her street clothes because she had a doctor's appointment. When the door closed behind her the conversation resumed. Rosa joined in and told her side of the story. 'It would be different if I had three clients in a row every day but this was something special. Magda wants them all for herself.'

Clara added, 'Magda would be happy if she worked here alone. She has a lot of clients because she works differently from the other women, Sylvia has a lot of luck, but Rosa is lucky if she has one client a day. And to top it all off, after Magda got angry with Rosa, she got picked up with Sylvia in a raid.'

'How did they manage to be free so quickly?' I inquired. 'They paid a bribe in the bus and got out before they reached the police station.'

'The women are charging between 2 million and 2.5 million and, like clockwork, the owner wants to raise the rent again, this time to 1 million.'

Sylvia came back from the doctor. Clara asked, 'What did he say?'

'Hormones,' she replied. 'I told you when menopause comes many women have hormonal problems. I told Señora Rosa the same thing but she hasn't gone to the doctor yet.'

Rosa called out from the bathroom, 'I stopped having my period a while ago.'

Sylvia said, 'Me too.'

Rosa left the house to buy some medicine for Petra. Clara confided, 'I would not be surprised if Rosa loved Petra more than her own children. Rosa has changed a lot since I first got to know her.' She recalled the innumerable times in the past when she had dragged her out of a bar in the early hours of the morning. 'They all thought I was her *machona* [derived from *macho*, signifying the woman in a lesbian relationship who takes on the male role], but I didn't care. She has had a tough life, but she has calmed down a lot. She used to neglect her own children, she didn't give a damn. She learned to care while living with me and seeing how I treat my own children.'

While eating lunch, I decided to make a last attempt to make an appointment to do a life story with Magda. Clara was going about her regular business. 'Señora Magda, I want to ask you a favour, you can say no if you like.'

'I don't know what you are going to ask yet', she replied.

'We have spoken a lot together and you are a woman who has a lot of experience in this world. I would like to do an interview with you putting all the things in order we spoke about for my book. I would like you to be in my book.'

'With my name?' she asked.

Clara interrupted, 'Of course not, she changes the names.'

Magda did not seem happy but she agreed to my request. 'After all, you have done so much for me this is the least I can do for you.'

The next time I came back I met Magda walking down the street. I was surprised to see her working so early in the morning. She accompanied me to Clara's house. I felt her resistance. I suggested we sit in the living room so we could have some time to talk alone. She insisted we sit at the table. Finally, we ended up in the living room. She sent out a message like 'Let's get this over with.' She also expressed it physically, sitting on the edge of her chair and glancing at the door at regular intervals. I did not want to insist, so I suggested we do it at a more suitable hour. She said, 'One o'clock would be better.'

'But the other women will be present', I replied.

'So what? They are all doing the same thing I do.'

When she left Rosa and Clara suggested I do it after she finished work at seven o'clock. I thought it was a good idea. Clara said, 'Magda gets really nervous if she is kept from working, it is better to do it after.' As on previous occasions, this attempt dissolved into thin air. The interview never materialized, convincing me for the very last time that, as much as I thought this was a suitable way of producing an ethnographic narrative, it was incompatible with the ways we communicated in relationships. I realized I was attempting to construct a moment of closure because I would be going home in a few weeks. Collecting of a life story could symbolize the end of fieldwork.

On my last visit, the women invited me for a farewell drink. But when the time came to gather together, they had to be called in from the street. Sylvia reminisced about the first time she saw television and what she used to do when she played hooky from primary school. She never finished primary school. It was at this last encounter that she told me about her husband's maltreatment of her. Her openness surprised me. This was the first time that one of the women besides Magda spontaneously began to tell me something about their lives.

Thirteen months had passed since I entered Clara's house for the first time. The lasts visits to Barrios Altos were as eventful and uneventful as the rest. There would be no out of the ordinary crisis bringing the fieldwork period to a dramatic end, but rather, my departure would be woven into the fabric of daily life.

I did return on two other occasions. The first followed shortly after I had left. I had the possibility of returning to Peru for a brief vacation. I visited the women on Clara's birthday. I will never forget the expressions on their faces when they saw me get out of the taxi. Nevertheless, as usual, it did not occur to them to come in to spend some time with me. Clara pulled them in from the street, more or less at my request. I had brought each of them a small present. It was only after three women asked me how much money I wanted for the earrings, that I understood their reluctance to accept my presents. They thought I had come to sell them these things, they did not realize I brought them a gift. Julia immediately told me to come back because she wanted to leave a present for me with Clara. I was unable to return on this visit, but it was a warm and memorable experience.

The second visit occurred one year later. I returned to Lima for a longer period and I had been putting off my visit for a while. I had been gone for so long and had become unaccustomed to this environment which had once been so familiar. When I visited it on a regular basis, I no longer experienced it as dangerous. However, being away for such a long time made me feel threatened. This feeling was strengthened by my friends, who thought it was a crazy idea to go there alone during these hard times. I eventually got over my apprehensions and reminded myself that, even when I worked there on a regular basis, many people thought I was crazy, so nothing had changed. I looked forward to seeing the women again and wondered what their reaction would be to my big belly, not a product of overeating but of being five months' pregnant.

When I got to the familiar corner, I saw Señora Sylvia, who looked tired and older than I remembered her. We kissed hello and I asked her if I would be seeing her later at Clara's house. She said she did not go there anymore because she had had a fight with Magda. I thought to myself, some things never change. I went down the street and passed a house which looked like Clara's but the brand new doors confused me. I could not believe this was her house because I could not imagine that her economic situation could have improved so dramatically for the better to allow for such home improvements. Sylvia saw my confusion and called out that I was at the right place. I knocked on the door. A chubby tall little Petra answered it. Juanita was sitting at a table and when she saw me screamed 'Lorena!'. We hugged and in the meantime I glanced around. It was not hard to notice the big new refrigerator in the corner of the front room and the newly tiled floor. The dining room set was also new. I went straight back to the kitchen and on the way I passed a new colour television. Magda greeted me with a big hug, Clara too. I kissed Rosa hello. They were surprised by my big belly. A few people thought I had grown fatter and I had to tell them I was pregnant. Magda and Clara told me they had recently been thinking of me and Hermana Marta had asked about me, too. Unfortunately, not many of the women were there that day. Nonetheless, things had not changed. They all still worked on this particular street in Barrios Altos. Señora Magda left quickly after my entrance. I had hoped I would have more time to speak to her, but she did not come back before I left. Juanita was visiting her mother and it was a coincidence I saw her because, as Rosa said, 'She has not come to see me for the last ten days.' She is married and has stopped working. She lives in another neighbourhood. I do not know if my face expressed the surprise I felt seeing all of Clara's new possessions. When things quietened down Clara cautiously gave me some clues. She had become involved in some sort of illegal scam; she suggested it had something to do with cars but would not give any details. The scam backfired and she ended up in jail for 15 days. Although things did not work out as planned, she was pleased the police did not confiscate the merchandise. Her story rang in my ears for several days after I left. I never got back to see her again. There were several personal circumstances which impeded my return, but I would be distorting the story if I did not admit that her troubles with the police also influenced my decision.

Clara was my backbone through the whole period of fieldwork. I trusted her 100 per cent. I knew if necessary, I could count on her protection. On the evenings I left Barrios Altos late at night she accompanied me to get a taxi, making sure I met no trouble along the way. She projected an image of a woman who would struggle as hard as she could not to get involved with the 'bad elements'. She gave the impression she would rather be poor than earn money illegally. All her efforts did not enable her to improve her situation. I am not judging what she did. Her motives are completely understandable. Perhaps it was her obvious attempts to conceal the truth, even though this could have been for my own protection, or perhaps my pregnancy made me feel more vulnerable; nevertheless, our relationship began to tremble at the foundation. I was no longer sure I could trust her as I had in the past, and I was extremely aware that without a guardian angel, this neighbourhood is very dangerous. In the aftermath, I realized I had internalized the lesson I was taught concerning the environment far better than I thought: once somebody steps over to the other side, meaning they get involved with the 'bad elements', then there is no turning back. My situation did not permit me to find out whether Clara's case upheld this axiom. Months later, I heard from a nun who had recently begun to work with the prostitutes in Barrios Altos that Clara allowed her to use her house to meet the women. Thus, Clara continued to let outsiders visit the women at her house. In all likelihood, few things had changed and her involvement in this illegal transaction was more likely a one-off affair rather than a new income-generating possibility. Nonetheless, my question still remains unanswered.

# 7    THE FUSION OF TRUTHS AND ILLUSIONS
## The Nightlife and Street Prostitution

## EL AMBIENTE

The district where nocturnal fieldwork took place contrasts sharply with Barrios Altos. With the continual deterioration of Lima's centre, many commercial and business enterprises have moved here, transplanting the heart of Lima's business sector into its midst. It also houses many of the tourist hotels. Its residential population primarily consists of inhabitants of middle- and upper-class origins, although small popular enclaves still exist. For many of the affluent inhabitants of Lima, this district has become the centre. During the day, the centre is alive with people attending to their daily chores, business activities or stopping for *almuerzo* at one of the restaurants. When night-time falls, the hustle and bustle takes on other forms. It is one of the entertainment sectors where many movie theatres and restaurants are situated. People come from all over Lima to enjoy an evening out.

It is also the location where a variety of types of prostitution are practised: male, female and transvestite street prostitution, prostitution in clubs, illegal brothels and massage parlours. Certain streets are infamous for clandestine prostitution. During the period of this investigation, the residents felt that clandestine prostitution was getting out of hand. Tired of the 'inconveniences', they complained to the Municipality and demanded it take action to resolve this 'prostitution problem'. To appease the residents, and out of fear this would blemish the district's image, a campaign commenced to eradicate prostitution. The details were published in the newspaper:

The Municipality, which has received numerous complaints from the residents of this district, has ... decided to initiate an effective campaign to eradicate the practice of prostitution in our city.

The personnel of the Municipal police and the residents belonging to the Communal Programme of Adult Participation (PROCOPAD) will write down the licence plates, the colour and type of vehicles of those who gather in the public streets who have dealings with female and male prostitution. This information will be published in the capital's newspapers and passed to the corresponding police authorities.

With this measure, the Municipal district council, expects to eliminate as quickly as possible this type of clandestine business which is an attack on morals, good customs and public health.

For A Clean and Safe City (*Comercio*, 6 August 1990)

Hence, with the help of resident vigilantes the Municipality intended to get rid of prostitution by threatening potential clients with public exposure. As might be expected, this plan of action caused another discursive explosion. But worse was the unnecessary panic it caused for prostitutes working in the neighbourhood. Its proponents considered it to be an original and creative way to tackle the 'problem'. Nonetheless, they were realistic. Of course, it did not eradicate prostitution in the entire city, but it did get rid of these 'undesirable elements' from their district.

A few months after the publication of the announcement, a municipal official told me the campaign had been extremely successful. He proclaimed that clandestine prostitution had declined by 70 per cent. Strangely enough, the women I knew still came regularly to the area. Were the women I knew included in the 30 per cent of the prostitutes who had not been driven away? Undoubtedly, it is more likely that this initiative was as unsuccessful as the many other initiatives that have been taken over the years. What makes this campaign unique is that it is the only initiative undertaken by a municipality without the involvement of the national police authorities. In contrast to a district like Barrios Altos, this municipality has more revenues. Therefore it can endorse self-initiated campaigns to combat the 'prostitution problem'. The campaign briefly exposed the district's particular nature to the general public. For those with a trained eye, prostitution is extremely visible. For others prostitution blends in with the goings-on of this entertainment district and remains invisible.

One neighbourhood characterized by this nocturnal schizophrenia is a central area of the district's nightlife, where I did my research. The Plaza Bolivar is well-kept, lined with restaurants and a few discos, where people of all ages come to enjoy a meal. But there is another group of people who frequent this street and their experiences in this plaza are extremely different. It is where they earn their money as waiters, bouncers, flower vendors, watchmen and prostitutes, or in illegal business transactions. Circulating in this group are other individuals attracted to the nightlife. They are regulars at one of the restaurants – young men who drink there most nights, the partners of the women or young women described as dangling on the border, implying if they did not drop out of the *ambiente* soon they would eventually end up prostituting. At one table a group of youngsters could be sitting finishing a meal and getting ready to go home. At the adjacent table, another group is drinking and conversing. Their evening has barely begun. As the night progresses, the streets and establishments belong more and more to the people of the latter group, who can be considered a part of the *ambiente* (the scene).

There is no clear-cut definition for the term *ambiente*. Yet the word evokes certain images. Those who somehow identify themselves as part of it (un)consciously make a distinction between themselves and the other people who frequent the area. To a certain degree it is a spatial concept. Its borders are drawn among several establishments. For example, women who are working will be chased away from some restaurants and in others their presence is accepted. There is also a tacit acceptance that being part of the nocturnal *ambiente* distinguishes their lives from the lives of those who do not belong to it. They experience a different slice of life when the average citizen is tucked warmly into his or her bed. They have more contacts with the underworld and are exposed to more risks, but because this is experienced daily it is not considered to be dangerous but as a part of life. If someone is picked up by the police, for example, no one is overtly worried. It is considered fate: a consequence of the life they lead. The discussion of the incident would revolve around the mistakes made rather than complaints about police injustice. Finally, friendships and relationships appear transitory. When things are good, two people seem inseparable. A small argument could end a relationship between two good friends. They will stop talking to each other, avoid sitting at the same table for weeks on end until, for some reason, without discussing the matter any further, they are reconciled. Paradoxically, although everything seems to be transient, many of the individuals belonging to the *ambiente* have been in it for years.

The outward appearance of the restaurant where we congregated in the early part of the night did not differ greatly from the others. Although it was not as elaborately decorated, it did not seem very different. Noteworthy is the rare occurrence of anyone taking a meal there. For the customer, it was a blessing in disguise because the quality of its food was dubious. The odours captured by one's nose did not originate from the kitchen but rather they emanated from the bathroom. Frequently we were forced to take refuge on the terrace in the cold, to escape the unpleasant smell. Nonetheless, at times it seemed invincible, following us into the outdoor air. The *cuba libre* (rum and cola), which I came to relish as a part of my night-time adventures caused severe hangovers to begin with. This was not a result of the quantity I consumed but rather because the rum used was diluted (*bambeada*) with a cheap, high proof, colourless alcohol. When we discovered the owner's little secret, my assistant developed a strategy. He firmly persuaded the owner to open up a new bottle in front of him and made sure he served all our drinks from the same bottle. The superficial appearance of this restaurant did not contrast sharply with the others, but with all its subterranean qualities it was marked as a location in the *ambiente*.

During the night, and particularly in the street *ambiente*, the borders between truths and illusions fuse together. This goes far beyond recognizing that someone is lying; it is the acceptance that different versions of reality are enacted without prioritizing one version above another. This is not as easy as it appears, because academics have an almost instinctual inclination to search for the truth. For example, after hearing a story which was obviously made up, I was inclined to believe a version which conformed to my own expectations of the truth. It was only during the writing-up process, after multiple readings of my fieldnotes, that I came to the conclusion I had no reason to believe one version above another. The different versions portrayed different versions of reality, each engendering meanings of femininity. I have tried to portray these different versions for what they are and have not attempted to erase the discrepancies in the presentation, but rather point to them, drawing the reader into the ambience, exposing the uncertainties without producing chaos or confusion and capturing the illusions before they disappear.

The way into the nightlife is marked by the next section, which maps out different versions of prostitution embodied by women who are part of the *ambiente*. This is followed by a section which draws us into its midst, unravelling the intricacies of love and relationships to further disclose meanings of femininity.

## NIGHTWORK

In general, the women working around the plaza presented themselves and their work as distinct from the other street prostitutes in the district, and to a certain degree this was true. Unlike street prostitutes, who routinely congregated on the same street, waiting for clients to pass by and charged relatively low prices, the women at the plaza had different strategies to attract a client. They strolled along the plaza or the nearby streets, putting on a working gait that subtly made their intentions known to the men sitting at one of the terraces or they sat together at a table at a restaurant on the plaza or, less often, they went to a disco which informally functioned as a pick-up joint. Some had contacts with the larger hotels in the neighbourhoods. They had more opportunities to encounter their favourite clients – foreigners and Peruvian men with money – and they asserted that they charged US $50. A night with a client could begin with a meal or going out to dance and eventually end at a hotel, with the couple often parting in the early hours of the morning. This type of prostitution is uncommon in the street and bore a greater resemblance to an escort service than street prostitution. All in all, this description served as my frame of reference for quite some time. It was only after I became better acquainted with the ins and outs of the plaza that I realized this version of reality was at the same time an illusion. The women's experiences were far more heterogeneous then they projected and I presumed.

Anita was one of the women who spoke the most openly about her work and drew many of her clientele from the tourist sector. She confided that she normally worked the hotels and not at the plaza, waiting outside until an interested guest came out or an employee called her inside. She seemed to accept her life, hardly complained and enjoyed the company of a client who treated her well. When she had problems with a client she put it down to being par for the course. She identified herself as part of the *ambiente* and accepted the consequences. She presented a version of the prostitute who knew all the ropes, engaged in a more glamorous form of prostitution, balanced almost effortlessly the split between her day and night and, finally, was extremely proud of all the things she had accomplished on her own by prostituting. This image solidified when she related her experiences working in the *selva* (jungle).

Some years before, one of her clients, an engineer, told her she was wasting her time working in Lima and could earn a fortune in the *selva*.[1] He introduced her to a friend who worked at one of the camps and organized the groups of women. After spending a night with her, the man offered her a job. 'It was damn hard work, I had approximately 50 men a night and I lost a lot of weight. Luckily, most of my clients were relatively good people, because some acted like animals. I refused drunks, they were so drunk and coked up they never finished, and they also treated the women the worst.'

'Was it difficult to readjust when you returned to Lima?', I enquired.

'No, I sat around gaining weight surrounded by all my things I bought with the money I had earned. I took pleasure in my things and relaxed.'

Anita reminisced about her favourite client, a fat Greek American who treated her well. 'I met him while drinking a cup of coffee on a terrace around the corner. When we first started to go out he didn't know what I did, but later he found out. He wanted me to move to Miami. He would give me an apartment and he would come to visit from Orlando where he lived. I was his *dama de compañía* [lady escort] while he was here. I spoke to his wife and his son. They all want me to come for a visit, his wife invited me, too.'

One night, she described her encounter with a French client from the previous night. The man and his friend asked her and two other women to go out dancing. As she put it: 'We felt like we were in a lottery, we had no idea who they would choose to be with for the night.' She was chosen and described the evening as very pleasant – wined and dined and the sex was good. During sex the telephone rang, it was Chantal, a girlfriend whom he kept talking to in the excitement of it all. Then he passed Anita the phone. 'Chantal asked me, did I like it?' She reproduced the sexually aroused voice she used on the phone, 'Yes, yes, yes, he is very good, yes, yes.' When they hung up he asked her if she would be interested in doing it with Chantal. She replied she would do it if he paid her. He agreed upon one condition, Chantal had to think Anita did it out of love.

In the morning they ate breakfast in his room and he took out a piece of paper and wrote down the numbers 12 and 13. 'Anita', he said, 'I want you to find me a girl of 12 or 13.'

Anita replied sarcastically, 'What about 14 years old?'

'No', he said, '12 or 13. I will pay US $500.'

Anita went on: 'Lorena, I swear, I went into the bathroom and nearly lost my whole breakfast. What a horrible man. When it was time to pay he gave me US $10. I refused to accept it.' The negotiation and threats began.

'I threatened to take his camera, even though that is not my style. He kept holding back. I said if he made any more trouble I would send one of my friends after him. I managed to squeeze out another US $40, but I was still not satisfied. After all, I spent the whole night with him. He said he didn't have any more, but with a few more threats from my side he coughed up 40 *Intis*. We left the hotel and he took my hand, but I pushed it away. I convinced him to buy me one of those expensive magazines and then slipped away as fast as I could, jumping on the first bus that passed by. When I got home, I went into my daughters' bedroom. They were sleeping peacefully. There was no way I could imagine ever sending my daughter to a man like that, but I guess a woman barely surviving in this economic crisis who was offered US $500 would have no trouble accepting it. He probably wouldn't even pay that much. Look, he only wanted to give me US $10.'

Our conversation was interrupted by three young girls sitting at another table. They beckoned her to come over. She replied, '*Ahorita*', then went on, 'Those are the girls I went out with last night. They want to know what happened. We normally exchange information about the clients between us: what they are like, what their quirks are, so we are prepared when we go out with one of them.'

Our conversation resumed. She asked me how I earned a living. I was sure someone must have told her, but I pretended I was surprised she did not know and used the opportunity to find out what she thought about my work. I explained, 'I am an anthropologist and I am doing a study on the nightlife and I hope it might help change the ideas people have of women who work.' I asked, 'What do you think is important to include in a study of this kind?' Her answer to my question marked out another border distinguishing herself and her colleagues from other prostitutes. 'Listen, the women who work here don't feel the recession like women who work in other places, in the brothels, for example. If we have one client the money can cover the following days. It is different for the other women. It is more difficult. The women who work in the brothels are harsher, more vulgar.'

I told her a bit about the working conditions in Barrios Altos. She replied, 'Those women need your work.'

'But don't you think all women who work have some things in common? The fact that their lives are based on lies is a heavy burden to have to carry.'

She agreed, 'That is one of the reasons I would never work on the street. I am afraid a relative might see me or if I approached a car and it turned out to be my brother or cousin. When I leave the district, I leave it all behind and I take on my role as mother until the next evening.'

Her answer could not conceal that she did not consider herself in the same situation. She seemed to agree with me only to appease me.

In general, Anita's prostitution tales reiterated that she was a prostitute of a different category. Thus she was a typical version of a prostitute in this area. I had no reason to doubt this until, one evening, I arrived at the plaza and Anita called me over to a table where she sat with a john. She invited me to join her and introduced me to him. Only after she had disappeared, leaving her handbag with me saying she would be right back, did I realize she had used me as decoy to slip out of the situation. The john complained about Anita. 'She wanted 5 million (a little more than US $10) and I offered her 3, but we haven't left yet. Do you smoke *pasta* or do coke?'

'No.'

'Your girlfriend doesn't do drugs either. Well if you want to we could leave now.'

'I am accompanied.'

'Are you sure?'

'Yes', and I beckoned to Roberto to come over. The man disappeared.

Besides finding the whole situation quite funny, chalking up one point for Anita for cunningly manoeuvring herself out of an unwanted situation and using me to reach the goal, it did surprise me that she took the time to negotiate with a client who offered the going rate for ordinary street prostitution. Whether she knew from the start she would refuse him, or whether she was having a hard time and had become less picky, in all probability Anita relied on clients from the street more often than she readily admitted. Although the crack which appeared in the varnish tarnished her image as a higher-class prostitute, making me wonder once again where reality ended and illusion began, this new piece of information did not change her image for me. She continued to be a prostitute who managed her work and family situation relatively well.

Even if Anita did rely more on Peruvian clients than she said, she gave a correct assessment of her economic situation in comparison with other types of prostitutes who worked on the street. For instance, Anita was able to buy several staple products like sugar and rice in bulk before the minister's announcement of the *paquetazo*. This was inconceivable for a woman like Jasmina, who also worked at the plaza and surrounding streets.

In spite of all our good intentions, Jasmina and I never got to know each other as well as we would have liked. Whenever Jasmina came to the plaza she rarely stuck around long enough to have a conversation and, if she decided to join us, her eyes never stopped wandering in search of business. She did not work every night, nevertheless she was there on a regular basis. Her four-year-old son was frequently sick and she did not want to leave him at night. However, the fact her son often fell ill would eventually force her to work. She needed money to pay for his treatment and medicine.

Jasmina was one of the poorest women who worked on the streets near the plaza. Her clothes were always clean but faded and she dressed a bit more provocatively than many other women, a measure she took to ensure that she would attract clients. Unlike many of the other women, who took a taxi home after a night's work, Jasmina waited until six o'clock in the morning to take the first bus back to the *pueblo jóven* where she lived. Even if there were no clients, or it was too cold and all the restaurants were closed, she would have to wait until the first bus arrived.

Tired of the uncertainties tied up with working on the street, she decided to look into a tip she had received about working at a massage parlour in the neighbourhood. The next couple of times I saw her, she kept talking about the massage parlour and was certain it would be the solution to her problems.

After being gone from the plaza for some time, Jasmina entered the restaurant, looking exhausted. I thought something terrible had happened to her since she sat there looking very subdued, in sharp contrast to her previous behaviour – jumping and dancing around. She showed me a ticket with a girl's name written on it and it turned out to be the pseudonym she used at the massage parlour. Then she told me what it was like. 'I haven't been home in four days. I work from nine in the morning to nine in the evening. I sleep there, but if I leave the house after work they won't let me in until the next day. The *mami* [madam] is a horrible tyrant. If you come late she fines you, if you bad-mouth someone, she fines you. You have to eat your *almuerzo* there and she subtracts the price from your earnings. An entrance ticket costs 15 million, and you only receive half. When you leave the room they search your bag to see if you have received a tip and if you have they take it away. Every time I said something about the *mami* it has gotten back to her. The other girls that work there are of all ages, they have more clients, they have more *engancha* [*enganchar* means to hook up or attract]. Right now I only have two or three a day, I could have more too, but the *mami* is making it impossible for me. I would fuck 20 a day, if I had to, it wouldn't bother me, but that *mami* is driving me crazy.'

Jasmina began to come to the plaza more often after she finished work to escape the massage parlour. She preferred the cold and the boredom to having to stay longer than necessary there. She did not keep it up for long. Pretty soon, she left the massage parlour and came back to the streets and then she virtually disappeared from the plaza for several months. I never got to say good-bye to her.

Jasmina made no attempt to cover up that she was a typical street prostitute. It did not matter whether her client was a foreigner or a Peruvian, as long as he paid. She charged the going rate, approximately US $10. For Jasmina, prostitution had no frills. It was a purely pragmatic way to earn her money to support herself and her child.

Cati, a woman in her mid-thirties, embodied yet another interpretation of the prostitute which crystallized in a conversation prompted by the '*Caretas* crisis'.[2] The journalist had also asked Cati for an interview. I used this opportunity to explain the difference between the journalist's objectives and my own. In response to this she posed a question which at first seemed a little out of context, she asked, 'Do you think the women who work here truly sacrifice themselves for their children?'

Extremely wary, I used her language and not my own to reply; I answered, 'Yes.'

'I disagree. I do not think the women working here sacrifice themselves.'

According to Cati, her own story illustrated the meaning of sacrifice: 'I used to work as an *empleada* [domestic servant], but I lost my job. When there was nothing left to eat at home, I left my children with my mother in southern Peru and began to work here as a prostitute. That is sacrifice. Do you know what it feels like not to have your children with you? But it is the right thing to do. They are getting older and maybe I won't be the one to tell them how I earn my money, but what if a neighbour finds out and forbids her children to play with mine and they start teasing them? No I don't want this for my children. I have visited several of the houses of the girls who work here. Do you really think they are sacrificing themselves? When they are home they talk about *fulano* [guy] this and *fulano* that, in front of their children. Anita, for example, when is she going to stop? She has been working the last eight or nine years. She has a daughter who is a *señorita*, do you think she is sacrificing herself?'

Just like Anita, Cati's perception of herself as a prostitute emerged when I talked about my work's objectives and specifically my desire to (in)directly contribute to defending the rights of prostitutes and improving their situation. Although her explanation opposed Anita's, they both thought the women working here did not need to benefit from the results of my work. In fact, she insinuates they are not worthy of it because they do not sacrifice themselves, as she does. They live with their children and appear to enjoy what they do and do not attempt to stop. Cati continued, 'Luckily I have other ways of making money, which I am not going to tell you about, but this is not my only income.' She repeated this several times, and I requested that she stop because she made me very curious. She did not disclose her other income sources on this occasion, but emphasized, 'I don't have to prostitute often, I only go with a client if he has a lot of money. In fact the police don't even know I prostitute.'

Cati enjoyed talking to us about love and boyfriends. She told us her escapades with her boyfriend and how she recently had to break up with him because he was a policeman and he discovered how she made her money. That is to say, not by prostituting but by selling drugs. It was too complicated to sell drugs and have a boyfriend who was a policeman, so they ended the relationship. 'Did he know you prostitute?', Roberto asked.

'I would rather have him think I sell drugs than do this.'

Roberto asked, 'You mean out of the two "evils", prostituting is worse?'

'Yes.'

I asked, 'When you retire would you ever tell your boyfriend how you made your money?'

'Absolutely not. I would rather sell drugs (I don't sell drugs to children) than do this because I don't like it when men touch my body.'

Cati maintained that prostitution acted as a front for her drug activities, and it was better the police thought she was a prostitute than a drug dealer.

Cati disappeared from the plaza because she received a tip the police were looking for her in relation to her drug activities. Every time the plainclothes police came to the plaza she coincidentally vanished, returning when things had calmed down. But this time, she seemed to disappear for good. Rumour had it that the police had picked her up for her involvement in a scam with another prostitute. Allegedly, they had stolen all his belongings. As the story goes, the other prostitute was picked up but Cati managed to escape and, as revenge, the woman fingered Cati. Since the people who hung out in the *ambiente* kept their distance from Cati because they did not want to be associated with her drug deals, nobody would tell me the whole story. I never found out whether and why she was arrested, if they had let her go or if she ran away before the police got to her.

Finally, I met Vanessa who fits the description of a young women dangling on the borderline. She was a 19-year-old woman who said she was studying book-keeping at a vocational institute and became the mother of twins at the age of 14 as a result of being raped. She hung out at the restaurant, waiting for her boyfriend to pass by during one of his breaks. He worked as a porter at a nearby disco and was said to be married and the father of one child. He broke her heart when he ended the relationship after finding out she was pregnant. She swore the baby was his, but he did not want anything to do with her. She sat at a table looking forlorn, writing poems to her lost love, and somehow always managing to have someone else pay her bill. Some people did not believe it was his baby because she had a reputation for sleeping around. Others did not believe she was pregnant, but only fat. Her stomach kept growing until, one day as she was approaching her seventh month, her stomach was completely flat again. She attributed the loss of her baby to self-neglect. She began to hang out more in the areas known for street prostitution. Someone overheard her negotiating prices with a client. Since I also distributed condoms here, I approached her one night and asked if she needed any, she said no, and emphasized that she did not work, she helped in the negotiations. Anita was also suspicious, she had the feeling Vanessa had started to work. Once they bumped into each other by the bathroom. Anita asked her if she was working and she denied it. Anita told her about her daughter, a good example of a girl of her age who was making something of her life. From that moment on Vanessa only greeted Anita at a distance.

## LOVE AND RELATIONSHIPS UNDER THE MOONLIGHT

Shortly after I started to visit the plaza, I came at the usual time, ten o'clock and met Roberto. He was seated with a young woman named Carmela. Roberto introduced me and we kissed hello. I sat down at the table and he told me straightaway about Carmela's life. 'Carmela is studying medicine, she is in her fifth year at San Marcos University.[3] She has two years to go.'

She added, 'When I finish I am going to Germany on a scholarship. My father is a German Jew who escaped from a concentration camp.'

During our conversation, I observed that Carmela watched me constantly. She was checking me out. I got the feeling Roberto had told her what I did.

It turned out I was right. Before I arrived, he had explained my interest in the nightlife. Carmela consented to do an interview.

Ernesto, a six-foot-tall black man who was always dressed in a suit joined us at our table. I had seen him previously several times and each time I could not help thinking he bore a strong resemblance to the stereotypical image of the (American) pimp. He was not. Rather, he worked as a chauffeur for a politician and he was a friend of many of the women who worked at the plaza. Since he was dressed up, I asked him if he had plans for the evening.

'Not tonight but tomorrow. Carmela, her boyfriend and I are planning to go to a *salsadromo* [a salsa disco].' Carmela invited me to join them. I told them I was not sure but if I did not go, there would always be another night.

Off Carmela went to work and told us she would be back later. In the meantime, a few more men joined our company and, as on many subsequent occasions, I became a victim of a conversation about football, tits and ass. Roberto and I went to take a stroll. He used this time to fill me in on the details of Carmela's life. 'She was raped at the age of 11 by a cousin and gave birth to twins. She has five children. Four are in a boarding school in the United States. She sends them US $4,000 a month. She was a novice in a convent for three years and made her money fucking the priests. She is 21 years old and has been working as a prostitute since she was 14 to support her children.'

To say the least it was an incredible story. It had made a deep impression on Roberto. I asked him, 'Why are you so sure she is telling the truth, she could be making it up?' He pondered a bit and decided I had a good point. Back at the table Ernesto had bought me a beer. It was two o'clock in the morning and I planned to go home, but Roberto advised against it. According to Roberto, Ernesto was interested in me. He would not only be offended but they needed to define their positions in reference to me. Ernesto was competing with Roberto. He bought me a beer because he wanted to be certain I would accept a drink from him, since Roberto had paid the bill. I was destined to stay longer and it turned out to be a good thing, too, because Carmela returned with her boyfriend Miguel and another friend Pedro who they told me worked as a bodyguard for the same person as Ernesto. At our subsequent meetings it became clear he did not work and his means of earning money, if he actually had any, were dubious.

A street magician known at the plaza performed his act. Carmela and I talked amongst ourselves. She asked, 'Is Roberto your boyfriend?'

'No he is not.'

'That's funny, he kept talking about his girl.'

'It's possible, because he has a girlfriend, but not me.'

'Roberto told me about your work and I am willing to talk to you any time. I will give you my address and phone number before you leave.'

She told me in telegraph style about her life. The rape, the money she sends to her children who are at a Mormon boarding school. 'My ex-husband is a Mormon.' She looked worried.

I said, 'Don't worry.'

'I have a lot of worries, my children are coming in August for a month, I won't be able to work. I have to save money to support them for the whole month while they are here.'

'Why couldn't you continue working, how would they find out?'

'They could feel it, and the people in the neighbourhood are always making remarks. I don't know what the neighbourhood knows but they find it very strange that I go out every night and come home in the morning.'

She talked about her boyfriend. 'The life I lead is tough. When you finally meet someone who truly loves you, you have to hold on to him the best you can.'

Another woman came in and sat down next to Pedro; nobody introduced us. Carmela showed me some scars on her wrist.

'How did you get them?'

'I did it during a fight with Miguel. I couldn't take it anymore and burned myself with a cigarette.'

It was four in the morning and it was time to go. While kissing everyone goodbye, Ernesto slipped me a piece of paper. I opened the paper – the silver lining of a cigarette box – outside. It contained a picture of himself with an inscription written on the back 'To my friend Lorena from your friend Ernesto.' He engraved a few words on the silver paper: 'Lorena, do you like me? I like you, Ernesto.'

Ernesto's present made me decide not to go dancing the following night. Even though I would miss a golden opportunity, as Roberto claimed, I found it way too early to get involved in the intricacies of having, or avoiding, an amorous relationship. Roberto tried to convince me to go.

'Carmela said she would look out for you.'

'Why would she have to look after me?'

'She knows you are new to the scene, she won't let anything happen.'

I stuck to my decision but worried that it would have repercussions. I realized afterwards I had nothing to worry about. Ernesto was known to be a *gringa*-chaser. It did not surprise anyone that he attempted to pick me up.

In the short span of an evening I learned a great deal about Carmela's life. The daughter of a German Jew, she studied medicine, worked as a tour guide and a prostitute, had five children and earned approximately US $5,000 a month. Somehow, I had trouble believing it all. It was hard to envision her managing the life she told me about and going to bed at six o'clock in the morning with a her bloodstream still full of alcohol or coke. I had entered Carmela's fantasy-rich world where the borders between truth, imagination and lies were often indiscernible. The most sensational, unbelievable things (almost, nearly) always seemed to have happened to her. Nearly every time I saw her she told a new tale to all of us seated at the table. I do not know how many times she had almost been attacked by a customer before coming to the restaurant or she had had a miscarriage. Her children in the US always had some kind of serious problem, one diagnosed autistic, the others physically abused by their grandparents. She kept running into horrible people from her past and always dropped a new piece of information about her study. Yet, in spite of her weakness for melodrama, she had a sweet and caring nature. She was a woman who desperately needed to feel loved. She looked after me, advised me to stay away from certain people who were known to be 'bad'. I came to appreciate her and was concerned for her happiness. She was full of surprises and often created a dramatic episode before our eyes.

The next time we came to the plaza, Carmela arrived shortly after, made-up and looking very pretty. Miguel would be coming to meet her. She whispered in my ear: 'He does not want me to work when he is here. He gives me money on those nights; a little, but it is money. It's all right, I have steady clients on the other nights. Some women give money to their boyfriends, I don't.' She implied these women kept the men and the men were *cafiches* (pimps). Something puzzled me, if Miguel's presence impeded Carmela from working, when did she work? Miguel showed up nearly every night.

In the meantime a very well-dressed black man passed by and stopped to talk to Carmela. Roberto made a remark with sexual overtones to which Carmela responded seriously, 'Roberto, I am a sexual racist.'

'What do you mean by that?' he inquired.

'I don't do it with blacks; brown skin like Miguel, yes, but not with blacks. They say theirs is as big as a donkey's. I have graduated from sexual university.'

I replied, 'You missed a few courses, such as black history.'

The subject changed and her eyes lit up when she told us about her one-year-old daughter and all the wonderful things she did and said. 'One day she picked up my skirt and she pointed below and asked what was there.'

I asked in disbelief, 'She is only one year old, how can she talk?'

'She can, she talks and talks, you should hear her. Miguel loves her.'

She went on, changing the subject, 'I have skipped a lot of school lately. I missed a lot of school last semester but I still managed to be one of the first ten in my class. I did an internship with one of the best doctors in Lima and learned more than I could going to university. My father is being operated on tomorrow for varicose veins at the Hospital Obrero [the hospital is situated across the street from the university]. I will have no excuse for missing classes because I have to visit my father.'

When Miguel arrived they retreated to a corner of the table making it their own. Carmela and Miguel kept making remarks about their jealous natures. In fact, I would venture to say their jealousy kept their relationship functioning.

The following evening we encountered a very perky Carmela who intended to make US $600 that night. Roberto said, 'I doubt you could make so much money in one night.'

'Okay, US $300, but it won't be easy because Miguel will arrive soon, and when Miguel comes', she told Roberto, 'he does not want me to work.

Normally we go to the hostel where he works, he gets a discount there or another hostel, but we want to rent a studio together.'[4]

Her eyes kept wandering, impatient to find some business or looking to see if Miguel arrived.

I asked, 'How is your father?'

With a serious expression on her face she replied, 'The operation went well but the second operation in August is the serious one. My mother wants me to go to Chiclayo for a week, to check our property. She does not trust my brother, but she is certain I won't steal from her.'

This new bit of information told me more about Carmela's background. She had already told me her mother studied medicine and was of Spanish descent. She boasted about the clinic owned by her mother's family. She told me she owned a refrigerated trucking business with her brother. Her tales about her family's financial situation were full of hints concerning her good background. They may have fallen down the social ladder, but she came from 'good stock'. The subject changed. 'My ex-husband, the father of my baby, came by. He wants a reconciliation. I don't want anything to do with him. After everything he did to me. It is his fault I work here.'

As she was anxious to roam the streets, we told her we would cover for her if Miguel came by. This proved unnecessary. She went off, only to return shortly arm in arm with Miguel.

Carmela's mood changed quickly, a result of her argument with Miguel. Before I knew it, Miguel was standing alone at the bar and Carmela was sitting at the table crying. I sat next to her and tried to console her. 'He doesn't love me, one day he says one thing and the next day he says another. He is a liar.'

'Of course he loves you.'

Two young men interrupted us. They obviously knew Carmela. 'Can we join you?'

Carmela replied, 'We are accompanied.'

They disappeared. Off she went to talk to Miguel again. I found myself sitting with Ernesto, Anita and Pedro. Miguel and Carmela's conversation slowly turned into another argument. Miguel walked away. Carmela, who had been drinking beer, took Miguel's *cuba libre* and chugged it down swiftly, which was an announcement that trouble was on its way. She went to the bathroom and took a very long time. Finally, the door opened, she staggered out and sat down at an adjacent table. We all thought she was very drunk, but then she announced she had taken all her pills for her heart condition. I went into the bathroom to look for evidence, so they could take it to the emergency room. I could not find any. Miguel found the empty bottle on the floor and off he went with Ernesto and Carmela to have her stomach pumped.

While waiting for them to return, a conversation evolved around the incident. Anita said, 'I don't understand why she did that, if she is not going to think of herself, she should at least think of her children, she has to think of her children.'

Roberto said, 'She didn't want to die, you don't go into the bathroom and come out and announce to everyone you took a bottle of pills if you want to die, she wanted attention.'

Anita: 'I told her several times, he is a married man, you have to accept what he can offer.'

I replied, 'But Carmela says he is going to get a divorce.'

'He is not going to get a divorce, he has five children, you have to accept what he gives.'

A fight developed outside, gunshots could be heard in the background. Pedro went to see what was going on. Anita advised me to stay inside, 'You never know when a bullet might hit you.'

I agreed. I offered her a cigarette; she accepted and said, 'You know I could be here all night smoking and drinking but when I am home I don't touch either of them. Pedro used to drink a lot before we got together. He changed. Ernesto too. Ernesto used to have a girlfriend who worked here and did drugs, he did them too. About a month ago he got this job and now he has straightened out.'

Pedro kept returning to our table, kissing Anita or biting her affectionately on her shoulder. He turned to me and said, 'I am going to marry her.' His behaviour contrasted with the conversation Roberto had overheard earlier in which Pedro aggressively told Anita, 'I am *criollo*, that's the way I am, if I say something you obey.'

This was the first conversation I had with Anita. Anita was approximately 40 years old. Pedro was at least ten years younger and had two children. She dressed very nicely, and kept herself in good shape. She told me about her children. 'Believe it or not, I have five. Two are in university, another is studying at an academy and the other two are at school. It really makes me happy to see all my children are on the right road, they are straight.'

Ernesto and Miguel's return interrupted our conversation. Carmela had come back with them too. Smiling, she sat down next to me. I hugged her. It was peculiar, after she left to go to the hospital and even when she came back, nobody dwelled upon the incident. Everyone acted as if nothing happened.

Both Carmela and Anita had relationships with men who were supposedly separated from their partners with whom they had children. Their marital status was not problematic. Being attached does not necessarily influence the decision to get involved in a relationship. It does, however, potentially place limitations on, or threaten the relationship.

Anita held certain values concerning relationships with married men and, in Carmela's case, a man with so many children. She disapproved of Carmela's determination to get Miguel to commit himself entirely to their relationship. Carmela was being unrealistic. He had too many children to demand that he abandon his wife. She claimed Carmela had to be happy with what she received. However, in her own relationship her demands were different. She insisted that Pedro take a clear position concerning his commitment to her because, as she repeated on several occasions, 'He is younger and has his whole future in front of him, I have no time to waste.' This was expressed at different moments, one of them after Pedro disappeared for several days.

Everyone asked her where Pedro was. Trying to sound indifferent, she replied, 'I don't know. I haven't seen him for four days.'

She did not refer directly to the possibility he had returned to his partner, but in our conversation her words implicitly expressed her concern. 'If I don't hear anything from him soon then it is finished. He should call even if it is only to tell a lie or give an excuse, but he should let me hear from him. If he doesn't show up, I am going to visit his mother. I am going to explain the situation to her and ask her what is going on. He has two children with a woman he used to live with, they are trying to persuade him to marry her.'

Anita and Carmela never admitted openly they suspected their partners went back to visit their wives and children. To avoid people's curiosity they would say their *maridos* went somewhere else to work. However, these words were meant to dissimulate their fear that their *maridos* had returned to their wives, perhaps even permanently. Perhaps Miguel really did go somewhere else to work, but it is just as likely he went home to secure his position there and then disappeared again.

The women did not display the vulnerable side of their relationships to others. As discussed in Chapter 6, a prostitute's relationship is continually scrutinized by outsiders and, as the following pages will show, also by people who are part of the *ambiente*. Their partner's love is always in question. Men are de facto defined as pimps. In fact, one of the worst things to say or imply to a prostitute is that she keeps her *marido*, because it implies that she not only works as a prostitute but she *is* a prostitute, making her relationship with her *marido* unauthentic. The fixed nature attributed to the partner, in the social representation of their masculinity, is actually far more fluid and shifts between the notions of *marido* and *cafiche*, depending very much on the man's attitude and actions.

Miguel's insistence that Carmela did not work when he was present reinforced the idea he was not a *cafiche*. If she got involved in a conversation with women working or men known to be clients he immediately became annoyed. On one occasion, Carmela gave a description of the new clothes she had bought for her daughter. Miguel abruptly left the table frowning. I asked, 'Why is he angry?'

She replied, 'He heard me talking about the baby's new clothes and realized I went to work yesterday.'

However unrealistic his demand, Miguel did not want Carmela to work, even though he never could have made enough money to support Carmela, her children and his own family. His obstinacy demonstrated that he was a man of principles. His jealous outbursts when he found out Carmela worked legitimized his identity as *marido* even more.

Carmela and Miguel seriously intended to make a life together. One evening she announced her plans to stop working. They planned to open a poultry stand on the market. After her announcement, she disappeared from the plaza for several weeks. I started to believe she had really left it all behind her. Ironically, their decision coincided with the announcement of the *paquetazo*, the worst imaginable time to start a new enterprise. Carmela had cut herself off from the only way she could earn money at the moment she needed it the most.

For some time after that, they frequented the plaza sporadically, but regularly and appeared happy. On one occasion, all dressed up and glowing, she announced she was going to have Miguel's baby. She told me earlier Miguel wanted her to have his baby, something they could share together. Shortly after, she miscarried. This was the third miscarriage since I had known her. The next time I saw her at the plaza, she showed me her engagement ring. They were planning to get married. She always dreamt about having a church wedding. However, her dream would be postponed for two years, the amount of time needed to finalize their divorces.

They came to the plaza to visit their friends. When Carmela conversed with people from her past Miguel became intolerant. He expected her to cut off all her old ties and forget about the past. This was difficult to accomplish because they always came back to her place of work to visit. Their proposed joint enterprise had still not materialized, but they had not stopped hoping it would happen soon. Carmela asserted she planned to combine the market stall with a job teaching German a few hours a week at an academy. She hoped these two incomes would be enough to support her family.

For approximately two months things seemed to go as usual. Carmela came to the plaza at nine o'clock, arriving from her internship, to meet Miguel, her study books jutting out of her bag. I began to suspect her of using the internship as a cover and that she had actually gone back to work. This evening she showed me one of the notebooks, pointing out the things she learned in class. It was impossible to avoid noticing pages filled with faded ink, dated 1960. Perhaps her mother really had studied medicine and this notebook had belonged to her.

Shortly after, Roberto ran into her on the street, made up and dressed in her work clothes. He asked, 'Are you planning to work?' She said, 'Yes, Miguel decided he loves his wife more than me.' The same night Carmela told another friend she had gone back to work because Miguel had lost his job. He knew about it and waited for her at the park until she finished. Roberto and I could not believe he would let her work and we were worried about his reaction if he found out. However, it turned out Carmela had told the truth. Miguel lost his job which left them with no other choice than for her to go back to work. The first few times I ran into her afterwards, she still denied she was working. She said, 'Nobody believes me, but I am not working, I am working as an intermediary.' Carmela and I shared a lot together, but she was ashamed to admit she went back to work.

Carmela's return to prostitution was completely understandable. However, Miguel's flexibility in regard to Carmela's work was surprising. He did not cause any problems, as he had in the past. He stayed in the neighbourhood and was there if she needed him. But he tried to stay out of her way until she finished. The change in his attitude, however, did affect the way people perceived him. This became clear in a conversation with Cati.

Roberto, Cati and I were sitting at a table when Carmela came by, kissed us hello, greeted Cati politely and refused our invitation to join us. I found her behaviour strange because, a few days before, they had appeared inseparable. When she left, I asked Cati what had happened. She said, 'I met Miguel on the street sitting on a park bench. We talked together. I told him he should be out looking for work instead of sitting on this bench. "You were different when you were working. You have five children, you can't just forget about them."'

I interrupted and said, 'Carmela has several too.'

She replied, 'Carmela only has one from a drug addict, who she kept even worse than Miguel. Every day, early in the morning she went to his hang-out to give him money for drugs. After him it was a watchman who worked at the plaza. It was the same type of relationship. Do you think her relationship with Miguel is different? They scream and fight and the following day it's over, that's not a relationship, is it?'

The conversation briefly focused on men kept by women. I asked, 'Do you think a women who contributes to the household is keeping her husband? Would you accept contributing to the household, perhaps even more than your partner if you had other work?'

She said 'That's different, but someone who lets you work in this doesn't really love you. Miguel should be working. He has five children.'

We said, 'But he lost his job for some stupid reason.' She replied in disbelief, 'He lost his job because he didn't show up for four days, Carmela persuaded him not to go to work. Why should I have to lie if they are my friends? I should be able to tell them what I think.'

I said, 'You know what I noticed. Every time anyone says exactly what they think, people stop talking to them.'

She replied, 'There is no place for truth in this *ambiente*.'

Cati's version of the fight shed another perspective on Carmela's image. She implied that Carmela habitually kept her partners, and was closer to a 'common street whore' than the woman from a good background whose family had fallen on hard times.[5] Moreover, Miguel's attitudes and behaviour towards Carmela's work defined his identity. His resignation to the situation challenged his image as the caring *marido* and attributed to him characteristics of a *cafiche*. A *cafiche* is a poor excuse for a man and is looked down upon. The crux defining this notion of masculinity in this *ambiente*, is not what stereotypically defines a pimp: a man who forces women to prostitute or has several women under his authority. This type of *cafiche* is almost non-existent. It is not violence or force that determines the definition of the *cafiche*'s identity, rather it is the fact he accepts money earned from selling sex. Within the general social context there are many unemployed men who have to rely on their wives' earnings; in this context, however, it is unacceptable.[6]

For a relationship to be labelled genuine, based on love and not on opportunism, the man must aspire to remove his partner from the work environment. In essence, he is responsible for remaking the women's gender identity, so that it conforms to traditional gender norms. The man is the breadwinner, providing for her and her children, and the woman becomes the housewife. In the realm of prostitution, this ideological illusion, and I deliberately call it an illusion because the majority of the relationships in the popular classes cannot even attempt to live up to this ideal, is striven for against all economic odds: the high rate of unemployment and a minimum monthly wage which is insufficient to satisfy a family's basic needs. The proof of the relationship's authenticity is determined by whether this goal can be successfully achieved. This is not merely an expression of wishful masculine thinking, the women share and contribute to this ideal too. Not all prostitutes work towards this objective but they do hold on to these values and weigh their decisions against them, even if the outcome might ultimately oppose the ideal.

For instance, some women are very pragmatic. They do not believe relationships exist in which the man can earn enough to support them and their children. Moreover, some men are willing to 'remove them' from the *ambiente*, but do not intend to support their children. Hence, a relationship would not alleviate the women's financial problems. In fact, it might even aggravate them because they would be expected to stop prostituting and could no longer earn money to support their children, which was their basic motive for prostituting in the first place.

Anita knew the gossip that circulated concerning her relationship with Pedro. People said he was a *cafiche* and, allegedly, she kept him. She fervently denied this allegation. Perhaps this image existed because Pedro never made any attempts to get Anita to stop working. Anita articulated her position on the subject of their relationship lucidly. 'I would never keep a man. When Pedro and I go to a hostel we split the bill. The day I decide to live with a man, I will leave my house with the clothes on my back and that is that. The man has to be willing to accept me and provide for me if he wants me to leave this work.'

'What about your children?', I enquired.

'They will be old enough to take care of themselves. I don't know how many times I tried to convince Pedro he should go to work, keep working. Many people who have money now, have worked their way up from the bottom. You have to keep working to get any where in this world.'

Since Pedro could never support her she had no intention of stopping working. Moreover, Anita would not easily give up working because of the satisfaction it gave her in relation to her children. It was her money which put her children through university. She took great pride in that.

Another woman I got to know placed clear demands on her *marido*. Ernesto had fallen in love, not with a *gringa* but with Angela, a street prostitute who worked on a street in the district. She had three children who lived with her mother and, a few months into their relationship, she was expecting another baby. Ernesto was ecstatic with the prospect of being a father. He assured me she had stopped working from the moment the relationship grew serious. They rented a room in a pension in the centre of the city. 'When I go to work, I tell Angela to wait for me there or I bring her to my mother's house to wait.' Just as their plans began to materialize, Ernesto lost his job but did not have the nerve to tell her. Angela kept asking him for things and he could not comply. This made him feel even worse. After a week, he finally told her. Angela moved back to her mother's and Ernesto planned to do the same when he could afford to pay the bill for renting the room. Angela went back to work, but stopped a few weeks later because she continually felt nauseous. She threatened to break up if he did not find work. Ernesto desperately looked for work to no avail. Angela refused to see him. Then his luck changed; he could lease a taxi, but he needed to leave a deposit, a considerable amount of money which he did not have. He finally managed to scrape the money together and started to drive a taxi. Angela and Ernesto's relationship continued.

Hence, men's identity as *marido* or *cafiche* is intricately informed by the meanings of femininity and their ability to contribute to remaking these meanings. This suggests there are notions of masculinity and femininity at play shared by men and women alike. Some of these notions are found in the domain of sexuality. What is involved in remaking a prostitute's gender identity is a rearrangement of her sexuality. Previously accessible to all men willing to pay the price, ideally it is supposed to be transformed into a sexuality exclusively practised with her partner.

When the women talked about their work they repeatedly emphasized the ordinariness of prostituting – a job like any other – dissociating the sexual from the way they earn their money. Their statements stressed the non-existence of their own sexuality in their work. Sexuality became a signifier of meaning through its absence. Concomitantly, the acceptance that a relationship is only authentic when the prostitute is removed from the *ambiente* implies that there is unspoken shared knowledge that a woman's sexuality is involved in the embodiment of the prostitute. Attempts are made to limit its influence in the definition of oneself as a prostitute, but nonetheless it possesses a forceful defining power. This became even more apparent in how it was used by the women to define each other.

Returning to Carmela and Cati's fight, Carmela presented a different version of the story. She claimed she stayed over at Cati's house with Miguel and Cati made a pass at him. Of course Miguel did not want anything to do with her. She did admit that Cati yelled at Miguel in public, claiming he was a *cafiche* and she felt she had no right to say those things in public. But her main explanation for their argument was Cati's sexual overture to Miguel.

On another occasion, Carmela quarrelled with Anita. She did not go into detail but rather presented a description of Anita to justify her anger. Before Miguel and Carmela got together, he was interested in Anita but she did not want anything to do with him. Carmela insinuated that Anita had changed her mind and wanted Miguel. She based her insinuation on an episode she claimed had occurred between Anita and her father. Anita allegedly made a pass at her father. Carmela said, 'My father is *bien mujeriego* [a real womanizer] but he told her he would never have anything to do with a woman like her.' She discredited Anita further by suggesting that she went out with other men under Pedro's nose.

I received another version of their quarrel from a mutual friend of theirs. Anita supposedly told Carmela's mother she kept Miguel. Anita denied ever telling her mother such a thing. In both cases, Carmela's explanation of her arguments with her girlfriends painted them as promiscuous women who unsuccessfully tried to steal her *marido*. However, the counter-versions indicate the root of the argument to be Miguel's identity. By challenging Miguel's image, Cati and Anita constructed meanings of femininity which implied that Carmela was a whore. Miguel accepted money derived from prostituting, an activity which demands that his girlfriend's sexuality be accessible to other men. Carmela defended herself by projecting the same image on to the other women, but even worse, her comments were taken out of the realm of prostitution and into their private lives, making them promiscuous women, one of society's standard definitions of prostitutes. Another incident occurred in which Anita negotiated her identity by projecting certain values on to another woman. This time Carmela was not the target, it was me.

After the argument, Anita and Carmela did not speak to each other for several weeks. Ernesto decided it was time to put an end to their fight and organized a party to take place at Carmela's parents' house. Ernesto and I were the first to arrive. Miguel would come after work and Pedro and Anita would come later. To say the least I felt very uncomfortable at the beginning of the evening. I did not particularly enjoy being treated by Carmela's parents as the guest of honour because of my advantageous social position – the white, European woman with a profession. Furthermore, I was confused about what I was allowed to say to her parents. Of course I knew never to mention Carmela's work, but she had told me so many fantasy-rich things about herself that I could not be sure what was fiction and what was reality. For example, in a conversation with her father, I asked him what part of Germany he came from, a relatively innocent question. He said he was not from Germany but his parents were born there. I felt I could not ask her parents anything without running the risk of destroying all Carmela's sandcastles. Lastly, Carmela's description of her family background disinte-grated before my eyes. Her house was extremely modest. The toilet, located outside the house in their courtyard, was a clear sign of their poverty. Other factors challenged the image she had been painting all along. Carmela did not seem to mind, she seemed happy that I met her family and I was in her house. Nonetheless, I felt schizophrenic.

As the night progressed I began to doubt whether Anita would show up, she eventually came, accompanied by Pedro and two other friends. The party went into full swing. Everyone, including her parents, danced and drank. Carmela's mother's obesity made it extremely difficult for her to walk and get off her chair, but it did not impede her from gracefully dancing in a sitting position. The jokes made about her father's infamous past as a *mujeriego* caused everyone to laugh. I crouched down beside her mother to have a conversation. She instructed me to marry a Peruvian and corrected me when I used the term *Ud.* (the polite form for you) instead of *tu* (informal you). She talked about Miguel. 'Miguel is a good man, he told me he wants Carmela to stop working the night shift at the hospital.[7] I tried to tell Carmela she should forget him because he is married.'

I said, 'Carmela keeps telling me how much she loves him, I don't think she could forget him that easily.'

Her mother agreed. Pedro came by and asked me to dance and I accepted. Afterwards, I asked Carmela to accompany me to the toilet to make sure their dogs did not attack me along the way. When I came back, Anita and Pedro were quarrelling outside. Carmela asked me to help her break up the fight. I agreed without thinking twice. When we got there Carmela said, 'Lorena, tell Anita you are not interested in Pedro.' I was flabbergasted. They were arguing about me. I tried to approach Anita but she screamed at me to leave her alone. Pedro called me to try to speak to her again. I retreated inside and told one of the guys what had happened. He had just happened to be sitting next to the two of them when the argument started about something else. Pedro decided to dance with me in the middle of it. 'They are using you as an excuse, don't worry about it.'

A few minutes later Miguel asked me to dance, I went over to Carmela and jokingly asked her permission. Miguel did the same and we all laughed. Carmela's mother went to talk to Anita and her father with Pedro. Anita went into the kitchen and I asked Carmela to come with me because I wanted to talk to her. I approached her and said, 'How could you think I would do anything to hurt you?' She admitted it was not my fault but Pedro's.

I said, 'How could you think he is interested in me? You are mistaken.'

'No', she said, 'he told me. This is not the first time this has happened at a party. Every time we are somewhere and he has a few too many, it is the same thing. It only shows he doesn't care about me, I am not worth anything to him. Lorena, you know I am a woman of the *ambiente*, I don't need this, I would rather be alone. Everything in my house I bought, no one bought them for me. I told him I want to break up, but he keeps coming back. He says if I leave him he will slash my face, he will shoot me. I say go ahead, I am not afraid. I want clarity. He has a future in front of him, I don't. I would rather be alone. Maybe you were innocent, but if he does this all the time it shows I am not worth anything to him.'

Pedro approached us and asked, 'Can I talk to Anita?'

I said, 'It is up to her to decide.'

She decided to talk to him and I went back into the living room. Carmela's mother could not hide her anger. 'This is not the first time they are arguing like that, it shows their lack of education.' A group of us left shortly after, when things had calmed down a bit, but it would take several days before they would be on speaking terms again.

The next time I was at the restaurant, Anita passed by and said hello from a distance, but she did not stop. Roberto said, 'She probably is with a client.' I said, 'I doubt it.' And for several months afterwards, Anita did not sit at a table where I sat and would only greet me from a distance, if she had to. I was used as a pawn in this argument between Anita and Pedro, but by maintaining distance towards me, Anita defined me as potentially dangerous as the other women in the *ambiente* and by doing so, became the chaste partner of Pedro.

In these arguments, negative qualities of sexuality enmeshed in work are projected on to the social setting to define the women's identity. The first thing this illustrates is that, although on one level the boundaries between work and their private lives are clearly demarcated, on another level, bits of their working identities flow into the social settings and act as signifiers defining meanings of femininity. Second, by projecting on to other women the promiscuous nature entangled in the label of the whore, they become the mirror image – the woman who in her personal relationships enjoys an exclusive sexuality, thereby severing this aspect of their work from their private lives and coming closer to conforming to the ideal gender identity.

The silence around the domain of sexuality is a chimera which conceals the hidden force with which sexuality informs meanings of femininity. This does not refute the assertion that the women dissociate sexuality from their work. On the contrary, their negation of their sexuality configures with the other meanings constituting the concept of sexuality. Sexuality and prostitution is a contested domain.

The nightlife in the street hosts a world that left me bedazzled. Unlike the other fieldwork locations, where lies were more often used as a strategic weapon, in this *ambiente* lies were truths that fused into illusions, making it difficult to distinguish one from the other. Regardless of their elusive nature, these different versions of truths superimposed layers of meanings, one on top of the other, the fragments merging together in the construct of femininity and the enactment of the prostitute.

In the world of the *ambiente*, where a multitude of relationships are woven into each other, a tendency exists to envision masculinity and femininity as clear-cut dichotomies, giving the individual apparently two alternatives to choose from. A woman is either a prostitute or she leaves it behind and becomes a non-prostitute – the wife of her *marido* – and the change in her status is meant to erase her past. A man's actions and attitudes label him as a *cafiche* or a *marido*. Finally, a woman's sexuality is posited as being accessible for others or kept exclusively for her partner. The episodes narrated above show these notions are used as fixed reference points to define oneself and others. In practice, the allocation of gender meanings is far more fluid and transitory than is explicitly recognized. Depending on the situation, a woman can be sexually accessible in her work and at the same time exclusive in her relationship outside her work. She can stop prostituting and be taken care of by her *marido*, and forced to return because of circumstances, with her *marido*'s approval. The former strengthens the *marido*'s identity and the later transforms him into a *cafiche*. A woman does not have to be a prostitute to be defined in terms of the same sexual notions, as Anita's argument with me revealed. Although these examples indicate that there are various con-figurations defining gender meanings and suggest there are numerous ways for women-who-prostitute to negotiate their lives, in practice these alterna-tives are not recognized because they do not conform to the ideal representations of femininity. The relationships between women and men embody meanings produced in the gendered enclosures, strengthening the idea that there are only two extreme alternatives to resolve their situation: either stay in and suffer or get out.

# 8 BETWEEN FOUR WALLS
## Embodying and Enacting the Prostitute

THE CRAZY HORSE: ANOTHER GENDERED ENCLOSURE

The Crazy Horse, the second place where nocturnal fieldwork took place, was located close to the Plaza Bolivar. Working at the plaza and in the disco was different, not only for the women, but also for myself. Every time I climbed the steps to the Crazy Horse, I felt as if I was entering a world which only existed between those four walls. It was not so much that different codes, values and norms distinguished the two places from each other, although the working conditions and the approach to work differed. Rather, this sensation was provoked by the way almost all outside stimuli were kept outside. The indirect dim lighting, which made it difficult to distinguish the persons seated at the far ends of the U-shaped bar, also had a way of preventing the street light from entering. The pulsating disco music, alternating with a few of the most popular salsa hits, effectively defeated any attempt to participate in or listen to a conversation taking place two stools further down. It also dampened any of the loud street noises that threatened to gain entrance through the open door. But it was more than just these superficial attributes. It was the unfailing predictability characterizing each night that contributed to this sensation. Visually, nearly every time I entered, the same scene met my eyes. There were one or two bartenders waiting to serve customers, five to ten women scattered in clusters along the bar, with occasional changes in the seating arrangement as a result of dissolved alliances or the presence of a male client. Virtually everything remained the same, except on the rare occasion when the bar was nearly empty, a sign that the women were having a good night.

There was a certain monotonous rhythm characterizing the nightly occurrences. It appeared as if nothing ever happened. The club was never packed. Rarely were all the women entertaining customers at the same time. There were no arguments in loud voices, drunken scenes, exaggerated sexual displays or anything else constituting the Limenean category of *escandalo* (scandal). It had a domesticated air. This sensation heightened after I made several visits to another club where approximately 50 women worked at the same time. This place was filled with clients, women would dance and do

176

stripteases on top of the bar, there was an abundance of drugs and the smell of sex was in the air. Compared to the latter, visiting the Crazy Horse was like attending a grandmother's tea party. Even the dress code was distinct. The women at the Crazy Horse rarely wore any garment which could be defined as provocative, overly sexy or whorish, while at the other disco the smaller the mini-skirt and the lower the *décolleté* the better. This does not mean the Crazy Horse was a tranquil, pleasurable and unproblematic place to work. On the contrary, a great deal went on, but most of it was in a subterranean mode leaving this overall picture intact.

The club's manager, Marco, had been working there for the past 28 years. He was an overly 'nice and pleasant' guy who initially made us feel welcome. In our conversations he never ceased to stress his firm but fair posture towards the women. He did not exploit them, like managers in similar positions elsewhere. He demanded the women present certificates of health, renewed every 15 days, and recently he had included the Certificate of Elisa in this. He swore he never bribed the police to keep them out of the establishment, he just talked to them and it worked. It slowly became apparent he kept up a façade, in all likelihood to keep me satisfied and off his case. In time, I would gather enough clues to realize that Marco did not live up to his image. He made life miserable for the women he disliked and he also had a way of making his sexual desires known. He did not enforce any type of health control. The few times the police came in while I was there, they left quietly. I assume it was more than gentle verbal persuasion which stopped them from raiding the bar. The more Roberto and I started to understand what really went on, although I must admit I never got the complete picture, the less he was interested in us. In fact, towards the end, his greeting transformed dramatically. Where, in the beginning, he would put on a big smile and greet 'Señorita Lorena' the moment she entered the door, he eventually replaced this with a quick look to see who was entering, returning to what he was doing and reserving the big smile for the moment he could not avoid talking to me.

The Crazy Horse has a peculiar history. Legend has it that the owner, who lives in the provinces and rarely visits the establishment, is actually against this type of club because it lowers its value. He has tried to change it, renovating the club in the early 1980s and converting it into a disco for couples. However, this attempt failed. Marco compared this period to working at a cemetery. Eventually, Marco received the green light to take the required measures to put the club back on its feet again. He called in some women he knew to work there and business started again. Everybody tells the same story about the club: the women, the two bartenders and the disc jockey. Nonetheless, when the owner came to visit, I could see there was another story. Several women looked nervous, trying to keep out of the owner's way because they knew he did not like it that women worked in the club, while a selected group sat in a corner with him laughing, conversing and drinking. The owner was obviously enjoying himself. He then disappeared and everything went back to normal. Jesús, the owner's brother, was present nightly to keep a watchful eye on his brother's earnings, but I never saw him lift a finger. He just sat there. He was a man nearing 60, with an eternally grouchy expression on his face, who chain smoked and drank whisky. His attitude did not even change after he started a relationship with a young prostitute who was obviously in love with him. Nobody knew what she saw in him and the general conclusion of the women was 'Love is definitely blind.'

Marco's attempts to create an exclusive atmosphere were counteracted by the faulty neon sign at the entrance and the smells emanating from the bathrooms. One of the tasks of the semi-uniformed doorman-cum-bouncer was to keep street prostitutes from entering because they were considered to be of a lower calibre. Marco complained constantly that there was a shortage of women, and of course the more women who worked there the more business there was. The exorbitant prices charged for each drink was one source of income, but the club also received a bar fee when the client left with a woman. I did not find out about the bar fee until the middle of my fieldwork. Certain women intentionally kept this information from me and others were reluctant to talk about it. When I did find out, I immediately understood why Marco became irate when the women would meet a customer outside the club and not bring him inside.

When a client entered all eyes either subtly or calculatingly turned towards the door for a moment. Depending on the outcome of this rapid appraisal, the women would then proceed to decide on their strategy. If the potential client was drunk, too young or did not appear to have any money (the women easily sussed out a client's financial situation, and exceptions were made for drunks if they were known to have money), then all heads would turn quickly back to their place to resume their conversation. If the customer was a woman's regular and known to pay well, he might be greeted immediately. However, the general etiquette called for the person's presence to be noticed, followed by waiting quietly to see if he would make an approach; or, if he situated himself close enough, and if he was considered a good catch, one of the women would eventually approach him. Drinks would be ordered. The women did not earn money on the drinks but they were expected to get the client to order several of the most expensive ones. Perhaps they would go off to dance in the back and from there seat themselves in one of the cushioned booths which offered more privacy. But even then very few sexual advances would be made. Several women rejected clients or temporarily left them if they made rapid sexual advances. They all disliked being kissed or caressed too much by a client, not only because they felt this showed a lack of respect, but also they got annoyed with clients who wanted too much without paying –'all touch and no pay', I was told, was unacceptable. Thus, at times the illusion existed that the client and the prostitute were dating. At other times, the women would abandon their principles and, for some reason, accept the client's caresses and tongue kisses. Normally, after a drink or two, the couple would leave. The women charged between US $35 and US $50 for approximately two hours. If they were to stay the whole night together, the prices were higher. But if the client decided not to leave with a woman, it was a common courtesy for him to give her a tip. I heard frequent complaints about clients who were cheap tippers or, even worse, those who spent the whole night with a woman without leaving a tip. The women shared this information among themselves, as well as who was known to treat the women well, whether a client had any special quirks or if he was known to make trouble when the time came to pay.

When a customer came in, I normally tried to nonchalantly make my self scarce. Basically, I did not want to be any type of competition for the women. Moreover, I did not think it was necessary to tell every Tom, Dick and Harry who entered my motives for being there. On several occasions, a client commented that I did not seem to be the type of woman who worked here. This situation made me feel uncomfortable, because I would not admit I was not a prostitute but I did not deny it either. Nonetheless, there were moments when I accepted a drink or a dance, or when I remained in the company of the women when a client approached them.

These scenes between the clients and the prostitutes, the empty moments when the women were waiting patiently, anxious and bored, were continually repeated. More often, during idle moments, I sat there with Roberto, usually at separate ends of the bar, and chatted or attempted to talk to the women. Zoila was the first woman I met at the club; Mariana was not a regular but for a short period of time came regularly; Gina and Suzanna normally stuck together like glue and were joined from time to time by Lola and Dolores; and finally there were Soledad and Esperanza. These were not the only women who worked at the Crazy Horse, but I have chosen to structure this chapter by placing these women in the foreground.

The conversations recorded in this chapter portray another part of the *ambiente* of prostitution. Concomitantly, it focuses on the performativity of the prostitute created in this space. This is a gendered space in which the prostitute is constructed through her interactions and only permits small particles of her private life to sieve through, that are in accord with the profile being performed. The sharp contrast between night-time work and private lives – a division nearly all women-who-prostitute experience – is felt even more acutely in the Crazy Horse.

## MAPPING OUT PROFILES

### Zoila and Mariana

I met Zoila the first night we went to the Crazy Horse. Roberto knew her from when she used to work as a cashier in a local restaurant. He was confident their acquaintance would facilitate our entrance into the club. He counted on her presence that evening. Shortly after we arrived, she came in. They exchanged greetings. Mine was met with a grunt. Then he introduced me, telling her I was working and travelling and I would like to get to know her better and he invited her to sit down. She accepted. The ice slowly melted with each compliment he gave her. 'You are the most beautiful woman in my life', exclaimed Roberto.

Laughing in disbelief, Zoila replied, 'I am sure you say that to every girl.'

The conversation was sweet-talk, and was repeated several times during the evening and on many subsequent ones. Everyone knew he was not completely sincere but it served to construct an affectionate relationship. Zoila made sure we realized she appreciated our company by emphasizing she normally ordered whisky, an expensive drink, when someone invited her for a drink. This time she made an exception and ordered a beer, implying that our conversation fell outside her work. Her curiosity concerning my presence was not satisfied by Roberto's introduction and she asked me what I was doing here.

'I am doing a study on women who work at night like yourself.' I explained to her how I thought things had to change.

She answered, 'Lorena, I am willing to help you in any way possible, why don't we go and have a coffee to talk some more.'

'Fine', I replied, 'but I would also like to speak to you some time alone.'

Roberto paid the bill, and we left to find a restaurant open at this time of night. I talked about my work and what I wanted to accomplish, and what I felt about the maltreatment of prostitutes. I must have made an impression on her because on other occasions, when she described my work to other women, she said that my work was aimed at defending the rights of women who work. The women were able to recognize what she said. Her re-wording of my work separated me from many of the other people who are interested in prostitutes for the wrong reasons, such as journalists.

Our conversation criss-crossed many terrains. She quickly rattled off a list of monthly expenses and the prices of the items she needed daily for herself, her nine and a half year old son and her two-month-old baby, whom she claimed the real mother had given her because she could not support her. However, after our first meeting the baby was often absent from our conversations and eventually she totally disappeared. Whether she really existed and why she needed to exist in the first place remains a mystery. Zoila was 29 years old, an abandoned mother whose husband left her nearly eight years before. Since that time she had lost all faith in men. That was the version she told me that night. On another occasion she told Roberto her mother married her off at a very young age to a much older man whom she did not love. Very cryptic about her past, she had a way of letting the other person fill in the details.

We talked a bit about the work. Her *nenes* (a colloquial term for baby which she used for clients; I never heard any of the other women use it) were all Peruvians. She did not like to work with foreigners because she could not speak any other language. She considered conversing, knowing what the client thinks, to be essential for her work. She charged US $50 and, unlike the other girls who worked there, after she finished with a client she usually went home.

We showed each other photos. She showed me a picture of her son. Time flew by and I had to go. We made an appointment to meet the following Monday at a restaurant close to the club. Roberto and Zoila accompanied me to get a taxi. The following day, Roberto told me that after I had left, Zoila asked him to go and get a bite to eat. 'You can't imagine how much I drank tonight, I didn't want to make it obvious to your friend. When I get home my baby will be waking up and I don't want him to see me like this.' Roberto interpreted her protective stance as a positive sign. I was less convinced, but took little heed because I thought it would pass with time. I should have taken this as a sign of how our relationship was going to be. She would always keep up a façade to show me she was a good woman or a good whore. Moreover, her motivation to talk to me was not solely a product of her belief in my work, but also because she wanted to have a relationship with Roberto. Although she would call me her *buena amiga* (good friend), a *persona excellente* (an excellent person), I think, more frequently than I could imagine at the time, she attempted to use me to try to get closer to Roberto. However, these are retrospective reflections. At the time, I evaluated the situation differently. I felt she had the tendency to choose what she decided to tell me and carefully conceal what was really going on. But I am rushing ahead. At that moment our relationship had yet to take root. Monday would be the official inauguration.

In our conversation that Monday, Zoila presented a performance of the prostitute, that is to say, the way she constructed her identity made it acceptable to herself, and finally how she enacted, reacted to and adapted gendered meanings of the prostitute in her life. This partial representation emphasizes her story of being a prostitute, only letting a thin ray of light shine on to her day-time experiences.[1] Even though I discovered several inconsistencies in what she told me and what I observed, her story constructs a particular profile – a shorthand abstract of how she interacted and presented herself in the Crazy Horse.

'I used to work in a Spanish restaurant and after that in a Mexican one, but what I earned did not give me enough to pay for the house, it didn't give me enough to pay for my child's education ... what should I say? ... it was a period when I was fighting with my family, so they threw me out of the house. I had nowhere to go ... I went to a girlfriend's and she brought me into this. I was taking an executive secretary course, but I had to stop. It was impossible to keep studying and work at night.

'At first, it upset me, why?, because not everyone you meet is nice. Many times you have to put up with a lot of things, because of the money, so let's just say it is not very pleasant. When I began, they painted a different picture for me, they told me it would be different, that ... well, plain and simple, you sleep with a man in exchange for money ... and nothing outside of that happens, you know? But as time passes, it's been about two years since I started working in this and ... what can I tell you? ... there are many men who are psychologically in bad shape. They have many problems at home and the woman who does what I do has to bear it.

'It still upsets me but now I also feel used. Of course there are also pleasant moments, you know?, yes, there are pleasant moments. A pleasant time can happen when you meet a person who takes you to dinner, who makes you forget the moment. Well not exactly, because he pays you to do it, but for a few hours you forget what you are doing. Of course it is nice if the man is good looking, but for me, and I think for a lot of the women, it is more important that he treats you like a lady, that's what I consider pleasant.

'There aren't always clients. Business in this place has declined, it must be because of the situation we are all going through, the economic crisis. Sometimes you leave once every 15 days and other times every night. It is relative, depending on the people who enter the place, depending on whether you appeal to the client, because when a client enters you just can't push yourself into the middle of things. Plain and simply, you have to adapt to the situation. If you please a person and he agrees with what you ask, that is the most important, then you can leave with him. Believe me, this can cause a lot of problems, especially with the Peruvians, because of the situation. They can't pay US $35 to go to bed with a girl for one or two hours and they offer you less, US $15 or US $20. But it isn't worthwhile to leave for less, why? because of the expenses at home, school tuition, everything ... you can't lower your prices. When they offer me less money, what I usually do is, if he appears to be a nice person, because I'll tell you, working in this *ambiente* you almost become a psychologist who studies people. So depending upon what the person is like, if he made a good impression at the moment, he converses with you, you might accept, but not for the amount of time he proposes, but for less. He pays for the time needed for the relation and for nothing more. After that you return to the club and leave again.

'I don't accept everyone. It depends. Let's say, when a person comes over to you and says hello, whether he is fat, short, bald, black, whatever he may be, from the first moment he has to have some class. But there are other people who grab you and say, "Hey, how much do you charge?" It depends. Like I told you before, there are people who make you feel good. You feel flattered ... and this person not only gives you what you want, but also some peace. He makes you forget the moment and you do not think about what you are doing. A woman who does this for a living who feels that her whole life is paid for by a man, would like to relax a little, at least the majority would, you know? That she could relax a bit from what she is really doing, it would be too devastating to always have to remember. Plain and simply, he treats you as if he was your boyfriend. But there are also people who treat you like a machine. Because they pay, you have to do this or that for them. In those situations what you normally do is, you enter the room, you begin to caress it, put on the condom and you make the relation. When you finish, you change and leave. Everything machine-like. But it is not always like that, other people caress you while you are making the relation, they make you feel like a woman. But with others, plain and simply, you treat them how they want and you leave. I will tell you something Lorena, I normally have more friends than clients. Why? because normally the people I know converse with me. Of course they give me a tip, a certain amount of money for the time they converse with me.

'There are a lot of men who don't like to use condoms. Plain and simply, you tell them ... it's here where you use a bit of psychology, you tell them it is to protect both of us. Plain and simply if you don't want to use a condom then we can't be together. Because what will I do if you make me have another child or if you are sick? It depends on the situation whether I use it or not. When you are with one of those persons, you know machine-like, well you take it, make the *nene* erect, and once it is erect, you put it on, sit on top of it, you move and he comes, that's all. But there are also people who do everything you want them to and you please each other, then it depends, sometimes you do and sometimes you don't. But like I told you the other day, I only go with one person a night so when I don't use a condom, the next day I get two injections, and that's all.[2] Normally, I don't use it with people I have been with before, who are nice to you. Of course there are risks involved, because as much as you like him, you don't know who he has been with before.

'Look, there are men who you appeal to so much you can control them, you can give them hell and they would still do anything you want because you appeal to them, they like you. But there are other men who like to dominate. So you have to adapt yourself to the situation. Why? because at home he certainly has many problems and he doesn't know who he could order around, so he comes here, and you, plain and simply, adapt yourself to his way of doing things. That's why I said that sometimes we almost turn into psychologists.

'I enjoy managing the situation. For example, one time I sat at the bar and a *nene* grabbed me from behind, "Hey, *negra* [black], how much do you charge?" So I turned around and said, "The same your mother charges, arsehole", and turned my back to him again. Because look it is one thing that he thinks he can do anything he wants, but he has to do it with respect. So he complained to the manager, and the manager came to me and told me what he said, and I said to the manager plain and simply, "Excuse me sir, do you really think I could say such a thing?" A little later the client invited me for a drink, I ordered a whisky. He sent me the whisky. I took it, went over to him and poured it over his head.

'It's important to be certain that you can trust the client because there are risks involved. If you don't feel you can trust him, even if he wants to give you all the money in the world, it is better not to leave with him. He could pull a knife, threaten to kill you. About a month ago I left with a *nene* and we were on our way to a hotel and he put a revolver to my head and ordered me to take off my clothes in the middle of the street. Plain and simply, I obeyed him and took off everything, he threw me out of the car and my clothes after me and left me there. A police car passed by, I asked for their help and they ended up stealing my money, my handbag and my watch. You can't trust the police for anything in the world.

'But in the club there aren't too many problems. Maybe two clients who drink too much will have a fight, or there are girls who are very rude who will fight with a client and the client has many problems and punches her in the face, but between the girls there aren't any problems. You adjust to it. We don't have many problems inside the club. Normally it's outside the disco, the women who work on the street who have the problems. The police don't raid the disco because everything is "arranged". So, they give them money, they bring them bottles of whisky, etc. There are no problems with venereal diseases either. The women on the street have more problems. In the disco we have to show them a certificate of health every 15 days. I go to a private doctor, my family doctor. What do I tell him? I tell him my husband travels for business and every time he comes back, I get a check-up to make sure he doesn't have anything. I have thousands of excuses to tell the doctor. My doctor can't find out what I do because he is my family's doctor too.

'I work six days a week. I told my son I work in a tourist restaurant and I have to work Monday through Saturday and that I can't miss a day of work. Sundays, nothing in the world would make me come here. If I had a good week, I spend what I earned with my son. The girl who works for me at home is off on Sunday. I take my son out for breakfast, for dinner, to the movies ... we go out the whole day. When there is no money, we stay at home, tell each other jokes and talk. Sundays are only for him. During the week, if I leave with a client, normally my limit to return to home is seven in the morning, I can't stay longer than that, no matter who the person is. I normally arrive home three, four, five in the morning. I get up, fix breakfast for my baby, send him to school, go back to sleep. In the afternoon I cook and his *almuerzo* is ready when he comes. The girl who works for me prepares everything beforehand, all I have to do is cook. My baby only likes the way I season things. He does his homework, I help him with his homework, we talk, I watch my soap opera and I go back to sleep. When I awake at eight or nine, I put him to sleep and go to work.

'You do this for your children. You sacrifice yourself so your children can have more than you had. Because you are alone, it is the woman who has to give him everything, education, everything necessary in his upbringing. I think we can be better mothers than any other women, we sacrifice ourselves for them a lot. That is my opinion. Look, if I had finished my studies and worked in an office, of course an executive secretary doesn't earn badly, but it is not enough to live on in Peru, it is not enough to give your child what he needs. It isn't even US $100 a month. Lorena, it is not enough! For example, if I only leave once a week, I earn more than double in a month. I want my child to have a profession, that he can have the best possible.'

Our conversation came to a close with me managing to get her to think about regulation and its consequences. Her answers showed me once again how little the women knew about it and how they only thought about its consequences when asked to. Zoila's thoughts concerning hazards and risks were restricted to aspects which affected her personally.

After our conversation we went to the Crazy Horse, where we met Roberto outside. The place was nearly empty. A punkish looking woman sat at the bar and greeted Zoila. Zoila introduced me to Mariana, and we started to talk while Zoila and Roberto played their customary flirting game. She asked me where I came from; I told her I was born in the United States. Her mother remarried and lived there and she wanted to get a visa to visit her. 'Do you have any connections at the Embassy?'

'No', I replied, 'I am afraid I don't.'

She told me a little about her life: 'I used to live with my father and I went to university, I studied interpreting – Japanese and English – but when I started to have problems with his wife because of the way she treated my little sister, I had to move out and I stopped studying. A friend of mine got me into this. I just returned from Bolivia. I worked there in a club, dancing mostly, god how I love to dance. We also drank with the customers and received a commission for every drink they ordered. God, I drank so much but I earned a lot of money. I didn't save much though. I was living with an Argentinean; he choreographed the shows. He wasn't living off me but he never had any money. He had to send his money back to Argentina, to his family. Basically we ended up living on my money. So instead of coming back with $6,500 I came back with $2,500. I really want to get out of this, I am sick of it. Sure it's good money, but I want to go to the States, and maybe I will get married there. What I would love to do is work my way up dancing to the States – Bolivia, Argentina, Uruguay – and get to the States and never work in this again.'

While we talked a man walked in who was pretty drunk. Mariana told me he was a bit crazy. He left shortly after with two women. Zoila said, 'He did that to annoy me, because one time he asked me to leave with him and out of respect for a friend because he was her client I said no, so now every time he comes in he looks at me and leaves with another. Last night it was Mariana, tonight it is with those two.'

'I really don't feel like working tonight', Mariana said, 'I think I will go home.' She turned to me and said, 'It's a pity we didn't have more time to talk to each other.'

'Don't worry,' I replied, 'I will be around for a while.'

For the short period Mariana frequented the club – she did not come that often because she preferred picking up sailors at the harbour or going to another club – we talked together nearly the whole night. In the meantime,

I joined Zoila's and Roberto's conversation. Zoila told me her last escapade with a customer. Just about then, Roberto and I decided it was time to leave. I had just said good-bye to Zoila, when a client walked in. I told her I would come back on Friday and asked her to speak to the other women. Half listening and definitely more interested in the client than what I said, she abruptly replied, '*Sí, sí, sí*', as her eyes turned once again to the gentlemen who had just entered.

On one of the following nights several women were enjoying a plate of chicken and french fries they had managed to persuade a very drunk customer to buy. Once again, Roberto and Zoila were not talking to each other. It was in part a game and in part serious. Recently, Roberto had been spending a lot of time becoming acquainted with Soledad. Zoila could not stand her and Soledad said the feeling was mutual. Neither of them were very clear about their reasons for disliking each other. Different styles, jealousy about Roberto, racial problems? – one was a *mestiza* from the Sierra, the other was black, all of these things might have contributed to the animosity they felt for each other. They stayed out of each other's way and always had a comment if Roberto or myself spent some time with one of them.

Zoila introduced me to the women sitting next to her and when I kissed them hello, one of them hit me on my behind. She caught me by surprise. Laughing she said it was a Peruvian greeting. I replied with a sarcastic grunt. Mariana came in and the other women retreated to the corner of the bar they normally occupied. Mariana's frequent trips to the bathroom and the constant sniffing as if she had a cold gave me the impression she was sniffing coke. It did not, however, influence our conversation.

Zoila told Mariana about her experiences of the previous night. 'You should have stayed, Mariana, after you left the place filled up, unbelievable. I got really drunk last night. I spent the whole evening talking to that imbecile ... you remember, Lorena, it was the guy I was with the other night. He is always good for a good tip. But he really pissed me off. Another client came in, one of my regulars who is good for some good money. He waited for me the whole evening and finally got tired and left. When it was time for the imbecile to go he slipped me a tip not even enough for the taxi fare home.'

Mariana complained, 'I am really getting tired of this, I want to fuck this whole month and earn enough to leave and work my way up to the States. I want to start a new life there, get married.'

'Why is getting married important to you, why not study?' I asked.

'Because it is missing in my life, I miss a life with affection. Of course studying is also important.'

Zoila changed the subject, 'I earned US $50 tonight, I really needed the money, I haven't been earning anything lately. Mariana you are alone, therefore you can afford to pay an expensive rent, but I have a son who has school tuition, private English lessons, karate, so I have a lot of costs.'

'That's the point, if I was to work in another job I would only earn 3 million *Intis* and that just isn't enough', Mariana replied.

She continued, 'Did you see Juan? Juan was a regular who was said to be the son of a senator. He was known to come to drink but never left with any of the women. From their conversation it became obvious that Juan regularly left with Mariana.

'I thought he never left with anyone', I enquired.

Zoila replied, 'Only with Mariana. He just left and said he would be right back.'

'I hope so, because he has my passport, he said he could get me a visa for America because he had connections. He has had it for the past two weeks and I haven't heard anything yet. He wants to go out with me as boyfriend and girlfriend.'

I said, 'Maybe that's why he has taken so long. He doesn't want you to leave.'

'I am not in love with him and he is probably the *bien machista* [typically very macho] type who the first three months everything is okay, he accepts everything and then after awhile turns into another person and starts hitting you. He is not the only client who wants something serious.'

Zoila added, 'There have been several clients who wanted something serious with me, but my problem is I have a child. I knew an American who wanted me to marry him. I was interested. I stopped working the whole time he stayed here. We went out a lot. At the end of the three months the only thing he could offer was to put my son in a Peruvian boarding school. I can't leave my son. My mother is too old to look after a nine-year-old. What man would be willing to take on the costs of another man's child?'

'But if you could work as well, not in this, in something else, it could work out', I answered.

'Sure it would work out but what we would earn together would not be enough.'

At that moment a black man entered. Zoila asked me if I had ever had a black lover. It never ceased to amaze me the prejudices expressed every time a black man passed by or black men and sex were mentioned. Especially in this case, because Zoila is black. I replied affirmatively. Mariana told us, 'A week ago a boat came in from Jamaica. I usually work at the harbour, when a boat comes in I am usually with one guy until the boat leaves again. Anyway there were two Jamaicans who wanted to be with me and my girlfriend. My girlfriend asked me whether I was really going to go with a black man. I thought what a stupid question. He was great and he said he is going to write me and invited me to visit when he gets back to Jamaica, that would be great.'

Zoila recalled the time she left with a black man, 'When it came down to making it [she illustrated the size of his penis by placing one hand at one end of the bar and extending the other hand to the other end, the measurements were enormous], I swear it was that big.'

I chuckled in disbelief.

'I swear, Lorena, it was that big, I told him I am very sorry but I am still a virgin for your size.'

A client came in and beckoned to Zoila. Zoila left our company and Mariana and I continued our conversation.

Mariana is 24 years old and has a four-year-old daughter who lives with Mariana's godfather. She decided to leave her daughter with her godfather and his wife – 'really good people, with a lot of money who adore my daughter' – when her mother moved to the US. When she became pregnant she wanted to have an abortion but her mother would not let her. Her mother promised she would help bring up her child. With her mother's decision to move to the US, Mariana was left alone with her child and she felt she could not cope with her on her own and gave her godfather and his wife temporary custody. She was scared that her godfather would not give her daughter back. 'They adore her, they want to adopt her, but I don't want that, I want her to know I am her mother.' She intended to take her back when she was in another situation. She felt her work did not permit her to live with her daughter.

Mariana was different from many of the other women working there. She was not working directly for her child. Her child was well taken care of. Nonetheless, she felt she was pushed into the business for economic motives. Unlike many of the other women, she came from a good middle-class background which she was not ashamed to talk about. Moreover, she did not seem ashamed of selling sex. She appeared to enjoy it. It was instrumental in improving her well-being.[3]

'I was living in Lince [a district of Lima] and one day I ran into an old girlfriend when I was working at a department store in the middle of Miraflores. I was working as a secretary. I quit university because my father stopped paying my tuition and we weren't on speaking terms. Moreover, I did not have any time to study because I was occupied from nine in the morning to nine at night, seven days a week. I finished work at four and then I went to a computer course. Then they changed my schedule and I had to work at night so I had to drop the course. One day, when I was working in customer services, I met this friend. We chatted, and when the store closed we went for a drink. She had changed a lot. We had a few drinks which loosened our tongues. She told me about her work in a night club. She started to work because her father went to Venezuela about two years before and they never heard from him again. She had younger brothers and a sister and had to help her mother. She told me how much she earned. I was very impressed. She earned nightly one or two month's salaries, I couldn't believe it. The money I earned did not stretch very far and I lived alone. I had to pay rent, for my food, for my clothes, you know: to eat well, dress well, for my fancies. Before my father gave me everything. When I used to work for him he didn't give me a salary, he gave me everything I wanted. Now I had to do everything alone. About three years ago I began to work in this. It upset me at first, not sexually because I already had sexual experience, but to leave with different men in the same night. I was a bit nervous at first, but when I had the money in my hand – you might think I am lying – you begin to like it in a certain way. You are able to resolve your own economic problems, it is a solution. I began to feel different. After three or four months, I felt different. I was financially better off, I could pay my expenses, do whatever I wanted with my life. In spite of the money I am not happy. I feel emotionally unstable. I don't feel good doing this, I want to do something else. I want to live with my daughter, have a home and a partner, do you understand – emotionally. Economically I am not badly off, I am not swimming in money, I am okay, I can support myself without any problems. But this isn't everything, I am looking for more. I am looking for something else, something which is going to make me feel stable. I don't have a peaceful life, Okay I go to the gym, it is a way of relaxing, I run, but later on I have to get ready for work. I have to change, I don't know what type of people I will meet, I don't know how it will go, till what time I have to stay up, if I will go to a hotel early or won't leave at all, you understand what I mean? Maybe it will be a waste of time or it could be an excellent night, but I always have to keep a good attitude. But I want to leave, I want to get out of this. If I don't get my visa for the States I want to go to Europe and work a year there, save money in a more or less short period of time and then go to my mother. One year in Europe and then the States. The day I set foot in the United States, I will never work again in a cabaret, I will never work again like this, of course I will work in something else to contribute to my mother's household, but in honest work, and I will study. I would love to go and work in Europe, I like the Italian men, I mean the European men. But if I do get a visa for the United States, then you know what I would really like to do? I want to go to Bolivia, pick up the things that I left there and for three months, not much longer than that I want to do shows, not nude shows. I would have some pictures taken in my beautiful dance costumes and leave, it would be my farewell to this world.'

Mariana's desire to leave the country must have been overwhelming. Shortly after our last conversation, she stopped showing up at the Crazy Horse. I assumed she was working at one of her preferred places. However, one day I found out what had really happened. She had left the country in a hurry. She had stolen US $3,500 from a Korean client and the police were after her. The police came to the Crazy Horse looking for her. Juan never returned her passport. She was travelling on false documents that expired in a week. She took Paraguay Airlines to Europe and was off to Spain where she hoped to meet up with her friends who, she told me on another occasion, had been working there for a while and had been earning good money. In general, the women working at the Crazy Horse were totally surprised by Mariana's actions. Of course they all knew women who stole from clients but they could never imagine Mariana doing it, and even more so stealing that amount of money. I, too, was surprised, but for different reasons. It made me realize how real her desires were to get out of Peru. It was not just an ongoing fantasy or strong desire, as it was for other women I knew. Mariana had, at least, accomplished the initial phase of her plan.


*Soledad*

We entered the Crazy Horse and I immediately sat down with Zoila. Seated next to her was a very shy woman whom I had never seen before. She gave the impression that she was a novice and Zoila had taken her under her wing. Zoila told me she had been working for years. However, in our following conversation she told me she recently started to work because her husband was in jail and she had no money to support herself and her children. Roberto immediately sat down next to Soledad and left the three of us alone together. Zoila said, 'Lorena, remember that guy who came in the other night? Well he finally left with me, he was excellent.'

I surveyed the bar quickly and asked her about a curly headed man who was standing there.

'Oh, him. He is the bodyguard of that guy over there. He goes everywhere with him.'

As Soledad passed by to go to the bathroom, she pulled me aside. She said, 'One day I want to invite you and Roberto to my house for *cebiche* [a Peruvian fish speciality].'

'That would be lovely', I replied.

'My house is modest but it has a huge heart, which is the most important.'

I went back to Zoila. A very drunk guy reeking of garlic interrupted our conversation. The other women kept away from him because he had an annoying manner. He asked me to dance. Zoila whispered in my ear, 'Tell him you ask 500,000 *Intis* for a dance.'

Timidly, I repeated what she said, he did not hear me. She repeated it for me. Marco came over to coax me to dance with him. He must have been a very important customer because Marco rarely got involved with the dealings between the clients and the women. Finally, the other woman went to dance with him. When she returned from the dance floor she said, 'And he can't even dance.'

Two men entered and they started a conversation with Zoila and her girlfriend. I slipped off to the booth and joined Soledad and Roberto. Roberto left and two men sat down across from us. One of the men suggested I change seats with his friend. Soledad replied, 'It's fine like this, thank you.'

We exchanged a few words, Soledad excused herself and said she would be right back. However, it was her way of getting herself out of the situation. So there I was sitting alone with them, I excused myself and went over to her. I sarcastically expressed my gratitude for leaving me there.

She replied dryly, 'I expected you to come over here.'

Soledad is about 28 years old and a Bolivian citizen. She came to Peru when she was 14, when she fell in love with a Peruvian. She had worked as a manager of a restaurant and in business, going to buy goods in Arica and selling them here.[4]

'Well, why did you start working here?'

'Because it earns more and besides, there is another reason I almost forgot, it gives me time to be with my child. I get home at four in the morning and sleep until nine and then I have all the time I want to spend with him until eight at night when I get ready to come here.'

Soledad has a son aged two and a half, and also takes care of her two Bolivian nieces, plus a woman who takes care of the children, and the woman's child. We talked about children.

I said, 'Until recently, when I thought about having children, I only wanted to have a daughter because I can identify easier with a girl.'

She said, 'I am very happy I have a son because men suffer less than women.' She described herself as a woman prone to tyrannies at home and always screaming, especially at the girl who works for her. Just then, a man entered the club. Soledad abruptly stopped talking, excused herself and went over to him. I used this moment to go to the bathroom. When I looked in the mirror and saw my face, it was telling me it was time to go. I asked Roberto to accompany me to my house in the taxi, but he said he could not because Zoila had just invited him to make love in a hotel and he had to come back afterwards to get himself out of the situation. He walked me to the taxi. When we left Zoila looked peeved.

The club was nearly empty. At the far end of the bar, a woman leaned against the wall who looked like Soledad but it was so dark, I could not be certain. Business was definitely slow and all the women were complaining. Zoila had just arrived back from a client. Roberto went over to the woman, who turned out to be Soledad. Zoila told me she had a fight with Soledad but when I asked for details she was evasive.

'Why don't you get along?'

'I don't like the way she acts', she replied.

Two guys came in and one of them was her friend. He pulled her aside to talk for a moment. When she came back she handed Marco some money (I realize now it was the bar fee. At that time I imagined the wildest things.) She left with her friend.

I went over to Soledad who was still seated next to Roberto. I acted as though I was offended because she had not come over to greet me. She told me she was offended, too. 'Why?', I enquired.

'Because I do not like the way Roberto behaved with Zoila the other night. He acted like a dog with his tail between his legs.'

I assumed she had observed Roberto's behaviour the night he explained to Zoila why he would not go to a hotel with her. They quarrelled. I became more and more convinced Zoila and Soledad were fighting about Roberto. Roberto decided to take a walk outside and Soledad and I were left alone for a moment until Marco came over, 'The client in the corner is asking for you.'

'What do you mean? I don't know him.'

'What do you mean you don't know him? You were with him last night.'

She turned to me and said, 'If I don't know the client I will be right back.'

Soledad remained at the other side of the bar for the remainder of the evening. Right before she left with the client, Roberto came back. She ran over to him and said, 'I requested a song and I am dedicating it to you.'

The song was about a man who was ugly and used women. On her way out she whispered in Roberto's ear, 'I bet Zoila dedicates prettier songs to you.'

Time passed and Soledad had been absent from the club for a while. Hence I was surprised to see her sitting there again, next to a woman who had recently started working. 'Hi Soledad, how have you been? Where have you been?'

She said, 'I have a *marido*, my *taxista* [taxi driver].[5] Therefore, I haven't been coming so often.' She took me outside to meet him. Out of a yellow Volkswagen beetle emerged a man with a very friendly face whom she introduced as Alfredo. She introduced me to him as a friend, 'a writer like Vargas Llosa'. We went back downstairs. 'You see I wasn't lying.'

'I didn't think you were', I replied.

'What do you think of him?'

'He seems really nice, he has a friendly face. How did you meet him?'

'I have know him for years but we just started to go together ten days ago.'

'Is he single?'

'Yes, I don't want anything to do with married men. He wants me to stop working, but he doesn't have enough money to support me. He works during the day as a cashier at a restaurant and at night he drives a taxi.'

The new woman joined us and we lifted our drinks for a toast. Soledad said, '*Salud, amor y dinero*' (Health, love and money).

The other woman corrected her, '*Salud, dinero y amor*' (Health, money and love).

I asked them if they thought money was the most important thing and added, 'I want enough money to be able to do what I want and not to worry.'

'I want to be rich, I want lots and lots of money', the other woman answered.

Soledad said, 'I want enough to be happy, to have everything I need.'

Her relationship with Alfredo would be short-lived. The next time I saw her, I enquired about her *marido*. 'So-so', she replied. 'He cares a lot about me, but it seems like when a man loves me I can't love him, but when I have to work so that the man will love me, I love him but he doesn't love me. I am thinking of going to a psychologist. What do they do exactly?'

I explained a bit. 'They don't give you solutions to your problems, they give you tools to solve your problems. Some go back to your childhood, others work in the present.'

To which she replied 'I have been working since I was six years old. Alfredo wants me to stop working in this. He wants us to start a business together selling French whisky. I am not sure. It is a good business but I am not sure if I want to take the risk. We are living together now.' A couple of weeks later, Alfredo was history. The relationship had fizzled out.

In all the time I was visiting the Crazy Horse business was never booming, in fact most of the women commented how different things had been in the past. One of the factors which played a role in the situation was the *paquetazo*. Business was definitely slow, yet there was no noticeable change in the women's behaviour with regard to the clients. Their interactions with clients were filtered through a screen of indifference. There were no outward signs that they tried harder to get or please a client. It was still common to hear a woman tell a story about how she managed to keep the client in his place, repeating the sarcastic remarks. There were two types of stories. One accentuated their control of the situation, while the other highlighted the fine time and the good money, making it into a most memorable experience. In both cases, they were implying that they were good at their work.

Soledad did not exactly fit this mould. She rarely talked about work. I never heard her recalling a pleasant moment with a client or bragging about how she dominated the situation. She painted herself as a women who only did what she wanted and nothing more, none of those *cochinadas* (dirty things) which usually meant certain types of kinky sex. If she did see more in her work than a distasteful means to earn a living, she kept it to herself. I rarely saw her smile.

Business reached one of its lows. Nonetheless, when I came in that evening Suzanna, one of the other women who worked at the club, told me Soledad had left with a client. Shortly after, she returned. She explained she had left with a client but he did not have any money. 'It was a waste of time. Luckily I ran into someone else, and although I did it for less, at least I earned some money. I need a lot of money.' Business must have been awful because Soledad always protested when a woman wanted to leave for less money. She claimed it made work for the others impossible. I remember when she was teaching a new woman the ropes, and a client offered her US $10. The woman wanted to accept the offer but finally declined because of Soledad's sermon.

Her anguish concerning her financial situation increased because of her recent move to the piece of property she had bought, far outside the outskirts of Lima. She was gradually constructing her house. Currently, they were still living in a hut made of *esteras*. She managed to trade two cement poles with a neighbour for a truckload of stones which she intended to use for the floor. She complained, 'I haven't even been able to raise one wall.' Living at such a great distance from the club affected her possibilities for work, and thus her income. She could not come as often as she wanted to and when she did work she had to wait outside until six in the morning to take the first bus back home. Nonetheless, her determination to improve her situation grew. On one occasion, she sat at the bar drawing up a grocery list and calculating prices. Someone offered her the opportunity to re-open and manage a restaurant which had been closed for a while. She only needed enough money to buy the required stock. However, this dream disintegrated just as quickly as it materialized. Shortly after, she announced she intended to go to the provinces to try her luck in the *selva*. It was always rumoured that in the *selva* or the petroleum camps a woman could make some good money. Soledad disappeared for a while. In less than a month she would be sitting in her usual place again.

I asked her, 'How did it go?'

'It was horrible. Our bus was held by terrorists for four hours.'

'What!?', I exclaimed, somewhat astounded.

'I went to the *selva* to a drug town, it was dangerous and there was no business, it wasn't worth it. Well at least I tried, now I know what it is like.'

'How were things when you got home?' I inquired.

'The bills were waiting for me. Luckily I am part of a *junta* (a rotating credit fund) and it was my turn so I could pay the bills.'

Although she would not come as often as she used to, Soledad would still come regularly.


*Suzanna and her Friends*

Suzanna and Gina rarely missed a night of work, except on the occasions they went back to their *tierras* (literally 'lands', it denotes one's birthplace) to visit their children. Gina's three children lived with her mother in the *selva* region, Suzanna had one daughter, and came from a southern provincial city situated relatively close to the capital. She owned her own house in Lima and lived there with her brothers. The other women pointed to Suzanna's accomplishment as if it was ideal. She was the only one among them who had managed to obtain such a material accomplishment with her work. Gina rented a room from Soledad. During the course of fieldwork she moved several times and ended up sharing a place with either Lola or Dolores. At times Gina and Suzanna appeared inseparable. In the club they always retreated to the same corner of the bar whispering continually or sharing the silence. Often they left together with the same client. And then I suddenly observed that they no longer sat together. Suzanna said that they just needed some space, and a short period would elapse before they would go back to their usual seating arrangement. Lola and Dolores often joined them. Dolores often stopped working for longer periods of time. It was said her *marido*, a retired marine officer, did not permit her to work when she was in Lima. Sometimes he sent her an allowance when she went back to her *tierra* to be with her children. She stayed away months at a time. When Lola was in Lima, she showed up like clockwork, working to save money so she could go back to her *tierra* for longer periods of time. She and Lola, Gina and Suzanna formed a clique. Perhaps their similar situations, living in Lima separated from their children, drew them together. Their lives were divided more sharply in two than those of the women who lived in Lima with their children. Soledad called them Marco's spies and would get really annoyed to see what she considered their arse-licking behaviour whenever Marco was nearby. Marco did spend a lot of time with them. I always wondered what secrets they shared together. Almost every time I was nearby the conversation circled around some highly sexual remark, but I never found out all the details.

Gina and Suzanna were tough cookies. After talking to Gina for the first time, I realized she was the woman who had hit me on the behind on one of my first evenings there. She was always inclined to put her hand where it wasn't wanted. Eventually, I responded to her action by repeating her gesture, which astonished her. On the first night I made an attempt to talk to them, they did not make it very easy for me. Suzanna expressed her unwillingness, among other ways, by changing one pseudonym for another. Changing her work name was a definite attempt to make herself totally disappear into anonymity, a trick the women used occasionally when the police entered the club.

Suzanna was known to be very popular or very lucky with the clients. She left often. Marco claimed her nickname was *Eléctrica* (electric) because there were nights she left six times, while the other women had difficulty leaving once. Gina had the reputation of doing *cochinadas* including anal sex. Both of them were shrewd when it came to evaluating or approaching the clients. And they hoped to be blessed nightly with a *gringo*. Suzanna rarely spoke about the clients affectionately. While some women went home after being with a client, she always came back to work some more. She seemed to look at every relationship in the nightlife in terms of what she could get out of it. That feeling never totally disappeared, even when she stopped asking me for imported shampoos or the like.

On that first evening together I had the strong sensation they intended to steal some money from my pocketbook, Gina grabbed my breast and I only received remarks such as, 'The only way you will find out what it is like is if you do it yourself', or referring to the client Juan, 'He has Aids, why don't you go off with him?' Nonetheless, as time passed, I came to cherish my relationship with Suzanna. Gina rarely let her guard down, but Suzanna and I started to appreciate each other. Perhaps the ice broke the night I came in with a bag of corn chips and we discovered our mutual love of salty things and devoured the bag together.

One night she asked me if I had any imported condoms. At this moment I had not yet begun with condom distribution. I told her the only imported condoms I had were for personal use. She pretended to act surprised to which I replied, 'Don't act as if you think I am completely innocent, you know I have a sex life. In these times everyone has to protect themselves whether you are working in the nightlife or not.'

She took two German condoms out of her pocket and showed them to me. 'The other women say I don't use them, but as you can see I do.'

This was not the first time that I was shown condoms without asking about them to counteract rumours concerning a woman's reputation. Hypothetically, not using condoms defines a woman as a bad whore. Throughout the evening several clients kept eyeing us, one of them came over and asked me to dance but I declined. Meanwhile his friend futilely tried to pay his bill with a credit card. He then came over and made an overture to Suzanna. Suzanna remarked that she had already seen him in the company of another girl.

'Don't worry', he replied, 'I will get rid of her.'

'I only accept cash.'

'How much?'

'US $50.'

'Can't we negotiate?'

'No!' She kept a firm stand. His friend came over and joined him and asked me to dance again while he put his arm around me and caressed my neck. Suzanna replied, 'She charges US $50 too.' She knew they couldn't afford it. And then he said something which turned my stomach every time I heard a client say it, 'You know, I really respect you women.' I took his arm off me. He went over to his friend, we knew he would not come back.

I said, 'I can't stand that line. If someone respects you there is no need to say it, you show it.' I turned to Suzanna and said, 'You know I was in your hands because you know I would not have left, don't you?'

'Yes,' she replied. She complained again about her headache. I suggested she go home, but she would not leave because she had not earned enough money yet.

The next time I came I brought condoms. Gina, Suzanna and Zoila sat together. Marco sat next to Suzanna holding her legs. I kissed everyone hello and asked Zoila how she was. 'Horrible. Last night I left with a client, a very old man, ugh, he was disgusting.'

Marco teased, 'I just proposed to Suzanna before you came in.'

Suzanna turned to me and said, 'Did you bring them?' 'Yes, let's go over to the corner of the bar and I will give you some.'

I opened my purse and gave her 20. She was happy. I enquired as to Soledad's whereabouts. She had not come yet. Gina came over, 'Give me mine', and demanded two more strips than she had asked for originally. 'That's just in case the thing is too big. The condom sometimes breaks.' Zoila asked for one a night, I gave her an extra five just in case they broke. I gave each of them a folder concerning the Aids information hotline, 'You can call them up to ask about anything you want to.'

When Gina left, Suzanna said, 'Don't give any to Gina, she just bought a box of 500, she doesn't need them. Soledad needs them, Zoila needs them but she doesn't.'

Her honesty surprised me but I doubted her motives. If I could have been certain she was not using condom distribution to favour some women and try to put other women at a disadvantage, I would have appreciated her advice more. Every time she began to tell me who should have and who should not, which would happen regularly from this moment on, I felt in a predicament. I could not accept her advice. But I could not show I rejected it either because she acted as if she did it on my behalf.

After the distribution ritual we went back to our seats. One of the bartenders said, 'Señorita, I am waiting for my present.'

I gave him and Marco one, too. I sat down next to Suzanna, but there was nothing going on. A conversation developed about Aids. Suzanna said, 'Everyone has to use them nowadays, not only us; Lorena, you use them too don't you?'

'Yes I do.'

'Well I want to use them', Gina said, 'just in case I remarry.'

Marco said, 'I never used them, never, never, never, I only do it with my wife.'

'But you are not married', I replied.

The other women laughed.

'Suzanna, did you ever test yourself?'

'No, when I get out of the business I will.'

Marco said, 'You should test yourself while you are working because if the police arrive and you don't have all your certificates in order they can pull you in.'

Marco said, 'Gina wants to see you naked.'

I replied, 'It doesn't surprise me.'

'Many clients say you have a beautiful body, many clients tell me that.'

'So, I guess I chose the wrong profession', I replied. Gina asked, 'What are the symptoms of Aids?'

I started to recall a few, 'Excessive weight loss, diarrhoea ... '

Zoila said, 'Why don't you call up that telephone number Lorena gave you, you can call from a phone booth and ask anything you want.'

Gina seemed nervous. She was silent for a moment and then said, 'I don't want to die.'

Jesús passed by. She stopped him and said, 'Lorena is in love with you.'

I replied, 'Don't pay any attention to her. Gina suffers from time to time from mental delusions.'

Everybody laughed and she said, 'You really got me this time.'

Satisfied, I replied, 'Finally.'

We talked about risky positions. I said oral sex – we used the term 'putting it in your mouth' – is not without any risk. The women were surprised. I explained that in other countries women have become so experienced they can put a condom on with their mouth without the client knowing or feeling it.

Zoila said, 'That is disgusting, I would throw up.' Gina said, using her customary graphic descriptions, 'But if you use a towel and every so often you spit out on the towel, isn't that enough? ... When a client comes on my chest I wash it off with very hot water afterwards.' She repeated it again.

I said, 'That is not a risky position.' From their reactions I realized they knew very little about prevention and the causes of Aids.

'The most risky position is anal sex.' Gina replied, 'Although I think money is very important, even if someone offered me US $500 I would not do it.'

Zoila exclaimed in disbelief, 'What did you say?'

Gina repeated herself. Zoila laughed. I asked her later why she was laughing. She maintained that Gina does do anal sex. Marco interrupted Gina and started to contradict her. Gina said, 'You should listen less to the clients and more to us.'

Someone asked, 'Is it true that the percentage among prostitutes is very high?'

I told them that it was still quite low but that that was even more of a reason to protect and take care of oneself now. Suzanna repeated what she said earlier, 'When I retire I will take the test.'

'When will that be?', I replied.

'Years from now.' Zoila put on an old woman's voice and acted as if she was approaching a client.

We laughed and I said, 'She will keep working even if she has to use a cane.'

Gina and Suzanna went over to different clients and Marco disappeared. I was left alone with Roberto and Zoila. It was time to go, but Zoila implied that she would appreciate it if we would stay a bit longer, until that very annoying, hyper client would disappear. He kept coming over trying to pick her up. He finally did retire from the establishment and we said goodnight to Zoila. She answered with a monologue concerning how she was a professional and she should not hate him but he should respect her. When she finished we left for the night.

Every time I came in Suzanna called me over to sit next to her. She claimed I brought her good luck. She began with her sermon how I should not give condoms to Gina and Lola and Esperanza, a woman who had just started working recently and was doing well for herself. Suzanna did not like her and tried to make her life miserable. I asked her why. She said 'Gina and Lola are abusing you.'

'What about Esperanza?'

'She makes me furious.'

'Suzanna, I am not going to use your criteria to give out condoms.'

She kept interrupting me, 'Okay, okay', trying to calm me down, 'just give them ten a piece to keep them quiet.' Trying to find out the truth, I went over to Zoila and asked her whether she thought there was someone trying to take advantage of me with the condoms, 'Is there anyone I should not be giving condoms to?'

'Yes, Gina.'

I went back to my seat and decided from that moment onward I would not make a great attempt to approach Gina about the condoms. With a look of contentment on her face, Suzanna confided, 'The other night I had a client who paid me $150. Don't tell the other women.'

We sat there for a few moments in silence. I had been waiting for the moment to ask her to do a life story with me. This seemed a good a time as any to ask her.

'Suzanna, do you have faith in my work?'

'What exactly are you doing?'

I was taken aback because, although I had told her a while ago why I was there, clearly it had not sunk in. I explained my objectives to her and the idea of the life story. 'I would like to do one with you.'

She was pensive a moment and replied, 'I think it is better if you do it with other women instead of me, I am not the right type for it.'

'Why?'

'I have left the past behind, me, I don't want to think about it, I don't think about the future, I just live in the present. I don't want to think about it because I don't want to recognize how I earn my money. I earn my money in an ugly way. I don't talk to anyone, I have always kept things to myself. I don't even talk to my mother, if she asks me too many questions I become annoyed, that's the way I am.'

'But Suzanna, don't you need to talk to someone once in a while, to unload?'

'If I need to talk to anyone I have the girls here, they are in the same scene as me.'

A little while earlier she said she did not confide in the other women here. I reminded her of what she had said previously, that she lies and does not tell them everything. She said, '*La mentira tranquiliza*' (lies soothe).

'So are you lying to me right now?'

'No', she replied.

I admired her honesty, but felt extremely sad. The calculating, business-like woman who I imagined her to be was her working profile, which covered over the pain and depression she felt about her life. She could tuck it away while she worked, but it emerged to the surface at the slightest moment dedicated to reflection.

Christmas approached and I asked her about her holiday plans. 'I am going home and will come back the following day. I will go back on the 29th and return to Lima for New Year's. I don't know what I will do, last year I spent New Year's at the club, I didn't have anywhere else to go. I will never do that again. Maybe I will find a party this year, I don't know. I am tired, I want peace, I want stability, but I am not going to a party so that I will get involved with some Peruvian who isn't worth it.'

At different times Gina participated in our conversation. She told us she was planning to go back to her *tierra* for a month. I kept my back turned to her. Experience had taught me not too pay too much attention to her because she usually threw it back in my face. I was surprised to see her interest in our conversation. She slid her stool over and asked Suzanna, 'But doesn't your daughter give you satisfaction?'

'She is not with me, no she doesn't. I want someone by my side who could give me affection and stability.'

'It's different for me, they give me joy so I don't need someone else. When I go home, I pick up the children from school, I clean the house. I do all the cooking, I don't let the girl cook. Sometimes about six-thirty or seven in the evening I go to bed because I am so exhausted. My children, who are nine, eight and six years old, gather around to talk to me and stroke my hair.'

'I am tired, I want to get out of this. I want to go somewhere else.'

'Why don't you?', I replied.

'It isn't easy', Suzanna said.

Gina said, 'Well I have faith in myself and faith in God, and one day I am going to leave. I am going to get my visa for the States, I have my connections and I will work in any type of work, it doesn't matter, as long as it is not this. I have been working two years in this and it is tiring, it drains you. Before, I used to sell food on the street. Suzanna has been working here for a year and before that she worked at another place.'

After the holidays, I noticed a change in Suzanna's attitude. She seemed fed up. She sat a few seats away from me trying to hold a conversation with a soft-spoken Canadian who only spoke a few words of Spanish and she only spoke a few words of English. He was the type of *gringo* who did not have sex with a prostitute. He came for the company. I called above the sound of the music to her, 'How are you doing?' Smiling at her companion, looking in his eyes (knowing he could not understand her), she said, 'I am sick of this', and continued to look at him with a big smile on her face. I never saw her act like that before. At one point she called me over to act as translator. I stayed there the rest of the night. She was only interested in one thing, the money. Every so often she would get bored and turn to me and say she wanted her tip, 'Ask him for my tip.' Then she would act interested again, followed by a demand for her tip. I had a hard time balancing both attitudes. Her lack of interest did not stop her from making sure he did not get ripped off by the establishment. The male employees had a tendency to try to squeeze as much money as possible out of the *gringos*. Even the disc jockey came over at regular intervals, shamelessly asking him for a hand-out. As the night progressed, Roberto and I talked to him more. He asked me what a good tip was. I asked Roberto who knew more on the subject than I did. Before he left he gave Suzanna the tip. She did not attempt to cover up her disappointment. She obviously expected more.

Although Suzanna thought about meeting her friends who were working as prostitutes in Spain, she also had her hopes set on meeting a *gringo* who would take her away from here. She decided to come to Holland and fantasized about visiting me there. She gave me instructions about the type of man I should look for: rich, honest, a worker. 'Should he be handsome?', I enquired.

'A little bit. Lorena, I will work in anything, and I won't bother you, don't worry.'

Sometime later in another conversation she repeated her intention to come to Holland, 'I heard you can make a lot of money working as a whore. You don't have to worry, I won't bother you, I will be sleeping while you are working and when you are up I will be working.'

I asked, 'Have you changed your mind? A while ago you told me you would not work as a whore.'

'Well if nothing else comes up I can always use it as a last resort. I can imagine how you will treat me in Holland, after all the things I did to you?'

'What things?', I innocently enquired, silently remembering how she and Gina had intended to steal some money from my pocketbook on our first encounter.

'All the times I talked fast so that you could not understand anything I said. You know I am going there to look for a husband.'

I nodded.

'Look, I have got money, money is not the problem, but I am still not happy, so what's the use of having money, if you don't have the things you want? I will be coming in August or September, don't be surprised.'

Things would continue as they always did. I would sit next to her and be her good luck charm. We shared corn chips together. She talked to me when she was interested and ignored me when she was not. She would ask me for her ration of condoms and tell me who I should and should not give them to. This routine would be interrupted every time a client came in who took an interest in her. Nothing changed. Whether she was sick of it all or not, Suzanna never missed an evening.

### Esperanza

One day Esperanza appeared in the Crazy Horse out of nowhere. She did not know anyone who worked there. There was no girlfriend who introduced her to it, which is the grand narrative of many of the women working in the *ambiente*. She maintained that once she had dated a Brazilian and they stopped for a drink at the Crazy Horse. 'I was so naive, I did not know what type of place this was. He told me this was the type of place where women accompanied men. So when I needed work I came here immediately. I have been working in this a month and a half.'

Esperanza was a petite young woman who had an expression on her face as if she was more prepared to be someone's younger sister than a prostitute. She said she lived alone with her four-year-old daughter in Chorrillos. Her mother and brothers lived in Rimac.[6] She had studied to be a travel agent and could not find work in it.

Suzanna and her friends did not receive the new arrival warmly. As I said earlier, Suzanna tried to make her life miserable and she succeeded to a certain extent, spreading rumours which questioned her innocence and insinuated that she had been working as a whore for some time. All this forced Esperanza to seek refuge in the company of Zoila.

Esperanza described the other women as cheats and liars and related an incident which had happened some nights before. 'A few nights ago a man came in with a few *gringos*. He always comes with different *gringos*. He wanted me to leave with him. I asked the girls whether he was all right. They said he was no problem. After we finished he didn't want to pay me, he said "Ask the Italians", those were the guys he brought to the Crazy Horse. I replied I wasn't with the Italians, I was with him. "You can do this to other women, but I am a first-class whore and you are going to pay me." He finally paid. The thing that got me is the other girls knew and they let me go with him without warning me he would give me trouble.'

Just then a client came in and she disappeared to the back with him. I sat next to Suzanna and when he came to pay their bill before leaving with Esperanza, Suzanna turned to him and made a nasty remark about her. Trying to demonstrate his indifference to her remark, he turned to me and said in a loud voice, 'You know your friend Esperanza is wonderful.'

Esperanza would pass the initiation rites with flying colours. At least that is my interpretation of her initial period working there. Sometime later, when I came in, Suzanna and her friends and Marco were talking about Esperanza, who had just left because she felt really depressed and did not feel like working. Everyone complimented her: the way she dressed, the number of clients she had and how she sometimes left twice a night. Their compliments implied that she was a good whore and, to my surprise, Suzanna was the most animated in the conversation. Financially speaking, Esperanza appeared to be doing well for herself. But she had a great deal of difficulty in adjusting to the work emotionally. She frequently felt depressed and did not feel like working. Originally she had planned to work six months, but she delayed her retirement. 'I am going to have to sacrifice myself a bit more before I can leave this work and work in something else. I spent a lot of money on my daughter and my family for Christmas.'

We were trying to have a conversation, nearly screaming to be heard above the music and then, in the middle of our conversation, the music stopped for what felt like an eternity, catching us screaming at the top of our lungs. We laughed. Esperanza said, 'This place is really ugly without music.' She had taken her daughter back to live with her mother because she could not bear seeing her. 'I come home and fall asleep with the television on.' She is a very religious woman and told Roberto that Mary Magdalene had appeared in her room several times. She was torturing herself and wanted help. She asked us if we could help her get in touch with a therapist.[7]

She described herself as an honest person who could not take advantage of anyone. She illustrated this with a story concerning a Chinese man (*un chino*) whom she had dated for several months. 'A good man who treated me well. He asked me to marry him and I felt pressured from everyone because he was economically better off than myself. But I could not do it. I didn't love him. There is only one man I truly love and that is my *marido*. But he is a drug addict. I had to leave him, drugs destroy everyone and everything.' There were several things that Esperanza wanted to talk to me about in detail, but we decided it would be better to wait until we were doing a life story.

When we walked into the Crazy Horse the place was totally empty except for Soledad, who sat alone in a corner of the bar. That was peculiar. On Wednesday nights there would be at least a few women present, but there was no one. I went over to Marco and asked, 'Where did everyone go?'

He said innocently, 'I don't know. Tuesday is my night off. I came in tonight and no one was here.'

I asked one of the bartenders and he replied jokingly, 'Maybe they are on strike.'

He stood close to Soledad, who answered my question cautiously, winking to tell me she would give me the details later. She replied, 'There was a raid, the others were picked up.'

I could not wait to hear the details and asked the other bartender what happened. He replied, 'I don't know, I just came back from Cajamarca.'

I asked, 'Was there a raid yesterday?'

'It appears so, they picked up three women.' He would not tell me any more.

So I asked the disc jockey and he said it was true. 'Six policemen came in and took Lola, Gina, Dolores and Esperanza.'

'But why now? Since I have been coming here there has never been a raid.'

'When they change the commander, they usually raid', he replied.

It amazed me how everyone had tried to keep it from me.

I went back to Soledad. The bartender frequently interrupted our conversation. She claimed Marco sent him over to spy on us. 'Why weren't you picked up?'

'It was not my time.'

I felt really bad for them and was concerned for Esperanza. But everyone around me reacted as if it was all a part of the game.

'Marco must be really pissed off that his girls – his spies – were taken in and I was not. I was with a client.'

Many rumours circulated concerning the incident. One of the other women said they were not picked up by the police but by the bomb squad. An unlikely story. Roberto had heard that since their release they were hanging out at a nearby disco because they were afraid of being picked up again in a raid. None of the rumours were true. They stayed away because they needed some time to rest. They had had to sleep in an upright position for two days.

'Gina, it is so good to see you, I was worried about all of you.'

'You heard?'

'Yes, I heard you were kept at the precinct.'

'Yeah, nobody came to help us. We would have probably been let out a lot earlier if someone from the club had come, but no one came.'

'How did Esperanza take it?' Gina confirmed my fears that she had taken it really badly.

'She won't be coming back. Dolores went back to her *viejo* [her old man, referring to her *marido*]. They kept us for two days. It was an ugly experience. We were locked up with transvestites and homosexuals. The transvestites took off their clothes, pissed and shit on the floor. It was horrible.'

'Did the police treat you decently?', I asked (this was an accepted code to ask whether they were sexually abused). 'Yes', she replied.

'Were you booked?'

'No, because we were picked up with so many people; there were girls that had nothing to do with it who were eating at a restaurant at the plaza, who were also picked up. We told them that we were eating at a restaurant when they picked us up and we had nothing to do with prostitution. That is why we were not booked. But I have to get a lawyer to take care of the rest. I have to get the papers out of their archives, don't forget I have children.'

I tried to find out more about Esperanza, but she could not tell me anything.

A few days later, Roberto ran into Esperanza waiting for a bus on a street corner. She told him her experience in jail was the push she needed to get out. She said she would never return. She ended their conversation saying she still intended to call me. She never did.


PERFORMING THE PROSTITUTE

The Crazy Horse provides a space where the embodiment and the enactment of the prostitute takes place. The women working there exercise a particular form of prostitution whereby the performance of the prostitute is repeatedly mediated through their interactions with the clients and acquires substance in their relationships with their colleagues and, temporarily, with myself. The Crazy Horse is not a stage where the players effortlessly remove their masks upon completing their performances. However, the women did not recoil from using a touch of melodrama when necessary, or creating illusions or lies when they saw fit. Rather it is another gendered enclosure that limits their room to manoeuvre.

This chapter has presented several profiles of women who enact and embody their performance of the prostitute differently. One of the things they all have in common is that they cannot go beyond the four walls which mark their movements. The wall's resilient nature bounces them back to their place, unless they make the decision to climb over and leave it all behind them.

Zoila's ambivalent posture towards the clients encapsulates two sides of her performance of her identity as a prostitute. On the one hand, through her actions and conversations, she attempted to belittle the clients. Sometimes this was aimed to show how bright and quick she was, at other times it was an expression of her contempt. Nonetheless, this was meant to show she was in control. On the other hand, she was an expert in creating good moments or the illusion of one for herself. These were memorable moments which made it easier to forget or deny what she was doing. She would retell choice segments of encounters with clients which reinforced this, or say how she had just let a good client slip between her fingers because she had misjudged the situation.

Mariana did not seem to have the least bit of remorse over entering the trade, even though she had various complaints. The money she made washed away much of the pain she felt about being a prostitute and she seemed to enjoy her encounters, particularly with foreigners. When she stole that money, she took her future into her own hands and gave herself the possibility of realizing her dreams. She was able to work towards her final goal: attempting to earn as much as possible before leaving the stage (and here the word 'stage' is apt, because she might have ended up dancing her way to the United States). She talked about her work in a completely different way from the other women who worked there and in her enactments she was the opposite of many of them. She did not let working as a prostitute paralyse her, or let it make her suffer too much. Nonetheless, she could not completely erase the sensation that the work gnawed at her well-being.

It is not a coincidence that I chose the pseudonym Soledad. Soledad means loneliness and solitude and the woman whom the reader has come to known as Soledad emanated this atmosphere. She accepted her work, did it and did not try to dress it up with baubles, bangles and beads. Her listless expression did not seem to affect her business too much, although her services were not as much in demand as other women's. She acted as if it was her destiny to be a prostitute, and this would be reinforced with each failed attempt to try to leave the Crazy Horse.

Suzanna and Gina's similar approach towards the clients did not result in many similarities outside that domain. Gina had developed the art of nastiness to perfection as her way of warding off any unwanted emotional intrusions within this *ambiente*. The one unspoiled spot, in which she momentarily let her guard down, was when she spoke about her children. Even if she had wanted to she could not conceal the significance that they had in her life. Suzanna evaluated her work with dollar signs in her eyes. But suddenly it seems that her calculator went on the blink. She profoundly felt that having money was not worth anything if she was not happy. And she was not happy. She wanted a man and, in the same calculating way that she headed towards her financial goal, she set out to prepare the field to get a man.

Finally, Esperanza could not shake off the anguish she felt at having been pushed through her circumstances to become a prostitute. This manifested in her depression and the visions she had of Mary Magdalene. In fact, she seemed to be portraying her at times. Whether she really was as innocent as she maintained, or whether it was an illusion is of less significance in her story than the pain she felt which made her interpret the police raid as a sign to get out before things got worse.

Each woman's profile, mapped out on these pages, is a different representation of their gender identities as prostitutes. Nonetheless, their performances start from common grounds which limit their potential in their work as well as their private lives.

It is as if the women adhered to an unwritten law which did not permit them to think in terms of improving or enjoying their actual situation. Things well within their reach, such as taking a few days off to spend outside Lima, or following a computer course, were rejected as alternatives and replaced with less tangible goals that, with any luck, could be accomplished in the distant future. They were immobilized when it came to trying to change their immediate situation because any observable change signified their acceptance of what they did. Hence, they consciously accepted the value-laden baggage they carried. Something they fought against, but at the same time they accepted, the marks it made in their lives, and they reconstructed it in the majority of their interactions.

Their portrayal of their private lives is accompanied by an undercurrent – that they live their lives with the constant awareness that their work is eating away at them emotionally and physically. Although they recognized that the money they earn gives them power, this is not enough to erase the message they transmitted about their lives, namely, prostituting is a sacrifice. The bits of information about their private lives which slipped into their stories often emphasized their suffering or the bad luck they always seemed to be experiencing. There was a tacit acceptance that a prostitute's life is doomed to go wrong and many of the anecdotes reinforced this premise. Even in the case where incidents were invented – for example I cannot be sure whether Soledad really was held by terrorists or not – these types of stories are generally accepted because it seems feasible that such things could happen to a woman who prostitutes. Of course, prostitution is filled with many more risks than other occupations, but the frequency with which the most incredible stories were told about a woman's life, brings me to several questions. Are women-who-prostitute so marginalized that they could only choose from options ranging from bad to worse? Is one of the reasons they accept prostitution because they have suffered more abuse in their lives than other women?

In conclusion, the women's performances at the Crazy Horse are, in part, reactions to the gendered enclosures between which they are situated, as well as a reflection of these same enclosures and, most importantly, the space where they create their gender identity. Although they manage to maintain their private and working lives as distinct entities, the gendered enclosures do not discriminate between the two realms. Their potency is felt in the way they portray both domains.

## AN EPILOGUE

Between initiating fieldwork and my return to Lima, the district underwent some considerable changes. Although the Municipality's campaign to eradicate prostitution was not successful, it did ultimately manage to change the nocturnal face of the district. To begin with, the park where male prostitutes congregated was closed and remodelled. During the weekend it offered cultural events in a small amphitheatre and a square was constructed where a weekly crafts fair was held. Its gates were closed each night. The Municipal police force (*serenazgo*), which started to function during my fieldwork, had increased in numbers. Although they had no legal authority to make an arrest, they were given the power to clean up the streets of prostitutes and bring them to police precincts. The number of raids increased. Subsequently, the Plaza Bolivar along with several other streets populated with street walkers and transvestite prostitutes, seemed to have got rid of its 'prostitution problem'. This is what the district looked like at a first glance. However, in reality, not much had changed; prostitution just went more underground.

One of the restaurants right off the plaza became the park's replacement for male prostitution. They sat there in groups or alone, eyeing pedestrians while sipping a Coca-Cola. There were fewer women working the plaza, but there was a new discotheque which young prostitutes used as their workplace. Older prostitutes strolled along the plaza's boundaries looking for prospective clients. Their presence was no longer accepted in the plaza's restaurants. I met Carmela again on the plaza's boundaries. She had come back to work after a period when she stopped working, was living with Miguel and had given birth to a baby boy – something they both wanted dearly. He left her and went back to his wife and five children. Anita still worked there, but I never ran into her again. Ernesto and Angela had a son. However, Angela had left Ernesto and their child for a woman. I found this out in a most unusual way. I was given a copy of one of the sensationalist tabloids. To my surprise, on the front page there was a picture of a smiling Angela with her new partner next to a picture of Ernesto with the caption, 'I want her back, no matter what.' This was the third article in a series of five which told the story from Angela's point of view and Ernesto's. Soledad worked the streets now, too. She had been ousted from the Crazy Horse and

Zoila left the Crazy Horse and worked on the plaza, but she fulfilled a different role now.

Right before I finished fieldwork, Zoila had been hospitalized with a peritonitis attack. Nobody from the Crazy Horse visited her nor did they take up a collection to help pay her medical expenses. When Anita came back from a visit, she said she was in bad shape. There appeared to be complications. At least that is what Anita deduced from the long line of stitches extending from one side of her belly to the other. After Zoila recovered, the extremely noticeable scar impeded her work as a prostitute. She situated herself at the plaza and became a madam (*mami*) for the young women who worked out of the discotheque. She teamed up with a drug dealer, strengthening the relationship between prostitution and drugs. How did I find this out? It was not on the evening I ran into Zoila on the street. She had gained a great deal of weight and her nervous twitch expressed her apprehension at seeing me. I found out through Vanessa. Roberto had run into her and advised her to call me because she was in trouble. Vanessa had finally crossed the border and openly worked as a prostitute at that discotheque. One of the drug dealer's henchmen had threatened her and physically attacked her. Since I had a lot of contacts with the feminist network which deals with abuse and violence, Roberto advised her to call me. However, Roberto's intuition had malfunctioned. He had become involved in something bigger than he could have imagined. The incidents were staged to force Vanessa to work for Zoila. When Vanessa realized this, she stopped calling and did not answer my phone calls. She accepted her fate. When Roberto realized what he had done he wisely disappeared from the plaza for a while. Rumours circulated that 'they' were after him.

The changes which occurred at the plaza were the consequence of the facelift the Municipality had given to the district. During fieldwork, nothing of this nature ever happened. Of course illegal transactions went on constantly; you could hear the gunshots from nearby and I even knew a bouncer who was killed by one of his drug connections. However, none of this had a direct relation with prostitution. It appeared that the Municipality's efforts contributed to the development of prostitution as an illegal and dangerous activity.

Gina and Lola still worked at the Crazy Horse. Lola became pregnant from a client and decided to keep the baby but miscarried, a result of the late nights and too much coke. Suzanna had finally accomplished what she set out to do. At least that is what seemed to be the case at first. She married an Italian and moved to Italy. At the time, I often wondered whether it was a marriage of love, convenience or whether she had been trafficked under false pretences or with her own consent. My suspicion increased when I returned to the Netherlands and heard that the majority of Peruvian (trafficked) prostitutes work in Italy. Did Suzanna go out of love? Was she taken there under false pretences or did she consciously make a step to get out and work in Europe? Unfortunately, I will never have the answer to these questions.

My return to the field showed the effects of the workings of the gendered enclosures on many different levels. The Municipality's solution to the 'prostitution problem' reflects the consequences of the state's regulation policy for clandestine prostitutes. I witnessed the change in the nature of prostitution as a result of a policy aimed at wiping out the 'illegal components'. Few positive changes had occurred in the personal lives of the majority of the women I knew, and in their working lives the situation appeared to go from bad to worse, all of which reinforced their 'well-grounded pessimism' (Scheper-Hughes 1992: 507) in regard to how they perceived their lives and the world around them. The events which took place between the fieldwork period and my return strengthened the pervasive illusion that the gendered enclosures do not permit women-who-prostitute to shed the suffering and marginalized image they embody and which surrounds them.

# 9  GENDERED ENCLOSURES AND GENDER IDENTITIES

## A BRIEF RECAPITULATION IN A THEORETICAL MODE

This book traces the process of the construction of gender identity of women-who-prostitute from two perspectives: the social representation and the self- or subjective representation. Part I relates the intimate relationship between prostitution, male sexuality and regulation – in the first place as discourses and, second, in practice. It delineates the construction of gendered enclosures and the embedding of gender meanings through history, and portrays their contemporary discursive manifestations. The gender meanings produced in these discourses melt together in the fabrication of an ambiguous, but nonetheless unequivocal social representation of the prostitute's gender identity, and accordingly the discourses are conjoined in this gender representation.

In Part II, the self-representation of gender identity is approached through the ethnographic narrative of fieldwork, highlighting the particularities enmeshed in the everydayness of the different fieldwork settings. Here, I seek to illustrate how gender meanings of femininity are constituted in daily relations, and how these, in turn, are subjectively enacted in the prostitutes' performances of their identities. These performances are distinguished by the differences existing between the settings, the conglomeration of socio-logical traits and circumstances, and the range of conformist and non-conformist attitudes enacted in regard to the discursive gender meanings: appropriation, resignation, resistance or defiance. Paradoxically, difference abounds, yet cannot erase the overall quality of sameness emanating from the women's performances, particularly the facets which bolster their no-way-out situation. These are intrinsically related to the options and choices available when faced with the discursive gender meanings of the prostitute.

Furthermore, this book makes a statement about the Western scientific binary of theory and practice and attempts to contribute to further weakening its grip on anthropological practice. This performance is acted out in my reflexive posture, starting from the premise that in the field my identity and my predefined objectives were in continual motion. In trying to resolve my theoretical quandaries, I attempted to direct or curtail interactions accordingly. Periodically, this evoked unforeseeable changes which altered the direction of research. This existential level of the research process is the enactment and embodiment of theory. Kondo's experience of fieldwork reiterates this assertion.

... the specificity of my experience – a particular human being who encounters particular others at a particular historical moment and has particular stakes in that interaction – is not opposed to theory, it enacts and embodies theory. That is to say, the so-called personal details of the encounters, and the concrete processes through which research problems emerged, are constitutive of theory, one cannot be separated from the other. (1990: 24)

The reflexive tone of the narrative contains two additional dimensions of meaning. The first are those meanings which spring from active participation in the fieldwork setting. Hence, as an actor, who I am, and my actions cause reactions and give first-hand immediate knowledge of relational dynamics and cultural meanings. Second, there are those meanings originating from the conflicts between my principles and methodology, and the research participants. For example, the conflict that exists between creating a sense of permanence for myself – an inherent characteristic of research – and the women's attempt to maintain an aura of temporariness, or the clash of masculinity and femininity embodied in my relationship with my research assistant. Although it is tempting to read these conflicts as part of a 'confessional tale' (Van Maanen 1988), their significance goes beyond demonstrating the performance of a fumbling anthropologist. Each of these conflicts is interpreted for the valuable insights it gives into cultural meanings. From this reflexive position the conflicts embody meanings.

In its entirety, the book interprets the construction and reproduction of gender identity as unfixed and fluid and maintains this assertion as the theoretical point of departure. It is here, as we will see below, when this assumption is placed against the central conclusion of the book, that a certain degree of theoretical discomfort evolves.

I conclude that the situations of women-who-prostitute are highly conditioned by pre-existing gender meanings produced in the gendered enclosures. Accordingly, their performances affirm these cultural meanings and actively contribute to preserving their own marginalization. The women-who-prostitute appear to enact and embody a fixed gender identity, albeit constituted by ambiguous fragmented notions, but nonetheless, with minimal space allotted for different interpretations. Many of their performances replicate aspects of the grand narrative written about them, upholding and recreating already existing dichotomies. Melhuus and Stølen recognize this fixed quality in gender imagery and assert:

... it may be that the very processes which serve to fix an image simultaneously obscure the ambiguities which underpin it. In other words the effect of visualization is to evoke unequivocal, easily recognizable images; images that are seemingly out of time and out of place – dislocated, disembedded, fetishized – and herein lies their power. (1996: 28)

In sum, the characterization of women's gender identities as appearing fixed is an illustration of difference and cultural specificity. It is an illusion concealing an extremely vigorous dynamic. If this process is so clear-cut, why should it be considered problematic? Basically, attributing a fixedness to gender identity implies a theoretical point of departure that rubs against the grain of the conceptualization of gender identity as multiple positions in a countless number of possibilities. To comprehend this dilemma, it is necessary to retrace a few of the theoretical developments which have taken place in recent decades.

With the deconstruction of the universal category of woman, various feminist assumptions and concepts directing feminist research were thrown overboard (Moore 1988: 10–11). One of these notions was universal oppression and its accompanying analytical model. This was replaced by an analysis which cracked open the concept of oppression to reveal gender relations of power in different configurations which depended on the specificities of the cultural and historical context and a notion of gender constituted by class, ethnic, race and sexual differences. With this development feminist researchers have been able to analyse women's lives to reveal the subtle and overt forms of resistance and the ways they appropriate and disown the hegemonic discourse, contributing to or freeing themselves from their subordination (e.g. Villarreal 1994; Steenbeek 1995). As feminist researchers, we have felt comfortable with this posture and we have bathed in the richness offered by the concept of difference, enabling us to write about women's agency, their manoeuvres and negotiations, without entirely losing sight of the social conditions of oppression.[1] A middle ground has been found which no longer victimizes women, neither projects them as superheroes in their own domains nor departs from their universal sameness.[2] Moore identifies this development as the current phase of feminist anthropology and characterizes it as 'a move away from "sameness" towards "difference", and by an attempt to establish the theoretical and empirical grounds for a feminist anthropology based on difference' (1988: 11). In her later writings she describes difference as delineating boundaries.

Difference(s) from others are frequently about forming and maintaining group boundaries ... Thinking about difference entails, then, thinking about identity and/or sameness. However, these latter terms are not themselves identical ... Feminist scholars, in particular, have been struggling with the question of how or to what degree women might be the same or similar without being identical. What is it, if anything we share? (1994: 1)

Hence, what was previously assumed to be fact, namely that women's life experiences are universally the same, has been abandoned and replaced by research that problematizes the relation between difference and sameness. Moore ascribes a relational quality to difference which accounts for the notion of sameness 'in terms of political discrimination, inequalities of power and forms of domination' (1994: 26).

Despite the recognition of the intrinsic relation between difference and sameness, it appears that there is a tacit tendency among feminist researchers, perhaps as a reaction to the past theoretical developments described above, to tip the scales and concentrate their use of this concept to elaborate what Hirdman calls 'feminist happy narratives' (1996: 1) of difference. She is not totally off track when she asserts that postmodern freedom avoids issues of subordination (1996: 32) and, I would add, centres on aspects which stress resistance and empowerment. Thus, although the tension that exists between difference and sameness is at the basis of many feminist queries, it is almost a taboo to articulate assertions concerning 'conditions of subordination' within present-day feminist academic discourse. It evokes memories of the essentialist, universal concepts that informed the feminist theoretical past.

Departing from this notion of difference, and concluding that the experiences of the women-who-prostitute are overshadowed by the sameness they share in their 'conditions of subordination', and that their self-representation seems to enact the meanings produced by the hegemonic discourses and does not display the appropriation of non-dominant discourses, this conclusion is not remnant of essentialism, but rather embodies one of the imaginable relational configurations that exists between difference and sameness. The fixed quality of gender identity is not assumed to be natural, but rather it is analysed to get to the roots of why it bolsters this illusion. Moreover, this fixed quality is constructed in a specific temporality and locality – the fieldwork setting which took place predominantly in the domain of work. It appears fixed in this domain but does not assume this conclusion is felt as intensely in other areas of their lives. It is therefore feasible that if this research had taken as its point of departure the women's homes, families or neighbourhoods, other subject positions would have moved into the foreground. Gender identity would appear more flexible and fluid and their performance as prostitutes would be one of the countless number of possibilities informing their daily experiences but not automatically circumscribing them. But when prostitution is taken as the point of departure the women's self-representations accord more readily with the meanings produced in the gendered enclosures. This demonstrates the forcefulness of these enclosures.

Gender identity is conferred with a topical quality that is concomitantly anchored in history. It is not pre-formed but performed in the immediate specificity of a context. Yet it is not totally arbitrary nor completely open to improvisation. It is constituted in the motion between agency and confinement which concurrently expresses difference and sameness. Butler defines gender as follows:

... gender ... is an identity tenuously constituted in time – an identity instituted through a *stylized repetition of acts* [author's emphasis] ... what is called gender identity is a performative accomplishment compelled by social sanction and taboo. (1990b: 270–1)

Further on she states:

The act that one does, the act that one performs, is, in a sense, an act that has been going on before one arrived on the scene. Hence, gender is an act which has been rehearsed, much as a script survives the particular actors who make use of it, but which requires individual actors in order to be actualized and reproduced as reality once again. (1990b: 277)

Butler's definition of gender fosters an analysis of how an actor enacts and embodies gender while at the same time is constrained in her movements by the gendered enclosures or what Butler calls 'already existing directives' (1990b: 277) and, as already stated in the Introduction, without falling prey to determinism. In addition, it contains an element of repetition which is a key component in constructing the self- and social representation of the gender identities of women-who-prostitute.

This definition allows for the persistent appropriation and enactment of pre-existing gender meanings in the performances of the women and buttresses the patterns of repetition which incessantly reduplicate discursive gender meanings and the solutions to the prostitution problem in the Peruvian setting. It would be difficult to find a more transparent example than the case of Peruvian prostitution to illustrate the significance of repetition in the construction of gender identity.

Recapitulating, there are two different strands, interwoven and continually in motion, that go into the construction of gender identity. The first are the gendered enclosures, in their manifestations as instantaneous and already existing directives, and in their continuous (re)production of gender meanings. The second is the individual's performance, her self-representation of her subjective position(s) which includes interpretations of gender meanings moulded in the gendered enclosures. In these subjective experiences the discursive notions are reworked, rejected or converge with other gender meanings. With this said, the task that lies before me for the remainder of this chapter is to synthesize this process of gender construction, relying on the accounts, analysis and narratives of the preceding chapters.

## GENDERED ENCLOSURES AND GENDER MEANINGS

I have used the notion of gendered enclosures metaphorically and literally signifying a marked-off space like Clara's house and the Crazy Horse, where interaction takes place and relationships are constructed through which gender identities are enacted and embodied in the women's self-representations. It has also been given a theoretical connotation, symbolizing the present and already existing directives which coax, inform and constrain prostitutes' actions to move in particular directions.

The first series of events and developments that enclose the performance of the prostitute are encountered in the history of prostitution with its accompanying debate. The institutionalization of the regulation of prostitution has serious repercussions in the women's lives. These events and developments are in constant motion with other gendered enclosures making the performances of women-who-prostitute different – culturally specific – from those of other prostitutes situated geographically elsewhere. Each gendered enclosure contributes a layer of particularity to their lived experiences, and regulation is the most dominant and determining of these enclosures in creating the specificity of their situation.

Poverty takes on a distinctive significance of enclosure in their experiences as prostitutes. An iron-clad relationship exists between poverty and prostitution as both discursive and experiential manifestations. It serves as one of the few accepted legitimations for choosing prostitution throughout history and in the media's contemporary representation of the prostitute. The women belong to the urban poor, and their experiences of poverty permeate their world view, the opportunities open to them and the way they negotiate their lives. However, its significance in the women's lives and as a constraining factor goes far beyond the push it gives them to become prostitutes. Chapter 6 illustrates the experiential relationship between poverty and prostitution. It shows how the women's enactments of the prostitute are continually fed by components of their identities as urban poor. Scheper-Hughes poignantly sums up the crux of living in poverty as follows: 'Flexibility is a prerequisite of survival. So is the ability to dance spitefully in the face of death' (1992: 477). The women working in this particular street in Barrios Altos have to be flexible in facing the insecurities encountered daily. Death, sickness and danger were situated close to the nucleus of their existence. They constantly had to accept the outcome of their precarious luck and to (re)adapt to their insecure economic situation, heightened by the *paquetazo* – the first and most extreme measure in the wave of measures to follow in the Fujishock. The bittersweet moments of pleasure and solidarity were never free of the problems of living lives pervaded by looming insecurity.

Although the nightlife *ambiente* tends to gloss over more thoroughly the private lives of the individuals and the significance of poverty therein, its undertone was felt constantly, not only in the recurrent conversations about price increases and the lack of money but also in these women's relationships and attitude towards life. Scheper-Hughes (1992) makes a distinction between strategy and tactics, defining tactics as more characteristic of the actions of individuals living in poverty. Strategy implies the ability to organize consciously and suggests a clear-sighted (collective) vision which supports an optimistic dream for the future.

[T]actics are not autonomous acts, they are defined in the absence of real power ... Tactics are defensive and individual, not aggressive and collective practices ... they do not challenge the definition of the political-economic situation. (1992: 471–2)

She continues, '[s]taying alive in the shantytown demands a certain "selfishness" that pits individuals against each other and that rewards those who take advantage of those even weaker [than themselves]' (1992: 473). One of the strengths in Scheper-Hughes' analysis is her matter-of-fact description of the social reality of poverty, particularly the impotence it creates in the experienced-based meanings of the urban poor. It is extremely difficult to describe behaviour and attitudes which are normally disapproved of by the status quo without transmitting the corresponding value judgements of existing stereotypes. She does this skilfully and her analysis of urban poverty in a Brazilian shantytown helps make sense of the less attractive dimension of daily life which I felt in the fieldwork setting in Lima and, specifically, in the interactions and relationships between individuals. Poverty is an enclosure felt by all the urban poor. However, when it is fused with prostitution it enhances the solitary position produced by stigma. The intricate relationship between prostitution and poverty is reiterated in Pheterson's account of a meeting of prostitutes from ten Asian countries. She states, 'Prostitutes rated stigma their number one problem. "Poverty we share with our sisters, but stigma robs us even of community support"' (1996: 145, note 2). The stigma of prostitution makes their experience of poverty different from that of other women.

To continue unravelling the gendered enclosures, male sexuality will be outlined below. The analysis of heterosexual male sexuality is an account of power and, specifically, its position in gender relations of power. The various versions of male sexuality presented in Chapter 3 remodelled essentialist notions such as the *macho* or male sexuality found in feminist and prostitute studies, but it could not dislocate the implications of certain vividly lived notions constituting men's sexual selves.

Despite the differences in men's subjective experiences of their sexuality, the experience of sexuality as virtually instinctual remains intact. This signifies that sexuality is outside their own control and implies that men accept their sexuality for what it is, denying the possibility for change because it is not socially constructed but rather biological. Labelling femininity is an expression in practice of this essentialist notion, fragmenting their sexual experiences into those enjoyed with social actors in the emotional realm of subjectivity, and those practised with sexual actors in which the notion of sexuality as virtually instinctual structures the encounters. This keeps prostitution in its place as a male prerogative even when it is not chosen as an alternative, and prostitutes as the most extreme representation of sexual actors. Male sexuality surrounds women-who-prostitute in a double bind. First of all, it informs the prevailing power relations of gender in terms of global meanings of masculinity and femininity, placing prostitutes at the lowest level in men's projections of femininity. Second, it conceptualizes the prostitute in purely sexual terms with almost no regard for her social identity nor the social conditions of her work. This strips the women of their agency, constructs fixed gender meanings and, finally, sustains their no-way-out situation. Pheterson also emphasizes the need to conceptualize prostitution within a social context. She affirms:

... [e]xamples abound of research designs which persistently treat the variable 'prostitute' as a fixed identity rather than a contingent social status, thus assuming prostitution to be a female trait or destiny removed from the dynamic realities of group relations and political power. (1996: 10)

These gendered enclosures – the discourse and debate on prostitution, regulation, poverty and male sexuality – have been essential in constructing the gender meanings constituted in the social representation of the prostitute historically and for their almost identical appearance now. As stated in Chapter 1, this is the outcome of inflexible, repetitive patterns which have led to the reduplication of practically identical events, meanings and identities. Disclosing the contents of these patterns will be another step towards undoing the illusion of a fixed gender identity.

### Repetitive Patterns and Gender Meanings

The history of prostitution is a history of repetition. It has been recurrently orchestrated by two discursive systems of thought: those of the regulationists and the abolitionists. These days, the abolitionist doctrine has been replaced by the sexual slavery theory, but its presence is still felt in the traces of abolitionism embedded in this present-day model. One of the substantial differences between the two is the position given to men and male sexuality. In the sexual slavery theory, the analytical foundation is the concept of patriarchy and a predominant role is ascribed to men. This theory exists side by side with measures aimed at solving the prostitution problem by control of prostitutes. Needless to say, the differences between the different doctrines vanish in regard to the position given to the prostitute. She is at the core of the problem and the key to the solution. This literally objectifies her agency, making it simple to view her as easy to manipulate, or so the history of prostitution has it.

The solutions proposed by the proponents of regulation reiterate its central argument, namely prostitution is a necessary evil and the prostitute is the instrument of control.

At the end of the nineteenth century, there was a call for regulation which, on the one hand, demanded a sanitary control of all women working as prostitutes. On the other hand, it proposed the creation of centres of prostitution, thus tightening the control of the health and law authorities. This was succeeded by the establishment of sanitary control in 1910 and different attempts to concentrate prostitution in one area, which only achieved success in 1923, when all houses of prostitution were moved to Jirón Huatica. This was followed by an attempt to remove the prostitutes from Huatica to a distant area where a brothel complex would be constructed. In the meantime, it was suggested that the disturbances could be diminished by sealing off all streets leading to Huatica from all forms of traffic except pedestrians. Huatica was shut down in 1959 without another area being designated as an alternative. In 1972, another proposal was made to construct a brothel complex at the outskirts of the town, with a capacity of 600 women and which would include health services and rehabilitation workshops. In 1982 and 1988 it was rumoured that the brothels of Callao would be removed to a remote area, but these proposals were never implemented. The brothels of Callao remain in the same geographical location and show no sign of moving anywhere. Finally, there is the 1993 proposal, suggesting the construction of a prostitution centre which would offer more employment opportunities, revenues for the municipality and a new law criminalizing clandestine prostitution. The 1993 plan intended to make clandestine prostitution in the centre of Lima a thing of the past.

Besides exhibiting their lack of originality, these proposals demonstrate the limitations of a system of thought that incessantly indicates the prostitute as the core of the problem and repression and control as the only solutions. Consequently, the prostitute's identity has a veneer of a fixed appearance, rather than being conceptualized as a set of social relations that involves the provider of sexual services, the receivers or buyers and the regulator[s], which are assumed to 'vary with history and the particular sites through which prostitution is practiced' (Truong 1988: 25). Prostitution is approached as unchanging and reduced to an ahistorical, essentialist phenomenon, fortifying the links between repetition, repression and subordination.

Another repetitive pattern sculptures the prostitute into the Other (as opposed to non-prostitutes). This is accomplished by funnelling the discussion of all social, psychological and economic factors into a model which explicates why certain women become prostitutes and implies why others do not. In addition, the positionality of women-who-prostitute is riveted into the world of prostitution. With the exception of the subject position of the mother, there is practically nothing that connects her prostituting experience to the worlds beyond prostitution. These types of conceptualizations fix the idea that some women are predestined to become prostitutes, preserving the nineteenth-century perspective towards women-who-prostitute as physically and psychologically different from other women, resulting in the dislocation and the disembeddedness of the gender identity of the prostitute.[3]

Lastly, the repetitive patterns form dualities, some of which take the form of dichotomies. Two pairs have had a particularly profound effect in carving out the performing space of women-who-prostitute: the control/danger and the sexual/social dyads. The division between registered and clandestine prostitutes transparently expresses the former. The registered prostitute is sketched in the image of the health-concerned mother, while the clandestine prostitute is dangerous and clandestine prostitution can be compared with a social tumour whose growth is out of control.

The division of the sexual and social is more complicated and takes on various guises. As mentioned earlier, it is found in men's construction of their sexual selves, splitting their sexual experiences into those which are pleasurable in the social and emotional realm, and those which give pleasure because they alleviate sexual pressure and satisfy their virtually instinctual sexual needs; experiences with prostitutes fall into the latter category. In addition, this division is replicated in the social representation of the prostitute's gender identity, first as a social actor who enters prostitution and is then transformed into a sexual being as a prostitute. On another level a distinction is made between women-who-prostitute for socially correct reasons 'for their children' and the sexually promiscuous prostitute who enters because she 'enjoys it' or 'for luxuries'. However, the split between the social and sexual goes deeper, demarcating boundaries of difference between women-who-prostitute and women who do not. Recalling the death of Marita Alpaca, Reaño's case took a different direction when Marita's alleged true identity was exposed to the public. The sexual inferences contained in the category 'prostitute' were used to argue Reaño's innocence or guilt. The social identity of Marita, which had been in the foreground for several weeks, became invisible.

Finally, there is the multi-faceted notion of sexuality constantly reproduced in the hypersexual representation of the whore, the ambiguity surrounding promiscuity, and notions of honour and shame, all of which are given a degree of significance in the prostitute's performance of her gender identity.

These dualities are at the basis of the social representation of the prostitute's gender identity – the official, written version – a version, as mentioned several times, which is fixed and resistant to the specificities of the context. Only a few observable differences exist between the historical and contemporary representation of the prostitute. Venereal disease has been replaced by Aids. In the modern version the descriptions of the women have become more elaborate, and honour holds a less prominent place, but its undertone is still felt, and the number of clandestine prostitutes has increased significantly. However, in general, the prostitute conforms to the notion of the Other. Whether she is the impoverished victim, the promiscuous woman as the whore, and the mother, as opposed as these subject positions may be, they all melt together in the fabrication of the social representation of the prostitutes' gender identities. These repetitive patterns contribute to the creation of a no-way-out situation.

As stated in Chapter 2, the no-way-out situation does not permit the prostitute to improve her working conditions, because any improvement implies the promotion of promiscuity. Rehabilitation is aimed at, but concurrently new measures are sought to improve regulation. Prostitutes are expected to please the client, but if they show pleasure they will be considered whores. However, if they treat him with indifference then they are criticized for being lousy whores. Strikes and demonstrations are either disempowered by the media or go unsupported because the self-empowerment of prostitutes would ultimately reinforce women's subordination. Other economic opportunities are virtually non-existent and the countless numbers of sewing classes which have been started and will be started in the future, to promote the rehabilitation of prostitutes, are doomed to failure because a seamstress could never earn as much as even one of the lowest categories of prostitutes. The relationship between the no-way-out situation and the gender meanings repetitively produced by the discursive patterns is clear and has far-reaching implications for the subjective embodiment of the gender identities of women-who-prostitute.

## GENDER IDENTITIES: SELF-REPRESENTATIONS AND SUBJECTIVITY

In the social sciences it is common knowledge that there is a schism between what is experienced and what is socially proscribed or sanctioned, in other words, social reality is defined by the discrepant relationship between discourse and subjectivity. According to the contemporary state of the art 'any social theory must account for the reproduction of dominant categories and discourses and for instances of non-reproduction, resistance and change' (Moore 1994: 52). Or, to rephrase this development from a different angle, 'individuals embody many different subjectivities. And, though hegemonic discourses may suppress, they never totally censor other expressive possibilities' (Cornwall and Lindesfarne 1995: 152). Villarreal describes this process through her definition of agency.

As agents, women re-transcribe different discourses, consolidate scripts and enlist interpretations in accordance with their practices, or adjust practices to comply to standards and their strategies differ in the degree to which each is willing to yield personal space or able to defend it. (1994: 26)

Hence the social scientist's discovery of the importance of the subjective dimension has led to analysis which reveals moments of appropriation of non-dominant discourses, instances of non-reproduction and a large dose of attention to practices of resistance, all of which are enacted in the subjective domain. This analytical current has led almost to the creation of a dualism of domination and resistance: where there is domination, resistance is lurking around the corner. Considering its theoretical weight in feminist anthropology, and the contrast this tendency poses to the conclusions in this book, it is necessary to deal with it briefly.

One theory which is most representative of this current is Scott's (1990) public and hidden transcripts. Scott has managed to take apart many stereotypical images of the oppressed and poor, but in doing so, has cast their actions in a realm of intentionality. In public, subordinates uphold relations of subordination but off-stage they act out a hidden transcript.

[T]he greater the disparity in power between dominant and subordinate and the more arbitrarily it is exercised, the more the public transcript of subordinates will take on a stereotyped, ritualistic cast. In other words, the more menacing the power, the thicker the mask. (Scott 1990: 3)

The hidden transcript 'is produced for a different audience and under different constraints of power than the public transcript' (1990: 5). Each hidden transcript is 'specific to a given social site and to a particular set of actors' (1990: 14). 'At its most elementary level the hidden transcript represents an acting out in fantasy – and occasionally in secretive practice – of the anger and reciprocal aggression denied by the presence of domination' (1990: 37). From Scott's perspective, my conclusion concerning the impact of the social representation of gender meanings on constituting the prostitutes' identities is an expression of the disparity in power that exists between the public and hidden transcripts. Accordingly, women-who-prostitute's adherence to the social representation of their gender identity is, on the one hand, proof of the degree of domination, but on the other, implies that their submissive stance is a front that conceals another scenario. Although the prostitute's performance is, on one level, the acting out of anger and aggression in response to dominant discursive notions, this does not automatically mean they construct hidden transcripts of resistance with all the implications this entails for self-propelling empowerment. I tend to think an alternative interpretation exists and rely on Scheper-Hughes to articulate it.

In writing against cultures and institutions of fear and domination, the critical thinker falls into a classic double bind. Either one attributes great explanatory power to the fact of oppression (but in so doing one can reduce the subjectivity and agency of subjects to a discourse on victimization) or one can try to locate the everyday forms of resistance in the mundane tactics and practices of the oppressed ... Here one runs the risk of romanticizing human suffering or trivializing its effects on the human spirit, consciousness, and will ... I have to argue a middle ground, one that acknowledges the destructive signature of poverty ... but one that also acknowledges the creative, if often contradictory means the people of the Alto use to stay alive and even to thrive with their wit and their wits intact. The goal of the *moradores* of the Alto Cruzeiro is not *resistance* but simply *existence*. (1992: 533)

This middle ground makes good sense. Setting the notion of existence alongside the concept of tactics elaborated earlier, frames the agency of the women in a dimension of temporariness, immediacy, intensely lived in the present with hope and dreams reserved for the future. It gives space for actions of resistance and moments of solidarity to exist side by side with moments that reiterate the unchanging rhythm of their lives. This was the feeling constantly transmitted to me in fieldwork encounters.

The women's performances continually deny the legitimacy of the notion of promiscuity and, as a consequence, denounce prostituting 'for all the wrong reasons'. They are continually working against the symbol of the whore in the construct of the prostitute. This is expressed in their attitudes, gestures and assertions that emphasize the ordinariness of prostitution – 'a job like any other'; it is reiterated in the domestic, chaste style of dress which scarcely differentiates these women from other women in their surroundings; it is heard in the virtual silence surrounding the subject of sexuality and the indifferent and even demeaning attitude they said they took towards their clients.[4]

Furthermore, their performances reject the social representation of the prostitute in other ways. First of all, they use normative values to distinguish themselves from other women-who-prostitute – the good and the bad prostitute. Second, in their continual enactment of the correct reasons for prostituting and in their perception of their work as a temporary circumstance, they put their lives on hold until the future, that is to say, until they leave prostitution behind them. Lastly, they negate plausible improvements for the immediate present. Thus, the self-representation of their gender identity creates difference through denial. Yet, this notion of difference is created by symbols and meanings shared by the women and illustrates the significance of sameness in the construction of difference.

This same gender performance, when held up against other discursive notions, is the embodiment of the social representation. The flip-side of the whore is the impoverished, more often than not abandoned mother who is forced to prostitute to guarantee her children's well-being and a chance for a brighter future. The power allotted to this sociological characteristic in the written, official version of the prostitute is recognized by the women, particularly when they use it in their relationships with clients to receive compassion and gain respect. In this sense, they comply with what is expected of them. Nevertheless, in the subjective realm, insofar as the majority of prostitutes are mothers, motherhood is given a priceless significance in the performance of their identities.

In essence, in the subjective construction of their self-representation, the women-who-prostitute relive and re-create daily the split between the mother and the whore. They disclaim the discursive gender meanings and concurrently affirm and legitimate them.

The relationship between men and women is a site that substantiates the hegemonic discourse of masculinity and femininity. Men's and women's affective relationships are evaluated for their genuineness, for their failure or success in remaking the gender identities of women-who-prostitute into ones that resemble those of non-prostitutes, whose sexuality is reserved exclusively for their *maridos*. The notion of promiscuity is, once again, crucial in defining women's gender identity and for differentiating one from another. Their affective relationships are defined against this notion and are continually being put to the test. Consequently, alternative arrangements which exist, for example, a relationship which permits a woman who prostitutes to continue prostituting or one that fluctuates between this type of relationship and the ideal, does not count as authentic because these relationships do not live up to the exemplary one which is expected to erase the subject position of the prostitute and replace this identity with that of the wife and mother. In other words, in their relationships with their partners they fervently express their rejection of the social representation by making a great deal of effort to demonstrate to their surrounding environment that their relationship cannot be categorized, like other prostitutes' relationships, as one between the prostitute and the *cafiche*. This is done by replacing this social representation with another, the legitimate one, that is only accessible to decent women. However, in most cases it is nearly impossible for them to achieve this goal, because the reasons they entered prostitution have not vanished and it remains the only lucrative way for them to support themselves and their children. Thus, in this context, the version of femininity they uphold is the mirror image of their subjective social reality, making it even more complicated for them to break out of the no-way-out situation.

Certainly, parts of their performances break this process of reduplicating gender meanings between self- and social representations when there is a dissonance between discourse and subjectivity. Lying can be interpreted in this way, as well as pleasurable experiences with clients, the control the women maintain in the prostitute–client situation, the power they obtain from the money earned and, finally, the isolated, sporadic, collective actions aimed to improve prostitutes' work situations. All of these instances suggest the enactment of a subject position as agents in command of their own situations. Yet these moments do not jolt the discursive gender meanings sufficiently to dislodge them from the critical position they assume in the social and self-representations of the prostitute. This is expressed in the fixed position given to the notion of shame in their gender identity. Feelings of shame are a direct result of the internalization of the social representation in their subjective experience – of being aware of all the negative things that are said and thought about prostitutes, and women-who-prostitute either appropriate them or deny them in the performance of their gender identities.

As stated above, for the majority of the women with children, the notion of motherhood has the greatest significance in their self-representation and is by far the most gratifying. This goes far beyond the simple phrase 'I do it for my children', which suggests that prostitution is a pragmatic and logical way to fulfil their maternal obligations. Of course, this dimension must be recognized in their decisions, nonetheless, it embraces more. Prostitution enables the women to enact and embody a subject position of mother which is not only a matter of being able to satisfy their children's needs but also enables them to give voice to motherhood in their self-representation of their gender identities – in the ways they define themselves as women. In an article which relates an interview conducted with a group of prostitutes from Callao, when one women was asked how she felt when she entered prostitution, she replied as follows:

*I feel like a real woman* [my emphasis] because I am struggling for my children who are going to school. I feel peaceful because they are never without food and education, that is essential. I am a woman and I got involved in this so that my children could be more than I am, so that they won't get stuck in the mud like me, to educate them. For this reason I am peaceful ... (Villarán 1987: 16)

Prostitution permits women to create a socially sanctioned gender identity. Moore toils with the concept of fantasy to explain how and why individuals assume certain subject positions. Although the concept of fantasy in daily usage contains connotations that suggest an unreal or fictive perspective on reality, and would imply that I would be making a moral judgement in regard to the women's lives, Moore's use of the term does not contain this significance. Rather it is grounded in social practice, albeit, as the following quote illustrates, in the more immaterial dimensions of social practice.

If we imagine that individuals take up certain subject positions because of the way in which those positions provide pleasure, satisfaction or reward on the individual or personal level, we must also recognize that such individual satisfactions have power and meaning only in the context of various institutionalized discourses and practices, that is, in the context of certain sanctioned modes of subjectivity. In addition, there is the question of the institutional power of dominant or hegemonic discourses, where there are very tangible benefits to be gained from constructing oneself as a particular sort of person and interacting with others in specific sorts of ways. (1994: 65)

The enactment and embodiment of motherhood by women-who-prostitute, is constituted by this multi-layered process of gender identity. In the first two chapters, various manifestations of the significance of motherhood in the dominant discourse were revealed: as the legitimizing factor in choosing to prostitute, as an honourable gender identity and in the ways women appropriate both of the components in this construct for their own benefit, or as a projection of their gender identity in crucial moments, such as during interviews with the press. However, the book is also filled with numerous examples which outwardly express or suggest the importance of motherhood on a personal level and the feeling of power this gives them.

The use of the term 'fantasy' is important here because it emphasizes the often affective and subconscious nature of investment in various subject positions, and in the social strategies necessary to maintain that investment. (1994: 66)

Recalling Esperanza's words when I enquired into her plans for retirement, she said, 'I have to sacrifice myself a little more', postponing the time when she would leave prostitution to continue to give her child and family what they need. Thus, prostitution enables women-who-prostitute to maintain the investment they make in the subject position of mother. They perform a negatively sanctioned gender subject position to be able to complete a positive one.

The subject positions of the mother and whore, usually representing two different individuals and functioning as mirror images in the social representation of femininity, merge with all their complexity and contradictions in the performance of the gender identities of women-who-prostitute. Maintaining the tricky balance of a double life is, in practice, a manifestation of the subjective construction of their gender identity. The slap in the face Señora Pilar gave to the schoolboy can be interpreted as a moment in which the identities were conflated in the same action – the shame and embarrassment she felt as a prostitute and the pride she felt as a mother. It is no wonder that women-who-prostitute find themselves in a no-way-out situation with few alternatives open to them. Their self-representations are constituted by subject positions deemed incompatible in the social representation.

## THE PRODUCTION OF FIXED ILLUSIONS AND THE POSTPONEMENT OF CHANGE

The process of subjective embodiment of meanings moulded within the gender enclosures together with other meanings derived from the individual's circumstances and experiences has led to the construction of an illusion of fixed gender identity of women-who-prostitute. This contributes to the processes of stigmatization and marginalization of prostitutes. Inasmuch as these performances of gender are suffused with already existing directives, the pursuable possibilities are limited. Women's agency has been highly informed by the gendered enclosures which repetitively mould meanings constituting the social representation of the prostitute. What has been called the women's no-way-out situation is a consequence of this process. This book records this historical process and demonstrates how it continues into the contemporary period. It indicates those notions that are most pervasive and most resistant to change. This idea of change refers to finding ways to destabilize the illusion of a fixed identity and start from an idea of identity as unfixed, multiple and fluid, thereby creating countless possibilities. This in turn will encourage modifications to the systems of thought that enclose prostitutes. It could possibly engender the conditions required for women-who-prostitute to improve their own situation in the ways they see fit.

The first area, desperately in need of a facelift, contains notions associated with the regulation of prostitution. Truong states:

Change must be induced from the relations within the institution of prostitution as they directly affect prostitutes. The question is how to reconcile prostitutes' interests with the interests of society at large ... The reality of prostitution today shows that political positions derived from abstract ethical principles are not useful for social change. (1988: 91)

The fact that prostitution has been considered a problem in need of a solution throughout history underpins the idea of the necessity of regulating prostitution. This has created a case of mistaken identity. The institution of the regulation of prostitution is confused with the institution of prostitution. Therefore, all solutions to the problem start from the former, which, by separating registered prostitutes from unregistered, bestowing an erroneous notion of illegality on the latter and organizing initiatives to improve the efficiency of control and wipe out danger, has constructed a distorted view of the social reality of prostitution. It is therefore not surprising that the solutions offered are doomed to failure because they do not take into consideration the majority of the individuals who prostitute, namely unregistered prostitutes.

The panorama of the institution of prostitution is totally distinct to its portrayal in the regulatory system and is defined by the multitude of actually existing varieties. Although it is not easy to reconcile prostitutes' interests with those of society at large, starting from this latter standpoint is at least a healthier beginning.

Just as the regulationists say that prostitution will never go away, this book has shown that it is very unlikely that regulation will ever be abolished. To guarantee any possibility of women-who-prostitute improving their own situation, somehow, something or someone must pull the plug on this antiquated system of regulation, its accompanying value-laden discourse of prostitution and its production of unyielding fixed meanings, because history has shown it has never and will never come to a halt through its own self-destruction. While contemporary anti-regulationists propose grand schemes of change but offer little in terms of the immediate situation, the authorities representing the regulatory system, or who are concerned with the problem of prostitution, invent 'new' strategies which could have serious direct effects on the lives of women-who-prostitute.

At the outset of this research project I opposed the regulation of prostitution and shared this standpoint with the majority of Peruvian feminists. However, the investigation and the writing-up process caused me to reformulate my position. I still contend that the regulation of Peruvian prostitution is, in its implementation and impact (among the various adjectives which could be used to describe it), ineffective, repressive and inefficient. Therefore, I agree with the Peruvian proponents of abolition. But, in accordance with Truong's proposed strategy of change, if change is induced from within the institution then *regulatory measures* cannot be *a priori* rejected as an alternative. Peruvian history demonstrates that the only collective actions by prostitutes were undertaken by registered prostitutes. Throughout history there has been no initiative by unregistered prostitutes.

There are several examples which illustrate that regulatory measures need not hinder prostitutes' struggles to obtain more rights. One of them is found in a provincial town of Ecuador. The sanitary regulation of prostitution has not prevented the women from organizing an autonomous association which has been in existence since 1982 (Rodas et al. 1991). Regulatory measures could have the potential to enlarge instead of reduce prostitutes' room for manoeuvre. If this sounds utopian, then at least, in the meantime, they should not obstruct this process. For it is regulation which keeps intact the distinction between the clandestine and registered prostitute. It is clandestine prostitutes who are hardest hit by the images constructed about prostitution, although in actuality, what is common knowledge concerning this group is based on regulationist hearsay.

I could end here with a list of long-term ideational and social changes required to destabilize the fixed image of the prostitute, such as are found in notions of male sexuality and the mother/whore dichotomy. Because as much as this book has shown the significance of the regulation of prostitution in fabricating this image and producing a no-way-out situation, it has also illustrated that the illusion of a fixed identity is far more complex and is not only a result of regulation, but of other socially rooted aspects as well. This fixed identity is constituted by ambiguous, conflictive notions. However, if I ended this book as proposed above, I would be doing the same as the old-time abolitionists who were unable to go any further than proposing a range of long-term social and ideational changes to prevent its propagation. Perhaps contemporary feminists do not call for the immediate abolition of prostitution because they are aware of the detrimental affect this would have on the lives of prostitutes, but they are inflexible with regard to accepting any measures which could structure prostitution, or any self-propelling actions taken by the prostitutes to improve their situation. And they continue to call for its disappearance. Therefore, as simple as it may sound, the situation of prostitution demands an approach that takes one step at a time and starts from the immediate circumstances, in order to create the elementary conditions required to stimulate change on various levels in society and, more specifically, in the lives of women-who-prostitute. This book is inspired by this conviction and hopes to contribute to achieving this objective.

# A RETURN VISIT: PROSTITUTION IN LIMA ANNO 2000

After being away from Lima for seven years, I returned for a three-month stay to start a new research project. This gave me the opportunity to present more elaborately my research results on prostitution. I had come to Lima with the idea that there had been no significant changes concerning prostitution since my departure. In my absence no one had informed me of any legislative or social changes concerning the subject. In the first month of my stay I did an interview for an article in the Saturday supplement of *El Comercio* (19 August 2000); I was told I would be participating in an effort to present a new perspective on the subject. I gave the author the benefit of the doubt, only to find my one and a half hour interview cut down to two quotes pulled out of context and shoved next to sensationalist photographs of street prostitutes. This experience strengthened my belief that virtually everything had remained the same. I gave a paper at a conference on the subject of hypersexuality and the effects of regulation (Nencel 2000a), and here once again there were no signs that I was mistaken. Then I gave a talk at the First National Seminar on Prostitution which was sponsored by the Municipality of San Isidro (Lima), several NGOs, UNIFEM and the Ministry of Public Affairs. This was definitely an event which, ten years before, when I started this investigation, could have never taken place and would never have been sponsored by so many prestigious institutions. In that sense, it was a first.

Listening to the other speakers proved to me once again that the regulationist mentality, the problem-oriented approach and all their negative consequences for women who prostitute are as alive today as seven years ago. I gave my talk (Nencel 2000b), illustrating how regulation creates values and meanings that enclose the women and gives them few alternatives. I pointed out how other discourses did the same and I stressed fervently the need to listen to what the women who prostitute say and at the same time create spaces where they can reflect on their lives and work, and have easy access to the information and services that they need. It was only when the first day finished and I was trying to find a taxi – during the national transportation strike – with a professional from the Ministry of Health, whom I have known since the beginning of this project, that I was informed that since 1996 women who prostitute are no longer obliged to be registered by

228

the police. Thus, the distinction between registered and clandestine prostitutes no longer exists. She told me how new ministry-run health centres were opened nationally for all SEX WORKERS (in accordance with the ILO, the Ministry of Health now called prostitutes sex workers), where they can receive advice, get check-ups and be tested for HIV, the results remaining confidential. All of these changes and others are a result of the law against Aids (Ley 26626 – La Ley ContraSIDA). Finally, each municipality has the right to develop their own policy in regard to the 'prostitution problem'. This last point is not a result of the previously mentioned law but a consequence of changes in an ordinance of the Municipality of Lima City. It all sounded so utopian.

After a brief moment of self-reprimand for not having found out about this earlier, I realized that my research had taught me a lot. This brief moment quickly transformed into a fascination with why and how it was possible that I did not know about these changes. What could this tell me about prostitution anno 2000?

Although many people knew about the Ley 26626, those who do not work with prostitutes knew little about the effect it had for prostitutes. Everyone who ever thought about prostitution thought that everything was more or less the same. More importantly, I realized I was witnessing the early signs of social transformation. Nonetheless, the new legislation had barely been felt in the social domain or in the lives and work of women-who-prostitute. The discourse was showing signs of fatigue but the changes had, as yet, hardly trickled down to the dimension of practice. Professionals' opinions on the subject of prostitution had barely changed; it still remains a moral issue and a social problem. Women prostituting on the streets are still being picked up and held by police and brought for testing the following day. Women working in brothels and clubs are being obliged to disclose their results of their HIV tests. All of these practices are forbidden by law but are still happening, as the lawyer and specialist in prostitution Victor Lora told me upon my inquiring. Thus, it was definitely an exciting moment to be there.

This excitement increased on the following day of the seminar when after the first speaker, a woman named Lily (this is a pseudonym for her pseudonym) came to the microphone and began to tell her story: a story nearly told entirely prosaically about a sex worker and sex work and her bittersweet life. It was an eloquent presentation. When she finished she sat down weeping softly, coincidentally in the seat in front of me. I thanked her very much for her presentation and, to my surprise, she thanked me too because she felt that my presentation the day before had given her support to get up there and do what she did. This was the first time a sex worker had spoken in front of 300 people of the 'establishment'.

After Lily had finished, the next speaker thanked her profusely, showing her the respect she deserved, following this with a presentation in which prostitution was described as, among other things, the loss of dignity and values. The seminar concluded with a workshop which was aimed at drawing conclusions from the two-day experience. However, during the presentation of the conclusions, the discussion stagnated around the use of the term sex worker and it was ultimately concluded that prostitution cannot be called sex work.

I was lucky to participate in and witness this moment, a moment which, in an optimistic mode, could be interpreted as the beginning of positive change for women-who-prostitute. However, I prefer to think of it as a moment when discourse and practice are temporarily out of sync. It is definitely an important moment because nothing like this has taken place for over a hundred years, but its outcome is difficult to determine.

# NOTES

## INTRODUCTION

1. Their disguises did not make them unrecognizable. One health worker with whom I talked afterwards told me she immediately recognized one of her patients.
2. See Chapter 9 for a more elaborate discussion of the idea of gender and performance.

## CHAPTER 1

1. Although this tendency still can be found today there is a growing body of literature in which, to a lesser or greater extent, prostitution and the construction of the prostitute are deconstructed within the cultural context in which they are encountered. See Walkowitz (1980) on English Victorian Prostitution; Mahood (1990) on Scottish prostitution; Butler (1987) on prostitution in the American west; Soares (1988) on prostitution in Brazil; Guy (1990) for Buenos Aires, Argentina; White (1990) for colonial Nairobi; and Corbin (1990) for France.
2. See for example, Muñiz (1888), Avedaño (1892), García (1899), Valdizán Medrano (1909).
3. The notion of control is fundamental to understanding the contemporary situation of prostitutes. See Chapter 2.
4. I consider this to be the first article written. However, the possibility exists (although it is unlikely) that other articles appeared even earlier.
5. Throughout the book, the author has translated all quotes appearing originally in Spanish.
6. It is interesting to note the regular use of gender-neutral words such as 'individual', 'human being' or the plural 'we', which, without exception, are used to refer to men.
7. It proved impossible to find a copy of the project referred to in the following passages.
8. A discrepancy exists between certain sources, who call Muñiz the prefect and other articles in which he is referred to as a sub-prefect.
9. The enthusiasm for this project was inspired by the then president, who had studied in England where regulation of prostitution was enforced. President Leguía wanted to copy the English model.
10. Muñiz also talks of four categories of prostitution: luxury, private home, brothel and streetwalkers (1888: 20). However, his descriptions are superficial.
11. Dávalos y Lissón stated elsewhere that there were 120 public prostitutes in Lima. He considered this number to be on the low side, especially when it was compared with 'the rest of the civilized cities of the world' (1909: 7).
12. I translated *casa de cita* (house of appointments) as 'bordello', drawing a distinction between the terms 'brothel' and 'bordello'. Dávalos y Lissón defines these houses as places where the clients and prostitutes drink and dance in the parlour, retiring at a convenient moment to one of the rooms. This type of prostitution slowly disappeared. Currently, the term is used for hotels which rent rooms by the hour to prostitutes.

What were called *casas de citas* in Dávalos y Lissón's time have been called *casas de tolerancia* (houses of tolerance) in the regulation.

13. The fourth category of prostitute appears to be a group of women who transgress acceptable gender boundaries. It is plausible that they were not prostitutes but were labelled as such because their sexual behaviour diverged greatly from that prescribed by the dominant morality. This subject goes beyond the scope of the chapter, but could be an interesting topic for a historical study.

14. *Mestiza* is the term used to designate a person of mixed racial origins, generally but not exclusively referring to Spanish and Indian.

15. A *manta* is a traditional cloak which was used to veil the face, predominantly by upper-class women, while walking on the streets or in public places.

16. The preceding February a Prefectoral Decree established that *casas de tolerancia* should be concentrated in one area and women who prostitute should be in possession of identification cards, registering their health status (Solano 1943: 290). The information I have collected shows evidence that this ordinance was ignored until 1923, when all houses of prostitution were ordered to move to Jirón Huatica. An earlier unsuccessful attempt to do this had been made in 1905. All houses of prostitution were ordered to move to Los Patos, a street in a very poor section of town near the government palace.

17. Callao is the harbour of Lima.

18. The version of Special Licences quoted here is taken from *Boletín Municipal* 1639, 1957, vol. 57, pp. 10–18. Until 1983 Special Licences were the responsibility of the Ministry of Internal Affairs. Only minor modifications were made in 1972, 1979 and 1982. In 1983 the department was transferred to municipal authority.

19. The Department of Venerology was in charge of the anti-venereal dispensaries. This department fell under the authority of the Office of General Health of the Ministry of Public Health and Social Assistance.

20. When I asked the commander of Special Licences what steps could be taken to remove oneself from their register, he replied that the names always remained in the register. Either Article 36 was never enforced, or it was revoked or found too cumbersome to put into practice. Thus registered prostitutes are inscribed indefinitely. However, it remains a ludicrous idea that articles of this sort were written. They disregarded the fact that the women were marginalized and an enormous stigma existed concerning prostitution. The suggestion that the women might approach neighbours to countersign such a document goes against the grain of the women's dignity and demonstrates the lack of respect given to women-who-prostitute.

21. In the 1991 version of the Penal Code, this article has been modified and made into law.

22. The vagrancy law was abolished in 1982 (no. 23506). This changed the situation for unregistered prostitutes because they could be held for no more than 48 hours, instead of for several months. However, they still were and are arrested for street-walking. The grounds which permit their arrest are unclear. Some say it is based on offences against public order. Others say it is out of habit; during the State of Emergency it was said to have been used as a pretext to pick up clandestine prostitutes.

23. References to eugenic doctrines are scarce in abolitionist literature. Nonetheless, there was a matter-of-fact attitude concerning the relation between venereal disease, prostitution and the race. With the exception of the report I have already mentioned, and an article written by Bambarén entitled *Enseñanza de la Eugenesia*, published as a pamphlet in 1952, I have found no other references on the subject.

24. See for example Bambarén (1937: 279).

25. The Russian treatment of the prostitution problem was commended for being the ideal model.

26. This is the last publication I found written by the NACP on the subject (Solano 1962).

27. Stein states that the number of inhabitants in Lima increased more than 125 per cent from 165,000 in 1900 to 376,000 in 1931 (1986: 13–14). Lloréns Amico describes Lima at the beginning of the century as a:

> conglomeration of neighbourhoods around a nucleus where the public and government buildings were concentrated. The neighbourhoods were surrounded by vegetable and flower gardens, just outside of the city there were fields and 'haciendas'. The majority of the population lived in *callejones*. These were places that were a chain of one or two room dwellings opening up to a narrow corridor with only one outside entrance; they could house between 50 and 200 people and were occupied by families on low incomes. (1983: 25)

28. The journalists ask the woman if she is a *madre de familia* (mother of the family). The connotation this carries cannot be conveyed in writing. It implies that a woman is fulfilling her vocation as a mother, housewife and parent. Thus the journalist was obviously being sarcastic.
29. The coarse words in other languages refer to the madams. Many of the madams were said to be Europeans who retired from prostitution to administer and rent rooms.

## CHAPTER 2

1. The subtitle is taken from an article which appeared in *Página Libre* (1 October 1990). This story is based on newspaper clippings from *La República*: 25 September 1990, 1, 4, 15, 21, 24 October 1990, 10 November 1990; *Página Libre*: 21, 24, 25 September 1990, 1, 4, 11, 12, 15, 18, 24 October 1990; *El Nacional*: 22 March 1991.
2. According to the Bishops of Lima the new project legalized prostitution. However, their statement showed their ignorance on the subject. As explained earlier, registered prostitution has been legal in Peru since 1910.
3. In 1982 and 1988, there was also talk of moving the registered brothels of Callao to a more remote area. However, these plans also came to nothing.
4. It is important to keep in mind that, since the abolition of the Vagrancy Law in 1982, clandestine prostitutes could no longer be imprisoned. This proposal could be extremely disadvantageous for the working conditions of unregistered prostitutes but, as in the past, it offers absolutely no guarantee that it will prevent the practice of clandestine prostitution.
5. A possible explanation as to why the location of the entrance was fundamental to their closure might be related to the fact that it is prohibited to situate a brothel too close to a residential community. Every so often the officials make an effort to enforce the law. However, I have been unable to find any other articles which support this speculation or offer other explanations.
6. An earlier attempt to unionize was made by a group of prostitutes in 1972. This was mentioned briefly in an article written in 1980 which gave a socio-economic analysis of prostitution (Salcedo 1980: 69, 71).
7. My attempt to track down more information on this committee, its members and documents were in vain. I was only able to find out the name of one of its members and unsuccessfully tried to contact him on several occasions. A trip to the Congress Archives did not produce any documents written by this commission.
8. See <http://hivinsite.ucsf.edu/akb/1997/oiepiint:>. 0.63 per cent of female sex workers are HIV positive. Compare this to the northern region of Thailand where 60 per cent of prostitutes are HIV carriers (personal communication with Han ten Brummelhuis).
9. The Anti-Venereal Centre in Lima was planning to approach clandestine prostitutes, but was prevented by financial and political problems (interview with the nurse in charge of the Aids programme of the Anti-Venereal Clinic).

10. These women's image takes on mythical proportions. They are said to exist in large numbers and are the immoral prostitutes. Often they are confused with women who work in high-class establishments, or they are defined as any female with desires for sexual experiences. Women who prostitute for luxuries justify the other category of prostitutes' existence. Compared to this prostitute, the average prostitute is a saint.

11. Kane (1995) defines hypersexuality as follows: 'hypersexuality is the mythic distortion of certain categories of persons such that their sexual behaviors are imputed to have an exaggerated dominance in character formation and symbolic import. Following this logic, female prostitutes are only discussed as sexual beings; their roles as mothers, wives, sisters or heads of households are usually absent from discourse.'

## CHAPTER 3

1. Parts of this chapter were published earlier in Nencel (1994, 1996b).

2. Despite the age of some of the articles used in this discussion, I contend that these studies represent a specific way of thinking still extremely prevalent in the analysis of Latin American masculinity.

3. This term was first used by Vance (1985: 10).

4. We discussed the possibility that I would do interviews with the same men to see what differences arose. The differences would not only be gendered but also based on professional training. As a foreign anthropologist I would pose questions accentuating different aspects. This would have enabled us to collect material from the same respondent from different perspectives. However, this methodological experiment could not be realized due to, among other things, the lack of time for both the respondents and myself.

5. It is curious that they not only attempted to conceal the fact that they were virgins, but some men recall it as if they pulled it off successfully. Imagine a 13-year-old boy going to a prostitute for the first time, acting as if he knows what he is doing. Did they really believe that an experienced prostitute would not be able to tell? I think this is more about the construction of their sexual selves, than an accurate account of the situation.

## CHAPTER 4

1. For further discussion on the developments and significance of reflexivity in critical or feminist anthropology, see Pels and Nencel (1991).

2. Originally this term was used to indicate first-generation descendants of Spanish parents. However, its contemporary meanings refer to a cultural prototype.

3. Recently, more attention has been paid to the inner-city slums by NGOs, but the efforts made in these areas are still insignificant compared to the development work being done in the *barriadas*.

4. This was the adjusted monthly minimum, it decreased consecutively in the following years dropping to US $34 by 1994. The minimum wage was not changed until 1996.

5. On a few occasions we visited another club in another district where at least 50 women worked and where there seemed to be a constant flow of customers. In comparison with the Crazy Horse, the club we frequented regularly, this club was enormous. The number of women working at the Crazy Horse rarely exceeded ten and there were very few occasions when all the women were entertaining a customer at the same time.

6. To facilitate this discussion I appear at times as if I went to the field with a list of feminist dos and don'ts. Actually these principles have structured my perspective and research approach since the beginning of my anthropological training. They were

never meant to be put to the test on every available occasion, rather, as a part of my world-view, they normally lie quietly until they are challenged.

7.  See Wolf (1996: 24–5) for a discussion of the dilemmas involved in reciprocity, particularly in relation to the notion of power.

8.  In a presentation at the '*Lova-Dag*' in Nijmegen, the Netherlands, I suggest that by embedding my research in a network of feminist organizations, the research can ultimately contribute to changes in ways of thinking and strategies planned in regard to prostitution (Nencel 1996a: 9).

9.  Additionally, as Wolf points out referring to Spivak's writings, the notion of 'letting women speak' suggests 'that First World feminists are once again wielding their hegemonic power to allow Third World subjects an audience' (1996: 26).

10. For other discussions on lying, for example in relation to fieldwork, see Bleek (1987), or, for the significance of lying in the everyday life of a Lebanese village, see Gilsenan (1976).

11. In Nencel (1993) I portray the choppy process of constructing knowledge in the field by presenting a dialogue between myself and two prostitutes without editing out the different detours made during the conversation. This was intended as a statement in relation to polished ethnographies which eliminate these from the outset, giving the impression that the world is a neat and logically ordered place, awaiting discovery.

12. See Marcus and Fisher (1986), Clifford and Marcus (1986) and, for feminist critiques, see for example Mascia-Lees et al. (1989), Stacey (1988), Pels and Nencel (1991).

## CHAPTER 5

1.  On several occasions I participated in their activities. It was not only enjoyable but it also broadened my insight into this neighbourhood as a whole.

2.  The reader will often find in the text references to ethnic origins and more specifically skin colour. Making nicknames out of physical attributes is very common. Thus, *gordo* (fat) or *negra* (black) are heard often. I have chosen to reproduce these aspects to try to capture the subtlety of this mode of differentiation. In some cases skin colour has more significance than others, specifically when white skin is mentioned. The implicit comparison between white skin and that of any other colour reflects the value-laden correlation between ethnicity and class.

3.  Because everyone had a different story concerning regulation, I was confused at the beginning of my fieldwork as to who was eligible to register. I was under the impression that any woman could register and practise prostitution. It took some time before I realized registered prostitutes only work at officially licensed brothels.

4.  In 1999, as I write, it is strange to think that Fujimori ever conformed to this image. His name has become a household word especially after the *auto-golpe* (self-coup) when he closed down Congress. He was not only re-elected but changed the Constitution to be able to reach that goal. Previously it was forbidden for a president to sit two terms consecutively. He has succeeded in changing it again and has been elected for a third term. Currently (2000) he is embroiled in one of the greatest scandals in the history of Peru.

## CHAPTER 6

1.  See Chapter 1 for a discussion of the duties that are the responsibility of this department.

2.  Joseph defines the culture of indirection in the Lebanese context as follows:

> ... the culture of indirection also affected my research methods and data. My neighbors usually gave direct answers in formal interviews. When speaking

informally about feelings, desires, beliefs or sensitive subjects, however, they often shifted to indirection, implicating others present at the interview ... in the critical areas of expressing their feelings. (1996: 116)

Although Joseph describes a different realm of communication the concept is still adequate because, in both cases, it is not the words but the silence and the intentions behind them which must be interpreted.

3. At the time of the *paquetazo* the dollar was set at 450,000 *Intis*.
4. *Comedores populares* have generally been established in *pueblos jóvenes*. Often they are a self-propelled initiative of the residents. Fujimori incorporated *comedores populares* in his Emergency Plan. All the NGOs working in poverty-stricken areas temporarily shifted their priorities to help organize them.
5. In the middle of December US $1 was equivalent to 530,000 *Intis*.
6. This was the first time I heard she only had one adopted child. She had previously given me the impression that she had three children.
7. The reader will encounter throughout the story of Carmencita the interchangeable use of male and female pronouns. This is not a grammatical oversight, rather it reflects the way the people in the neighbourhood talked about her. Female pronouns were used more frequently but were often switched to male pronouns.
8. At this moment of time US $1 was approximately 550,000 *Intis*.


## CHAPTER 7

1. There are various oil, gas and engineering projects located in this geographical area. Large camps are constructed for the group of predominantly male employers. Many of these enterprises organize groups of prostitutes to come to the camps temporarily to serve the employees.
2. See Chapter 4 for further elaboration.
3. San Marcos is one of the state universities which has an extremely leftist tradition.
4. All individuals who live at home are obliged to rent a room at a hostel when they want to be together with their partners.
5. There were other signs that Carmela's glamorous image of the prostitute was an illusion and she most probably received the normal street rate for prostituting. I realized this after I found out she strolled the streets approaching passing cars to look for clients, one of the most common forms of street prostitution.
6. A woman who prostitutes will never label her partner a *cafiche*, even if she does keep him. He will always be her *marido*. This discloses another layer entangled in the fluid construction of the *marido-cafiche* relation.
7. I am not sure if we were talking in code, that is to say, did we both know Carmela did not work at a hospital or did her mother seriously believe she did, or think I did? I had heard, from Anita, that her mother knew that Carmela was a prostitute. Carmela and Anita quarrelled because Anita supposedly told her, and Anita denied doing this.


## CHAPTER 8

1. What I have called a conversation was actually an introductory interview intended to be a prologue to a life history. The circumstances under which it was conducted were extremely difficult. It took place in a partially covered terrace of a restaurant, which could not prevent the traffic noises from mingling in with our conversation. The terrace also served as a pick-up joint and, indeed, our conversation was interrupted twice by men seeking our company. Additionally, it was difficult to find an inconspicuous place to put the tape recorder to tape our conversation. These

elements did not contribute to creating an optimal interview setting nor did I feel at ease. My discomfort grew when I realized that the interview was not going in the direction I wished. Zoila steered away from talking about her private life, and I had difficulty finding a way to make the subject more accessible.

I have reworked the chopped-up interview pieces into a narrative. This textual twist creates the impression that the interviewee chose to speak about each subject and considered the same issues as relevant as I did. Actually, the reverse is true. Zoila would not have begun to talk about half of this had I not posed a direct question on the subject.

2. Injections are used commonly as a type of 'morning-after pill'. Additionally, many prostitutes used penicillin as prevention for venereal diseases. It appears that Zoila was referring to these two injections. It was only when I asked her directly whether she used condoms to prevent Aids, that she gave an answer. She replied with a desired answer, 'Of course, but quite honestly I don't know much about the subject.' Zoila primarily associated condoms with birth control and venereal diseases and not Aids prevention.

3. Mariana's story has been embellished with parts of the life story I did with her. I have created the effect that she told me all the details in our conversations at the bar.

4. Many people go to Arica in the north of Chile or to Tacna, in south Peru, to buy imported products known to be cheaper there and deal in contraband. It can be a lucrative way of earning some extra money, if you don't get caught.

5. Many of the women have 'their own *taxista*', a steady driver who takes them home every night. It is a safety precaution because they run less risk of being assaulted, harassed or blackmailed by different taxi drivers who would find out where they reside. Soledad was not the only woman I knew who had a brief relationship with her taxi driver. Several women had, including Zoila, who had the reputation of always getting involved with her *taxista*.

6. At another time she spoke about living with her mother in Rimac. Then all of a sudden her mother and brothers moved to her house in Chorillos because it was bigger. There is something intangible concerning where the women live. Either they and/or their families are extremely mobile or their residences are changed depending on how it suits the story.

7. Esperanza knew we were trying to arrange for women to be able to use the services of therapists who were interested in working with women-who-prostitute and, above all, would not pre-define prostitutes as abnormal, asocial or the like. It was not easy to find anyone who fitted this description.

## CHAPTER 9

1. My use of the term 'we' is meant to include feminist researchers who structure their work starting from the notion of difference.

2. See Moore's (1988, 1994) review of this theoretical episode. For the Latin American context, see Stevens (1973), who invented the term *marianismo* as a reaction to and to counteract the overemphasis on the term *machismo*. I refrain from using this concept, not only because of this theoretical objection, but also because it has been and still is used rather carelessly. While difference has emerged as a central theoretical concept, *marianismo* is still used as a universal analytical category for Latin American women despite the fact that this concept was developed in a specific Mexican cultural context. Its relevance for the Latin American setting must be investigated and cannot be assumed, otherwise the same mistake will be repeated as in the case of the concept of *machismo* (see Chapter 3). For a similar critique of this concept see Melhuus and Stølen (1996).

3. See Pheterson (1996) for a brief discussion of Lombroso's *The Criminal Woman and the Prostitute*, and Bell (1994) and Corbin (1990) for their discussions on Parent-Duchatelet. Corbin states that Parent-Duchâlet's quest aimed to 'accumulate sufficient knowledge to allow the authorities to exert their power more easily' (1990: 16). Both authors have been influential in the discussion of prostitution world-wide. Mention of their work is found in many theses reviewed for this study. Remnants of this perspective, in which prostitutes are dissected to reveal their social, economic and psychological similarities, have been used throughout this century and are still felt today. See, for example, Flores (1936), Estupiñan and Marcos (1958), Ismodes Cairo (1967), Hernández Aguilar and del Pozo (1967), Pareja Meneses (1989).

4. In regard to Scott's concept of hidden transcript, it would be interesting to analyse the possibility of a hidden transcript which exists in the client and prostitute's relation.

# BIBLIOGRAPHY

Abu-Lughod, L.(1993) *Writing Women's Worlds: Bedouin Stories*. Berkeley: University of California Press.

Acker, J., K. Barry and J. Esseveld (1991) 'Objectivity and Truth: Problems in Doing Feminist Research', in M.M. Fonow and J.A. Cook (eds) *Beyond Methodology: Feminist Scholarship as Lived Research*. Bloomington: Indiana University Press, pp. 133–53.

Archetti, E.P. (1992) 'Argentinian Football: A Ritual of Violence?', *International Journal of the History of Sport* 9(2).

Avedaño, L.(1892) 'Reglamentación de la Prostitución', *La Crónica Médica* 9(98).

Bambarén, C.(1937) 'Disertación del Dr. Carlos A. Bambarén', *La Crónica Médica* 54(891).

Bambarén, C. (1952) *Enseñanza de la Eugenesia*. Lima.

Barrig, M.(1982) *Conviver: La Pareja en La Pobreza*. Lima: Mosca Azul.

Barrig, M. (1993) *Seis Familias en la Crisis*. Lima: ADEC-ATC.

Barrios, M.C., A. Perez Roca, G. Bravo, M.A. Muñiz and L. Avedaño (1892) 'Informe Emitado por la Sección IV de la Academia en el Projecto de Ordenanza sobre la Prostitución', *La Crónica Médica* 9(103).

Basurto, C.F. (1941) 'Criterios para Canalizar la Prostitución', *La Crónica Médica* 58(935).

Behar, R. (1993) *Translated Woman: Crossing the Border with Esperanza's Story*. Boston, MA: Beacon Press.

Bell, D. (1993) 'Yes, Virginia, There is a Feminist Ethnography', in D. Bell, P. Caplan and W.J. Karim (eds) *Gendered Fields: Women, Men and Ethnography*. Routledge: London, pp. 29–43.

Bell, L. (ed.) (1987) *Good Girls/Bad Girls: Feminist and Sex Trade Workers Face to Face*. Seattle: The Seal Press.

Bell, S. (1994) *Reading, Writing and Rewriting the Prostitute Body*. Bloomington: Indiana University Press.

Bleek, W. (1987) 'Lying Informants: A Fieldwork Experience from Ghana', *Population and Development Review* 13(2).

Brock, D. (1989) 'Prostitutes are Scapegoats in the AIDS Panic', *RFR/DRF* 18(2).

Brunt, L. (1996) *Stad*. Amsterdam: Boom.

Bustamente Ruiz, C.(1941) 'Atisbos sobre Lucha Antivenérea Integral', *La Crónica Médica* 58(935).

Butler, A.M. (1987) *Daughters of Joy, Sisters of Misery: Prostitutes in the American West 1865-90*. Chicago: University of Illinois Press.

Butler, J. (1990a) *Gender Trouble: Feminism and the Subversion of Identity*. New York: Routledge.

Butler, J. (1990b) 'Performative Acts and Gender Constitution: An Essay in Phenomenology and Feminist Theory', in S. Case (ed.) *Performing Feminisms*. Baltimore: Johns Hopkins University Press, pp. 270–82.

Cáceres, A. (1990) 'Fieles o Mentirosos?', *Debate* 12(62).

Cardich, R. and F. Carrasco (1993) *Visiones del Aborto: Nexos entre Sexualidad, Anticoncepción y Aborto*. Lima: Movimiento Manuela Ramos and The Population Council.

Cavalcanti, C., C. Imbert and M. Cordero (1985) *Prostitución: Esclavitud Sexual Femenina*. Santo Domingo: Centro de Investigación para la Acción Femenina.

Champa, J. and E. Acha (1986) *Perú Desde el Margen: Dos Testimonios*. Lima: PUC, Facultad de Ciencias Sociales.

Chavez Diaz, E.A. (1955) 'La Prostitución y Estado Actual de la Lucha Antivenérea en el Perú', Tesis de Bacillerado, Universidad Nacional Mayor de San Marcos, Facultad de Medicina, Lima.

Clifford, J. (1986) 'Introduction: Partial Truths', in J. Clifford and G.E. Marcus (eds) *Writing Culture: The Poetics and Politics of Ethnography*. Berkeley: University of California Press, pp. 1–28.

Clifford, J. and G.E. Marcus (eds) *Writing Culture: The Poetics and Politics of Ethnography*. Berkeley: University of California Press.

Collier, D. (1978) *Barriadas y Élites: De Odría a Velasco*. Lima: Instituto de Estudios Peruanos.

Corbin, A. (1990) *Women for Hire: Prostitution and Sexuality in France after 1850*. Cambridge, MA: Harvard University Press.

Cornwall, A. and N. Lindisfarne (1994) 'Introduction', in A. Cornwall and N. Lindisfarne (eds) *Dislocating Masculinity: Comparative Ethnographies*. London: Routledge, pp. 1–10.

Cornwall, A. and N. Lindisfarne (1995) 'Feminist Anthropologies and Questions of Masculinity', in A. Ahred and C. Shore (eds) *The Future of Anthropology, its Relevance to the Contemporary World*. London: Sage.

Creatividad y Cambio (1984) *La Prostitución: Posición del Movimiento EL POZO Frente a la Prostitucón Reglamentada*, pamphlet no. 11. Lima.

Dávalos y Lissón, P. (1909) *La Prostitución en la Ciudad de Lima*. Lima: Imprenta la Industria.

Day, S.(1988) 'Prostitute Women and AIDS: Anthropology', *AIDS* 2.

Delacoste, F. and P. Alexander (eds) (1987) *Sex Work: Writings by Women in the Sex Industry*. London: Virago Press.

Delpino, N.(1990) *Saliendo a Flote: La Jefa de Familia Popular*. Lima: Fundación Friedrich Naumann.

Edwards, S.S.M. (1993 ) 'Selling the Body, Keeping the Soul: Sexuality, Power, the Theories and Realities of Prostitution', in S. Scott and D. Morgan (eds) *Body Matters: Essays on the Sociology of the Body*. London: Falmer Press, pp. 89–104.

Ennew, J. (1986) 'Mujercita y Mamacita: Girls Growing Up in Lima', *Bulletin of Latin American Research* 5(2).

Estupiñan, S. and J. Marcos (1958) 'Un Milenario Problema: Prostitución y sus Aspectos en Lima', Tesis de Bachillado, Universidad Nacional Mayor de San Marcos, Facultad de Medicina, Lima.

Flores, E.B. (1936) 'Algunas Consideraciones sobre la Prostitución', Tesis de Bachillado, Universidad Nacional Mayor de San Marcos, Facultad de Medicina, Lima.

Fuller, N. (1997) *Identidades Masculinas*. Lima: Pontificia Universidad Católica del Perú.

Galvez (1892) 'El Projecto de la Ordenanza sobre la Prostitución', *La Crónica Médica* 9(99).

Gamero, J. (1990) 'Sueldos y Salarios: Caida en Picada', *Que Hacer* 66.

García, A.C. (1899) 'La Prostitución Reglamentada', *La Crónica Médica* 16(251).

Gilsenan, M.(1976) 'Lying, Honor, and Contradiction', in B. Kapferer (ed.) *Transaction and Meaning*. Philadelphia: Institute for the Study of Human Issues, pp. 191–219.

Gutmann, M.C. (1996) *The Meanings of Macho: Being a Man in Mexico City*. Berkeley: University of California Press.

Guy, D.J. (1990) *Sex and Danger in Buenos Aires: Prostitution, Family and Nation in Argentina*. Lincoln: University of Nebraska Press.

Hernández Aguilar, Z. and T. del Pozo (1967) 'Rasgos Psicologicos Predominantes en las Madres Prostitutas', in *La Familia, La Infancia y La Juventud en el Desarrollo Nacional*. Lima, pp. 373–93.

Higginson, A. (1937) 'Acción Nefasta de la Prostitución Reglamentada', *La Crónica Médica* 54(891).

Higginson, A. (1941) 'Conceptos y Realidad Peruana en la Lucha Antivenérea', *La Crónica Médica* 58(935).

Hirdman, Y. (1996) *Key Concepts in Feminist Theory – Analysing Gender and Welfare*, Working Paper 34. Aalborg: Feminist Research Centre in Aalborg.

Ismodes Cairo, S.(1967) 'Estudios Sobre la Prostitución en Lima', in *La Familia, La Infancia y La Juventud en el Desarrollo Nacional*. Lima, pp. 349–79.

Joseph, S. (1996) 'Relationality and Ethnographic Subjectivity: Key Informants and the Construction of Personhood in Fieldwork', in D. Wolf (ed.) *Feminist Dilemmas in Fieldwork*. Boulder, CO: Westview Press, pp. 107–21.

Kane, S. (1995) 'Hypersexuality, Aids and Crime: A Series of Exaggerations', paper presented at the annual meeting of the American Anthropological Association, November, Washington, DC.

Kondo, D.K. (1990) *Crafting Selves: Power, Gender, and Discourses of Identity in a Japanese Workplace*. Chicago: University of Chicago Press.

Lal, J. (1996) 'Situating Locations: The Politics of Self, Identity and "Other" in Living and Writing the Text', in D. Wolf (ed.) *Feminist Dilemmas in Fieldwork*. Boulder, CO: Westview Press, pp. 185–214.

Lloréns Amico, J.A. (1983) *Musica Popular en Lima: Criollos y Adinos*. Lima: Instituto de Estudios Peruanos.

Lugo, C. (1989) 'Machismo y Violencia', in A. Koschutzke (ed.) *Y Hasta Cuándo Esperaremos, Mandan-dirun-dirun-dirun-dán: Mujer y Poder en América Latina*. Caracas: Editorial Nueva Sociedad, pp. 219–30.

MacLean y Estenós, R. (1942) *Sociología Peruano*. Lima.

Mahood, L.(1990) *The Magdalenes, Prostitution in the Nineteenth Century*. London: Routledge.

Marcus, G.E. and M.M.J. Fisher (1986) *Anthropology as Cultural Critique: An Experimental Moment in the Human Sciences*. Chicago: University of Chicago Press.

Mascia-Lees, F.E., P. Sharpe and C. Ballerino Cohen (1989) 'The Postmodernist Turn in Anthropology: Cautions from a Feminist Perspective', *Signs* 15(11).

Medina, C. (1892) 'Reglamentación de la Prostitución', *La Crónica Médica* 9(100).

Melhuus, M. and K.A. Stølen (1996) 'Introduction', in M. Melhuus and K.A. Stølen (eds) *Machos, Mistresses, Madonnas: Contesting the Power of Latin American Gender Imagery*. London: Verso, pp. 1–33.

Milliones, L. (1978) *Tugurio: La Cultura de los Marginados*. Lima: Instituto de Cultura.

Montaño, W. (1943) 'Los Aliados de la Prostitución', *La Crónica Médica* 60(964).

Monzón, A.S. (1988) 'El Machismo: Mito de la Supremacía Masculina', *Nueva Sociedad* 93(enero-febrero).

Moore, H. (1988) *Feminism and Anthropology*. Cambridge: Polity Press.

Moore, H. (1994) *A Passion for Difference*. Cambridge: Polity Press.

Muñiz, M.A. (1887) 'Reglamentación de la Prostitución', *La Crónica Médica* 4(48).

Muñiz, M.A. (1888) 'Reglamentación de la Prostitución', *La Crónica Médica* 5(49).

Nencel, L. (1993) 'El Genero como Sentimiento Comunicable: Compartiendo el Espacio con Prostitutas en Lima, Peru', *Debates en Sociología* 18.

Nencel, L. (1994) 'The Secrets behind Sexual Desire: The Construction of Male Sexuality in Lima, Peru', *Etnofoor* 7(2).

Nencel, L. (1996a) 'Shaking Foundations: Feminist Epistemology and Methodology, Guiding Principles or Hindrances?', *Lova-Nieuwsbrief* 17(2).

Nencel, L. (1996b) 'Pacharacas, Putas and Chicas de su Casa: Labelling, Femininity and Men's Sexual Selves in Lima, Peru', in M. Melhuus and K.A. Stølen (eds) *Machos, Mistresses, Madonnas: Contesting the Power of Latin American Gender Imagery*. London: Verso, pp. 56–82.

Nencel, L. (2000a) 'Entre la hipersexualidad y el silencio. Manifestaciones e imaginarios de la prostitutción en Lima', Paper presented at the conference 'De Amores y Luchas. Diversidad Sexual, Derechos Humanos y Ciudadanía', 13–15 September, University of San Marcos, Lima.

Nencel, L. (2000b) 'Doctrinas sobre la prostitución y sus consecuencias para la agencia de mujeres que se prostituyen', keynote presentation at el Primero Conversatorío sobre la Prostitución, un espacio de reflexión en busca de soluciones. 27–8 September, Municipalidad de San Isidro, Lima.

Nencel, L. and P. Pels (eds)(1991) *Constructing Knowledge Authority and Critique in Social Science.* London: Sage.

Pareja Meneses, A.(1989) *La Prostitución y su Problematica.* Lima: Polen Editores.

Parker, R. (1992) *Bodies, Pleasures and Passions: Sexual Culture in Contemporary Brazil.* Boston, MA: Beacon Press.

Patch, R.W. (1974) 'La Parada, El Mercado de Lima: Un Estudio de Clase y Asimilación', in L.J. Bartolomé and E.E. Gorostiaga (eds) *Estudios sobre el Campesinado Latinoamericano: La Perspectiva de la Antropología Social.* Buenos Aires: Ediciones Periferia SRL, pp. 229–76.

Pels, P. and L. Nencel (1991) 'Critique and the Deconstruction of Academic Authority', in L. Nencel and P. Pels (eds) *Constructing Knowledge: Authority and Critique.* London: Sage, pp. 1–21.

Personal Narrative Group (1989) '"Conditions Not of Her Own Making"' in The Personal Narratives Group (ed.) *Interpreting Women's Lives: Feminist Theory and Personal Narratives.* Bloomington: Indiana University Press, pp. 19-23.

Pheterson, G. (ed.) (1989) *A Vindication of the Rights of Whores.* Seattle: The Seal Press.

Pheterson, G. (1996) *The Prostitution Prism.* Amsterdam: Amsterdam University Press.

EL POZO (n.d.) 'La Prostitucion, un Microcosmos de la Explotación de Toda Mujer en Nuestra Sociedad', unpublished paper, Lima.

Prieur, A. (1998) *Mema's House: On Transvestites, Queens and Machos.* Chicago: University of Chicago Press.

Riofrió, G. (1990) '¿Asistencia Social O Asistencialismo?', *QueHacer* 66.

Rodas Manzo, R., M. Briones Velasteguí and T. Cordero Velásquez (1991) *Nosotras, Las Señoras Alegres.* Ecuador: Abrapalabra.

Rosaldo, R.(1989) *Culture and Truth: Remaking of Social Analysis.* Boston, MA: Beacon Press.

Salcedo, J.M. (1980) 'La Prostitución: Ese Turbio Espejo de la Realidad', *Debate 8* junio (Lima).

Scheper-Hughes, N. (1992) *Death without Weeping: The Violence of Everyday Life in Brasil.* Berkeley: University of California Press.

Schrijvers, J. (1991) 'Dialectics of a Dialogical Ideal: Studying Down, Studying Sideways and Studying Up', in L. Nencel and P. Pels (eds) *Constructing Knowledge, Authority and Critique in Social Science.* London: Sage, pp. 162–79.

Scott, J.C. (1990) *Domination and the Arts of Resistance: Hidden Transcripts.* New Haven, CT: Yale University Press.

Soares, L.V. (1988) *Prostitution in Nineteenth-Century Rio de Janeiro,* Occasional Papers No. 17. London: University of London, Institute of Latin American Studies.

Solano, S. (1936) 'Comite Abolicionista Peruano', *La Crónica Médica* 53(876).

Solano, S. (1937) 'Dos Años de Propaganda Abolicionista', *La Crónica Médica* 54(891).

Solano, S. (1943) 'Legislación Antivenérea del Perú', *La Crónica Médica* 60(964).

Solano, S. (1944) 'Fines Eugénicos en la Lucha Antivenérea', *Segunda Jornada Peruana de Eugenesia* (Lima).

Solano, S. (1962) 'En Conmemoración del XXV Aniversario de la Fundación del Comite Abolicionista Peruano' (Lima).

Solano, S., C.A. Bambarén, P. Martinez y La Rosa, A. Higginson and M. Carrion Matos (1941) 'Ley Antivenérea', *La Crónica Médica* 58(935).

Stacey, J. (1988) 'Can There be a Feminist Ethnography?', *Women's Studies International Forum* 11(1).

Steenbeek, G. (1995) *Vrouwen op de Drempel.* Amsterdam: Thela Publishers.

Stein, S. (1986) *Lima Obrera 1900–1930, Tomo I.* Lima: El Virrey.

Stevens, E.P. (1973) 'Marianismo: The Other Face of Machismo in Latin America', in A. Pescatello (ed.) *Female and Male in Latin America*. Pennsylvania: University of Pittsburgh Press, pp. 88–101.

Stoller, P. (1989) *The Taste of Ethnographic Things: The Senses in Anthropology*. Philadelphia: University of Pennsylvania Press.

Taller de Testimonio (1986) *Habla La Ciudad*. Lima: Municipalidad de Lima Metropolitana/Universidad Nacional Mayor de San Marcos.

Tamayo, G. and J.M. Garcia Rios (1990) *Mujer y Varon: Vida Cotidiana, Violencia y Justicia*. Lima: Raíces y Alas, Sea y Tarea.

Truong, T.D. (1988) 'Sex, Money and Morality. The Political Economy of Prostitution and Tourism in South East Asia', PhD Thesis, University of Amsterdam: Faculty of Political and Social-Cultural Sciences.

Ugarteche, O. (1992) 'Historia, Sexo y Cultura en el Perú', *Márgenes* 5(9).

UNESCO (1995) 'Seoul Declaration for a World Without Sexual Exploitation', International Experts Meeting on Violence, Sexual Exploitation of Human Beings and International Action (Memo).

Valdizán Medrano, H. (1909) 'Contribución de la Reglamentación de la Prostitución', *Gaceta de los Hospitales* 6.

Vance, C.S. (1985) 'Pleasure and Danger: Toward a Politics of Sexuality', in C.S. Vance (ed.) *Pleasure and Danger: Exploring Female Sexuality*. Boston: Routledge & Kegan Paul, pp. 1–27.

Van Maanen, J.(1988) *Tales of the Field: On Writing Ethnography*. Chicago: University of Chicago Press.

Verlarde Vargas, E.S. (1957) 'Los Barrios Altos de Lima', in C.E. Paz-Soldán (ed.) *Lima y sus Suburbios*. Lima: Universidad Nacional de San Marcos de Lima.

Villar, L. (1858) 'La Prostitución en Lima', *Gaceta Medica de Lima* 2(40).

Villarán, R. (1987) 'Cosa de Hombres', *La Tortuga* 21.

Villarreal, M. (1994) 'Wielding and Yielding: Power, Subordination and Gender Identity in the Context of a Mexican Development Project', PhD thesis, Landbouw Universiteit, Wageningen.

Walkowitz, J. (1980) *Prostitution and Victorian Society: Women, Class and the State*. (Cambridge: Cambridge University Press.

White, L. (1990) *The Comforts of Home: Prostitution in Colonial Nairobi*. Chicago: University of Chicago Press.

Wolf, D. (1996) 'Situating Feminist Dilemmas in Fieldwork', in D. Wolf (ed.) *Feminist Dilemmas in Fieldwork*. Boulder, CO: Westview Press, pp. 1–55.

Wolf, M. (1992) *A Thrice-Told Tale: Feminism, Postmodernism and Ethnographic Responsibility*. Stanford, CA: Stanford University Press.

## NEWSPAPERS AND MAGAZINES

*Caretas* 7 July 1990; 16 December 1993.

*El Comercio* 6 August 1990, 19 August 2000.

*El Diario* 22–26 February 1982; 16 July 1982.

*Hoy* 17 September 1987.

*El Nacional* 22 March 1991.

*Ojo* 18 and 24 September 1972; 15 February 1982.

*Página Libre* 21, 24–25 September 1990; 1, 4, 11–12, 15, 18 October 1990.

*Perspectiva* 14 March 1982.

*La Prensa* 25 February 1982.

*La República* 25 September 1990; 1, 4, 15, 21, 24 October 1990; 10 November 1990.

*Semana* 7, 30 September 1990.

*Sí* 12 March 1990.

*¡YA!* (1949) 1, 3, 6, 8, 9, 12, 14.

## ARCHIVES

Archivo de la Municipalidad de Lima
Archivo de Senado
Boletín Municipal, 57, 1639, pp. 10–18, 1957.
Codigo Penal: Ley 4868
Derogación de la Ley de Vagancia: PRoy: 300/85-s. corre con 42/ 8s-s. Ind: G-2, Reg. Just.,
      pag. 118, part. 55
Ley de Vagancia: Expediente numero: 1376

# INDEX

*Index compiled by Auriol-Griffith Jones*